To

MW01093128

Good luck with your
Story. I hope you enjoy
the Book!

Best Wishes
God Bless

Terry
Sheriff Terry Ashe

BY SHERIFF TERRY ASHE

WITH TERRI MERRYMAN

Foreword by CHARLIE DANIELS

ASHES OF

BLUEBIRD

A Sheriff's reflection on a lifetime of tragedy and triumph, gunplay, murder, and politics.

PUBLISHED BY WESTVIEW, INC., KINGSTON SPRINGS, TN

PUBLISHED BY WESTVIEW, INC.
P.O. Box 605
Kingston Springs, TN 37082
www.publishedbywestview.com

The stories in this book are true. Some names and identifying details have been changed to protect the privacy of the characters within.

ISBN: 978-1-937763-38-1 Perfect Bound
ISBN: 978-1-937763-39-8 Cloth with Dust Jacket

First edition, July 2012

Good faith efforts have been made to trace copyrights on materials included in this publication. If any copyrighted material has been included without permission and due acknowledgment, proper credit will be inserted in future printings after notice has been received.

The author gratefully acknowledges permission from the *Lebanon Democrat* and especially photographers Bill Cook, Bill Thorup, Allen Ricketts, Dallus Whitfield, and Richie Bouton to reproduce from their print and photo archives,.

Printed in the United States of America on acid free paper.

For Jesse, Beth, and Ron -----
Your love and support sustain me.

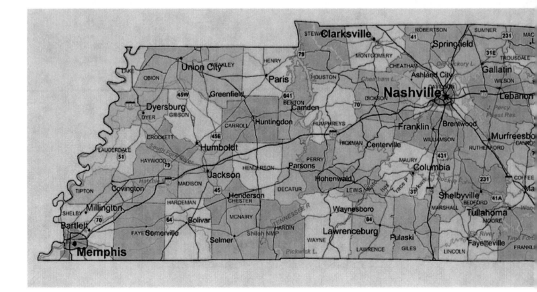

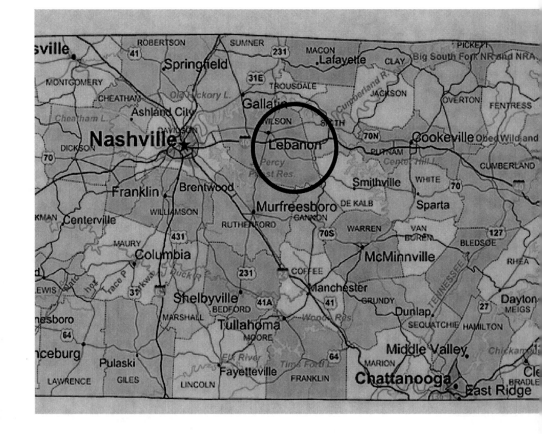

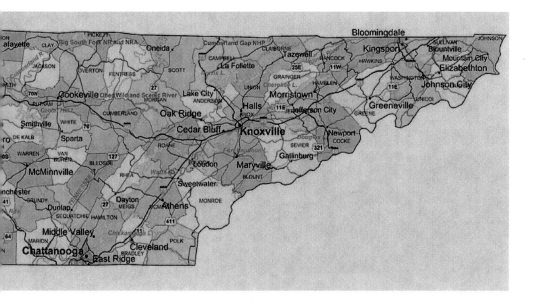

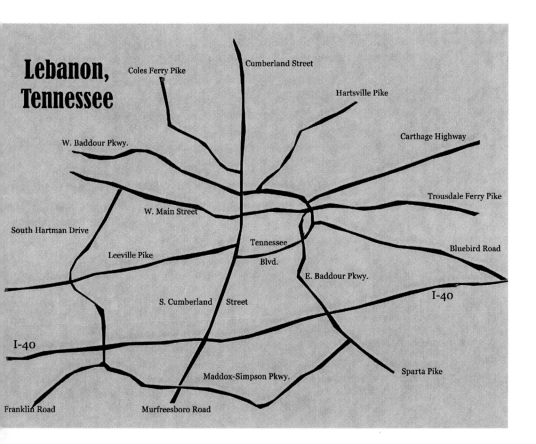

Lebanon, Tennessee

Coles Ferry Pike

Cumberland Street

Hartsville Pike

Carthage Highway

W. Baddour Pkwy.

Trousdale Ferry Pike

W. Main Street

South Hartman Drive

Bluebird Road

Leeville Pike

Tennessee Blvd.

E. Baddour Pkwy.

I-40

S. Cumberland Street

I-40

Maddox-Simpson Pkwy.

Sparta Pike

Franklin Road

Murfreesboro Road

ACKNOWLEDGMENTS

I'd like to thank all the many fine men and women in law enforcement who have been my team members through the years, helping me gather evidence, catch the bad guys and obtain justice for the victims of crime. We share these stories as we have shared our lives day in and day out. Thank you all for your help with some of the toughest cases on record. I couldn't have done it without you.

My family and my extended family and friends have put up with me and my plans for this book for so long. Thank you for keeping the faith that it was going to happen.

This book would not have been written if I had not been elected sheriff. I owe so much to my wonderful network of supporters who have put signs in their yards, donated to the campaign, organized rallies, and most importantly, stepped into the voting booth and pulled the lever beside my name a total of 103,690 times in nine elections. I'll be forever grateful for your kindness and loyalty.

Special thanks to Terri Merryman for her talent and efforts in bringing these stories to life.

Charlie Daniels, you're not only one fantastic entertainer, you're a hard-working, goodwill ambassador for our wonderful community. I'm so proud that I can call you my friend. Thank you for all you've done to help us make Wilson County one of the best places to live in this great country!

Charlie Daniels

www.charliedaniels.com

Photo Credit: Deppisch Foto

TO MY FRIEND TERRY
GOD BLESS

YOU'RE
THE BEST

FOREWORD

I have lived in Wilson County Tennessee for more than four decades. It's the place above all others where my wife Hazel and I choose to spend the rest of our lives.

Wilson County is just east of Nashville, for the most part peaceful, friendly and a great place to raise a family and run a business and we moved our headquarters for the Charlie Daniels Band there over twenty years ago.

I've known Terry Ashe since he was just a young man serving his first term as Wilson County Sheriff. We've been friends for years and talked a lot, but Terry never talked about his days in Viet Nam during the height of the conflict where he saw so much death and, but for the grace of God he would have died himself.

He never talked about the shoot outs, the bullet riddled patrol cars, the breakneck pursuits nor the threats to his life by a gang of local thugs.

He never talked about his lifelong and burning desire to clean up his old neighborhood where bootlegging, prostitution, gambling and drug dealing were open and rampant.

There was so much about the man, who kept the peace in my neighborhood and so much about the county I call home that I didn't know until I read his book.

The *Ashes of Bluebird* is the life story of a country boy, a patriot, a family man and the longest serving Sheriff in the history of Wilson County, Tennessee --- a man I'm honored to call my friend, Terry Ashe.

--*Charlie Daniels*

PROLOGUE

I've heard it said that right before you die, your whole life flashes before you. Since those uniquely qualified to confirm or deny this rumor aren't around anymore, we'll never know for sure. But if it's true, maybe the phenomenon is the result of sheer terror doing a number on the brain.

Perhaps every joy, every pain, every regret you've ever felt is downloading into the deepest part of your heart, making one last curtain call before the lights go out.

Whatever caused me to flip frantically through my memory banks that night must have been making up for lost time. This matter-of-fact feeling that my death was imminent was not exactly a first for me, but it was rare. Of all the life-threatening predicaments I had ever faced — having stared into the business end of every kind of weapon — this was one time my instincts were screaming at me; I was not going to survive this night.

I never would have imagined that my life would end where it began, on Bluebird Road.

Just east of this blight, kids feel safe to run and play after dark. It's where I learned to ride a bike, hitch up a team of plow horses, and throw a curveball with my brother. East of our farm stands the little white clapboard church where I was taught to pray — a skill I would practice every day of my life, especially during times like this.

How ironic — how absolutely *so like me* was it — that I was going to die on this road where I had spent so much of my life?

Memories of my father were on this road — memories of a Ward Cleaver brand of working man who loved his wife and kids and worked at a factory all day, just to walk behind a team of work horses and plow a field when he got home. A sweet, honest man who deserved better than the hand he was dealt. A gentleman who didn't deserve to be cut down in the prime of his life. I always imagined that Dad was looking down on me with a smile, very proud of the choices I had made and the man I had become, proud that I had fulfilled my childhood dream of becoming a sheriff.

I couldn't allow myself to think about all of this now. I had to concentrate on the task before me and think of the deputies I had brought along as backup. They all had families too — fathers who were proud of them, wives who sent them off to work with a kiss goodbye, children who bragged to classmates that their dad wore a badge.

On this night, they deserved to go home to those families as whole as they left them, and I had to see to that.

The gravel crunched beneath my boots as I crept from my car alongside the thick hedgerow lining the path to the little rundown shack. It was unlikely that I would be seen or heard since the clouds obscured the moonlight and the noise coming from the house was deafening as I got closer.

The people who lived next door had been calling my office since sundown complaining about the music, loud laughter, and other unidentified sounds that were roaring from this joint. I had to take action, and this crowd needed to see that I meant business … again. This apparently was a re-start of a business that had burned — one of a half-dozen of the illegal establishments that had been set ablaze by rival bootleggers and gamblers, only to rise from the ashes and move down the road to taunt me.

Throughout my career in law enforcement, I had been called many times to investigate this place and a dozen just like it lining Bluebird Road. The abandoned and re-purposed hovels housed gamblers, moonshiners, dog fighters, drug dealers, and hookers. That was on a peaceful night.

Police never patrolled this area without backup, as the more "sinister elements" moved in to mark their drug trade territory with weapons local law enforcement couldn't begin to match.

In the decades since our family farm was split in half by Interstate 40, this western end of the street had gained a nasty national reputation — a notorious embarrassment to any elected official foolish enough to think he could make a clean sweep of the rusted out single-wide trailers and boarded-up shacks and call it a day.

I had been elected sheriff on the promise that I would clean up this area for good, making it safe for the rest of the neighbors who were law-abiding, hard-working, blue collar people with mortgages, kids, well-kept clapboard houses and clipped lawns. These were taxpayers who had to dodge staggering drunks and flying bullets as they drove down this road to get to church on Sunday morning.

It was high time something was done, and it was time the high sheriff did it. That would be me. I had found out many years before that this was one campaign promise that was going to be very difficult and very dangerous to keep, but I had no intention of breaking a promise to anyone — least of all, to myself.

One big raid wasn't going to do the job. I was going to have to devise a plan that would make life considerably uncomfortable for these criminals, and I would have to make small, consistent efforts over a period of months. In the weeks following the election, I was consumed with the idea of making Bluebird Road the respectful and safe neighborhood I remembered.

With my deputies parked nearby to watch my back, I would burst through the door like a bull, using my double-barrel shotgun or my M-16 rifle as a battering ram. I would turn over jukeboxes, smash bottles, and break tables, chairs, and pool cues in half. The business owners and customers were violent and usually armed. Add drunk to that résumé, and you can get some idea of the type of element I was up against.

The purpose of this show was to let them know that I was a combat veteran, I was armed to my chin, and I wasn't afraid to come out there by myself to do what needed to be done.

I would soon learn that my efforts were akin to using a teaspoon to dip water out of a sinking canoe.

Within hours of making arrests and shutting down one joint, we would learn another had sprung up to take its place, leaving the entire department frustrated, disheartened and angry. The good people who couldn't afford to leave their homes on this road had long since given up hope that it could change for the better.

All of this was getting the best of me on this night. I didn't realize my emotions were beginning to cloud what was normally my conservative judgment regarding safety. As I made my way down the long path to the house, I was careful to scan the front yard, which was packed with cars of every description. License plates from out of the county and out of state were attached to everything from new luxury cars to old rusted-out pickups. I was thinking that if all those people were in that tiny house, it must certainly look like a fraternity prank in there, and my deputies and I were going to be dangerously outnumbered.

I recall thinking it was odd that no one was hanging out in this lot, drinking and talking as they sometimes did around these types of places.

I carried a .12 gauge, sawed-off, double-barrel shotgun securely across my chest with my finger on the trigger as I gingerly crept along. The deputies were parked all along the road, quietly hidden away in the shadows awaiting their cue from me.

About fifty yards from the house, I was ready to give that cue when an ominous-looking, black mass of a man sprang from the bushes to my left. In the darkness, I could barely make out who or what it was, but then my eyes fixed on the signature bowler hat of old Legs Stinson.

Legs, a nickname he came by honestly at 6 foot 7, was a towering fixture in this neighborhood and had done his fair share of shooting craps, betting on the ponies and drinking, and had even been caught up in an arrest or two in his time. He was a friend to law enforcement, however, and the gentle giant kept me informed as to what was going down on any given night in the 'hood.

Long before there was an organized Neighborhood Watch program in place, there was Legs Stinson, and on this night he had come here — or should I say he was sent here — to save my life.

"Sheriff, you don't need to be goin' down thea now. They gonna kill ya tonight," Legs whispered with urgency in his voice I'd never heard before.

"They brung ovah some fellas from Memphis and they done set it up to kill ya. Dey waitin' in thea for ya now. Please don't go down thea, Sheriff!"

Legs had a vice grip on my elbow as he begged, desperately trying to keep me from taking another step toward what he knew would be the last raid I would ever lead.

Not a man in the habit of bullshitting, most tips from Legs were usually right on the mark. And if he told us who had moonshine and where they were hiding it, we could take that information to the bank, or more importantly, to a judge to get a warrant. I knew he was telling me the truth at this moment, and I was humbled that he thought enough of me to risk his own skin to save his friend from getting his head blown off by a gang of hit men from West Tennessee.

But I was determined to move forward if Legs let go of my elbow, because my mind was certainly not in the retreat mode. The fact that I was probably in some gangster's crosshairs at this point didn't enter into the equation.

For a moment after hearing Legs' warning, I wasn't giving *anything* that much thought. I felt the heat rising to my head. I was furious.

My anger fueled a part of me that I've always known was buried deep down in there somewhere — that "crazysumbitch" battlefield mentality that can blind a man beyond reason when the adrenaline is pumping.

I wanted to run toward the house as fast as my feet could carry me, screaming at the top of my lungs, firing my shotgun into the air, acting out every bit of the old "guns ablaze" cliché, but I took a deep breath and snapped out of it. I had to think of my deputies. Upon hearing the gunshots, they would have to come out of their hiding places to protect me and would be killed in a crazy, confusing hail of fire.

This volatile situation had to be brought down a notch, or it was going to look as if Al Capone had thrown up in the parking lot.

Legs stared at me and was probably thinking I had suffered a stroke, as he waited for me to make my decision. I managed to nod my head in a feeble thank-you to the man who was attempting to save me to fight another day. Giving my elbow one last nudge, Legs turned and ducked back into the bushes near a ditch where he had hidden his car.

Once I saw him drive away, I continued to move forward as if he had never appeared.

I don't know why I continued to move toward my guaranteed demise for as long as I did, although I'm sure being totally pissed had a part to play in it.

Suddenly, I just stopped. A cold chill ran over me as if self-preservation were trying to freeze me in place. I stood there for a moment, then began slowly to back my way out in the same tracks I had made going forward. Somehow, the trip backward seemed longer.

Once inside my patrol car, I radioed the deputies to tell them the impromptu raid was off for the time being. The words stuck in my throat. The way I saw it, calling off the raid when we were *"thisclose"* was as good as going on the ten o'clock news and announcing that I had broken my promise to the people who put me in office. I would have to think of another way on another day.

At least I would be alive to draw up an alternate plan of attack.

While I was extremely disappointed that I hadn't accomplished what I had set out to do, with every beat of my pounding heart, I was thanking God for sending an angel in the form of a six-and-a-half-foot-tall African-American affectionately called "Legs."

In the following weeks, our intelligence confirmed what our accurate informant — the makeshift angel — had told us: professional hit men from Memphis were waiting inside that house with automatic weapons and shotguns, ready to blast me out of the county as I burst through the door. We had been called to the house, not by angry neighbors as we had assumed, but by the very people who had paid for the hired guns. It was a setup — a setup I survived only because the hand of God was firmly in the mix as it had been in so many of the tragedies and triumphs of my life.

So here it is, a book that has been in the making for more than half of my life. A collection of memories from just a few of those tragedies and triumphs. The story of a small town sheriff who has seen more than his share of close calls, heartbreaking cases, and the worst humanity can dish out.

It's an intimate look at how I miraculously rose from the ashes — on and off of Bluebird Road.

The Ashes of Bluebird: Audrey and Joe, Terry and Ron

CHAPTER ONE

Three generations of Ashes lived on Bluebird Road. My family was the last to leave.

It's just like so many rural roads in this country where there'll be a thriving high crime area on one end and a blue-collar, law-abiding, farming community on the other. The eight-mile stretch connects Wilson and Smith Counties in Middle Tennessee, and before the interstate highway was built, the only way to go from east to west was by Highway 70, which intersects with Bluebird Road in the city of Lebanon.

That part of the road, west of our farm, was the section littered with whorehouses, dope dens, bootleggers' houses, and gambling joints. Shootings, rapes, and murders plagued this area, and the crime spree bled over into the surrounding counties for years.

For five decades, the political payoffs and the head turning had sustained this mess. Locally, those in law enforcement called it Dodge City, but its national reputation — and indeed it had one — compared its appeal to mobsters rather than cowboys. Elsewhere, this little section of our state was known as "Little Chicago." More on that later.

With jobs being created in Nashville after the war, money was pouring into these establishments, and they were flourishing.

This blighted area couldn't be avoided in day-to-day life since it was traveled daily by anyone going to and from work, shopping, attending church, or visiting relatives who lived closer to the city. When I was a child, my mom was always uneasy traveling this way when we had to go into town. It seemed so odd to me that just by driving a few miles from our peaceful, quiet farm, we would have to be concerned about our safety — even back then.

My Paternal Grandparents:
Mr. and Mrs. Henry Ashe on their wedding day.

The Homeplace

Ronnie and Terry

I was born just after World War II near the last three or four miles of this road, located closer to Smith County. This part of Bluebird Road, to this day, is dotted with picturesque farms, churches, barns, silos, and pastureland. We milked cows, raised tobacco, grew a big garden, and got eggs from the chickens and wool from the sheep. My dad also worked at an airplane factory in Nashville to supplement our income; so essentially, he worked two full-time jobs.

We loved our old farm. In so many ways, and on so many levels, the farm folk were far, far away from the dangers just down the road. The little country churches on Bluebird gave the people of the community a refuge from all that waited outside this protective neighborhood cocoon, offering vacation Bible school for the children and afternoon picnics and gospel singing concerts for the adults. Just off Trousdale Ferry Pike was a deep area in the creek where these churches would baptize the faithful.

The roadway was mostly dirt and gravel, and if it needed repair, it was done by the people who lived on it. Most all the houses were wood clapboard with painted shutters, and the barns were sometimes larger and had more decorative detail than the homes. I think barns and silos back then were a source of pride for the farmers; it was like having a big, fancy sign on a place of business.

When I was a little boy, I thought the big red barn beside our house was the largest building in the world. My brother and I would love to play in there with the sweet aroma of the fresh-cut hay and the feed; that old barn smell is so hard to describe but so familiar to anyone who grew up on a farm.

We milked cows twice a day by hand — before daylight and after school. It was hard work, but it was a terrific way to grow up, and that fact wasn't lost on me. I knew somehow deep down in my soul that these were indeed the good ole' days.

My brother Ron was two years older than me and we were inseparable, except when it came to choosing sides for ball teams at church. Since I was the youngest of all the boys in the neighborhood, I was the last to be picked. My brother was a great athlete in every sport and was usually the first choice of any team captain who wanted to win. Ron tried to help me develop a wicked curve ball to make me a more acceptable ball player. He had the patience of Job.

Everyone in the area had a good hunting dog — for squirrels, rabbits, and raccoons — and most had a cat or two living in the barn to help with the mouse population. I had a dog named Trigger. He was part collie, part shepherd and part Heinz 57, and Ron would take the two of us hunting with him sometimes on the weekends. Old Trigger could tree a squirrel quicker than any dog I ever saw, but mostly that speed was better put to use chasing us around the yard as we played tag or hide 'n seek. Trigger couldn't wait for me to finish my chores after school and focus on playtime.

My dad, Joe Ashe, and my mom, Audrey Gregory Ashe, were good parents who treated us like gold. Like so many homemakers of that era, Mom cooked on a wood stove and scrubbed clothes with a washboard and galvanized washtub in the kitchen.

Once a week, I took a bath in that same little tub. Our house was modest, but Mom kept everything clean and orderly, which was no small task with two young boys, a husband, and a dog parading through on her freshly mopped floor.

The Happy Homemaker

Mom was a beautiful, talented, and high-spirited lady. And, she was a Gregory. The Gregorys are noted in this part of the state as being loyal members of very large families. It was an inside joke that you had better not say anything unkind about a Gregory within earshot of anybody, anywhere, because chances are, you would offend a cousin. Gregorys can either be very strict, religious, or very rowdy,

party types. There are a few in-between types, but they're rare. Any of them, man or woman, will fight at the drop of a hat when they think they're right or they're protecting their family. Mom showed that side of her personality many times to others when we were growing up, and I was always amused by it.

I don't know if Mom had ever pursued a career before she met and married Dad, but she enjoyed being a homemaker and mother, and her love for her job showed in everything she did for us; it seems she was always doing something for her family in the little house she adored.

The dining room doubled as Mom's sewing and quilting room, and she kept a quilt under construction hanging from ceiling hooks in there. I was always amazed at the bright colors and beautiful artwork Mom would create using her old fabric scraps. Where she found the time for her hobby, I'll never know.

Somehow, as if by magic, the quilting scraps were put away, the table cleared, polished, and ready for dining when we entertained V.I.P.'s like the preacher or out-of-town kinfolks.

There was nothing like the sight of three or four different kinds of vegetables, meats, and desserts lined up on the sideboard when guests joined us for dinner.

Mom would bring out her lace tablecloth and her mother's dishes while we brought out our best manners on those days, especially when the preacher came to visit.

Outback

We had all we needed and everything we had was a necessity. We wasted nothing. We were "green" before we knew how cool it was to conserve our resources. We were also "roughing it," but we weren't aware of that fact at the time.

In back of the farm house, there was a long, well-kept path which led to the springhouse — our only water supply. Water flowed into this rock structure from an underground spring that ran all along Bluebird Road. The water was fresh tasting and ice cold. We kept a dipper in a bucket full near the kitchen; it was handy to grab a sip when we would come in for a break from working in the hot sun.

Along that same path behind the house was another necessity, the outhouse. It was called a two-holer, meaning there was one adult-sized cutout on a bench inside and another smaller hole on the bench for the little bottoms of my brother and me. If there is anything colder in the winter than an outhouse, I haven't found it.

Beyond the outhouse was the pile of coal. That's where we kept our fuel for the big hearth. One of my chores was to grab a scuttle-bucket of coal in the morning and each night after supper to stoke up the fire in the winter. Down the path from the coal pile was the chicken coop, our main source for meat as well as eggs Mom used for cooking and bartering.

If the outhouse was a bad place to be in the winter, then the chicken coop was the worst place to be in the heat of the summer. Besides the rank smell rising in the heat, without fail, there would always be a chicken snake in the coop, and I would have to get rid of the slimy creature.

Nothing was allowed to mess with our chickens. When my cat Bobsey killed several of our little chicks one spring, my brother broke the news to me that Dad had apparently carried out capital punishment without as much as a trial. All I remember of that morning is that Dad walked out of the house with his trusty old .22 caliber rifle. I thought he was going to do some target practice.

I never saw Bobsey again after that.

In the summer, people would share work along Bluebird Road, helping each other harvest hay, which was always put up in bales and loaded onto a wagon out in the field. It was backbreaking work.

Tobacco was another money crop that required all the help a farmer could get. Back then, it had to be set out by hand and, when it was ready, cut and hauled up into the tobacco barn to dry. Once dry, around the time school started in the fall, another skilled set of hired men stripped the tobacco and got it ready for market. It was tedious and time consuming, but well worth the effort. A farmer and his family could live a long time on the income from just one year's tobacco harvest.

The hired hands helping us with all of this each year were mostly black workers my dad had known all of his life. Mom cooked a big midday meal for the field hands daily, and they ate at a long table on the back porch as if they were holding some kind of summit. I would always eat out there with them because I enjoyed their funny stories and was afraid I was going to miss something.

Mom would have put a stop to my story time if she had heard any of these saucy tales, many of which I didn't understand, but I laughed along anyway.

My Grandmother, aunts, and friends at the country home on
Bluebird Road. Ron is front row far left; I am front row
second from right (with baseball glove).

Age of Accountability

On Sundays, without fail, my brother and I would sit in the pew in our perfectly starched white shirts as Mom played the piano at Saulsbury Church. My granddad was one of the founders of Saulsbury and helped erect the building where it still stands today. Dad came to Sunday services some of the time, but the elderly preacher, Brother Albert Jewell, made him doze off. Looking back on the situation with adult eyes, I think that was embarrassing for Dad, so he chose to do his snoring at home.

Saulsbury Church only had about three dozen members, but the congregation seemed determined to continue an odd custom; men sat on one side of the sanctuary and women sat on the other. That was apparently the seating arrangement at the majority of the country churches, and no one questioned it.

This is the church where my brother and I accepted Christ into our lives at a Monday night revival meeting — a decision the two of us had discussed at length the day before.

It was a hot, sunny, Sunday afternoon and the sky was the brightest blue I have ever seen. It looked as though heaven was as close to the ground as it could be. My brother and I ran to a plum tree out in the orchard after lunch with a plan to pick our own dessert, since the tree was packed with fruit and ready to be harvested. We climbed almost to the top while swatting at the bees and wasps swarming around us, which were apparently competing with us for the sugary treats.

I was only eight years old, my brother had just turned ten, and we had developed a strong curiosity about Jesus. Something in that day's sermon piqued our interest, and we began to discuss the man who died on the cross.

We were brought up hearing and talking about Jesus as a matter of course, so this was a natural subject for us to ponder as we sat in the tree and sampled the ripened plums. We eventually came to the conclusion that we wanted to go to heaven when we died, and to that end, we needed to make a decision to join the church and be baptized.

The next night, in that hot, humid, little country church, my brother and I went up to the altar to join hands with the preacher and dedicate our lives to Christ. That was the second time I ever saw my dad cry. I glanced at Mom, who was playing the piano and crying so hard that it was a miracle she could see the hymnal in front of her.

Several other boys and girls were saved that night — a successful revival for our little community church. The morning of our baptisms, church members lined the banks of a nearby creek and sang "Amazing Grace" as we were led into the water for the ceremony.

Life was so good and so uncomplicated that year.

Everywhere we looked and everywhere we went, my brother and I were surrounded by friends and family. Gregorys, Hacketts, and Ashes — they were all around us, and we were embraced by people who loved us and cared about our souls, our wellbeing, and our future.

I wish all children could feel as happy and loved as we knew we were that summer.

If every child experienced the joy we felt at that moment in time, I know my job as sheriff would be so much easier today.

The Coon Hunters

My dad loved to go 'coon hunting. I remember he would round up some of his old service buddies, grab his hounds and his rifle and go up into the hills to build a campfire on crisp, fall Saturday nights.

They'd pull out a bottle of "possum grape" wine, and as they listened to the dogs wail and run around, they'd tell war stories and talk politics until the wee hours. Meanwhile, all the wives gathered in our living room to play cards and talk about their husbands. Sometimes, my brother and I got to go along on the hunt, but when there was homework to be done, we stayed behind with the women-folk and listened to the gossip. As we would soon find out, our living room was the safest and most exciting place to be.

Mother always switched on the yellow light bulb hanging over the porch swing to light my dad's way home from the hunt. When he got home, he would always turn out that light as he entered the front door.

One night, very late, or perhaps it was in the wee hours of the morning, that light was still on; Dad and his buddies had not yet returned from their hunting trip. The wives of the men were concerned, and one of the neighbor ladies showed up at our front door with her three little daughters to wait it out. The women talked, and I could tell by the tone of their conversation that they were getting upset.

The next thing I knew, Mom was coming into our room to wake us up and load us into the lady's car. All of us children rode in the back seat, trying to stay awake as the women drove down Bluebird Road, getting angrier by the minute and looking toward the beer joints and the honky-tonks, trying to catch a glimpse of my dad's old black Dodge truck.

I didn't realize at the time that they were tracking these men who were *hunting*, all right; hunting on the wrong side of town — and *not for raccoons*.

Soon, we were on the square in Lebanon. The woman parked the car near a tavern, which was located across from the old sheriff's office and jail. Mom, who barely waited for the wheels to stop rolling, left the car like she was being shot from cannon.

Then I saw the evidence she had just spotted — Dad's truck parked right in front of the bar. Beside it, several more trucks were parked in a neat row — all with dog cages in the back — as if there were some kind of 'coon hunters' convention taking place nearby. The dogs were wailing and barking like crazy, disturbing anyone within earshot of the town square. That's how the women were tipped off about the whereabouts of their husbands. The sheriff had called one of the wives of the men, telling her that the hounds were making so much noise near the tavern that the prisoners in the jail were complaining.

I knew my dad was in trouble — man, did I know it — even at my young age. I watched as my mother approached the tavern with a power-walk move reserved for the Olympics. There was a big picture window in the tavern and I could tell by what I saw throughout the smoke-filled room that this was not going to end well.

There was my dad, dancing with some woman I had never seen before. Beside them, the neighbor lady's husband was cutting quite a rug with some floozy.

My mom was only five feet tall, but she burst through the door of the tavern like a ten-foot rocket. Within minutes, she had emptied the tavern, dragged Dad out by his ear, and returned the square to a state of peace and quiet. Done and done.

The 'coon dogs were sold off the next day by all of the men in the group.

As far as I know, none of those men ever made it out 'coon hunting again, although I'm sure they spent plenty of time, literally and figuratively, in the empty dog houses.

Priorities

I'll never forget when we traded in the oil lamps for electric lights. Oddly, it seemed to be a bigger deal for the farmer than for the homemaker, in our case.

A bulb hung down on a single wire from the ceiling in the living room, and that was the extent of the much anticipated, life-changing event for us. For the livestock out in the barn, however, living better electrically was all the rage. My dad strung a wire from the house to the barn to power a big light along with a radio the size of a suitcase. From that day forward, there was music at all times in the barn. Dad said it helped the cows give milk. I think he learned this trick from his dad, a veterinarian. Today, my animals enjoy the same luxury. There's a radio playing out in my barn right now, and my farm is home to some very contented cows.

My granddad, Henry Ashe, was a brilliant jack-of-all-trades, and was a quite an entrepreneur in his day. He did a little bit of everything to bring in an income, but farming and his veterinary practice were the most important. They just called him a "cow doctor" back in those days. Most people addressed him as "Mr. Henry" or "Doc" when they passed him on the street. We called him PaPa.

I traveled with Granddad throughout the county as he made his farm calls and watched him deliver calves and colts in every kind of situation imaginable. I was always amazed at how his work made such a difference and, for a while, I thought I wanted to be a veterinarian when I grew up. That is, until I met the sheriff.

A Little Boy's Hero

Wilson County Sheriff Howard Griffin was my dad's good friend and would drop by our house two or three times a week on his way home. The two buddies would sit on the porch if the weather permitted and talk about politics, tell old war stories, and generally shoot the bull like old buddies do to get their minds off the daily grind.

The sheriff always wore a neat jacket with a tie and drove a long, shiny, black patrol car. He charmed everyone with the mild-mannered goodness of a real Southern gentleman, juxtaposed with a rugged but business-like appearance.

He was only about 6 foot 2, but to a little boy, he seemed as tall as a mountain. He would come through the front door with a smile and a nod to all of us as he took off his hat — a hat that should have been white, because in my mind, he was the good guy I would see in the cowboy pictures whose goodness always overcame evil.

Just like in the movies, Sheriff Griffin carried his gun in a worn, brown holster, and I was intrigued by it; I always wanted to get an up-close look and maybe even a demonstration, but was too shy to ask, of course. I couldn't talk when I was around him; I could only manage to stare at this man I admired. He was doing what he loved, in the community he loved, and I wanted to be just like him.

His many visits to our home to sit on the porch with Dad were mighty powerful, and made all the difference in my life.

As fate would have it, I would grow up to share not only Sheriff Griffin's career choice, but another goal of this fine man: Sheriff Griffin had always said if the courthouse would let him, he could clean up Bluebird Road.

I didn't understand at my age what he meant by the "courthouse." I just remember that I couldn't grasp why my hero couldn't do anything he wanted to do since he was the high sheriff. As it turned out, the whole discussion of turning Bluebird Road into a safe neighborhood was moot for Sheriff Griffin.

He never got the chance.

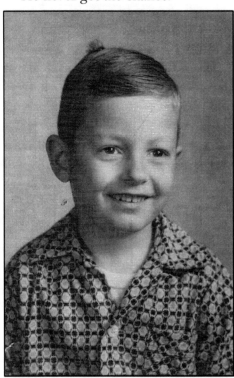

I was only six when Dad answered the old crank telephone one April night to learn that Sheriff Griffin, his closest friend, had been shot to death while serving a warrant.

It was the first of only three times I would see my dad cry. Domestic situations are the most dangerous for law enforcement, and I never responded to one in my career that I didn't think of how my hero died — not at the hands of a notorious outlaw, and not cornered in a shootout with robbers holding up a Wells Fargo truck. Sheriff Griffin was shot in the heart by a farmer who was angry because his estranged wife had come back to the house to retrieve her belongings.

Sheriff Griffin had accompanied Mary Jane McMillan to her house with a moving crew and an execution warrant, an order from the judge assigning certain pieces of property to the petitioner in the divorce. Mrs. McMillan had obtained this warrant in the legal separation for some of the couple's furniture and other small household items. The truck driver and his helper had the truck half full when Herbert McMillan started arguing about what his ex-wife was taking from the house.

As Sheriff Griffin pored over the papers to check the items listed in the warrant, McMillan pulled out at .25 caliber pistol and shot the Sheriff twice in the heart at close range.

It happened so quickly that the sheriff didn't have time to react. My hero died instantly and fell on the hearth in the bedroom of the farmhouse. McMillan then turned the gun on everyone else in the room, critically wounding his wife and shooting the driver of the truck in the leg.

All this carnage was witnessed by the couple's seven-year-old son, who ran to the neighbors next door for help. Pretending to be the caring husband, McMillan never left his wounded wife's side as he rode in the back of the ambulance he had calmly called following the shooting spree. He was arrested and booked upon arrival at the hospital.

It was the third time Sheriff Griffin had been to this home with Mrs. McMillan to get her belongings, and there had been conflict between husband and wife each time. When the sheriff left his house with the warrant that evening, he told his wife, Rosalind, that he "intended to see about it for the last time." Prophetic words from a lawman and husband headed out to serve the last warrant of his life. He was only 40 years old and left behind a wife and three sons who depended on him; his retirement was only a few months away.

Death With Retirement Near

—Photos by Leslie Power
WATERTOWN, Tenn.—Sheriff Harold Griffin lies sprawled on the hearth of a farm house, his pistol still in his holster, after he was killed by a single shot through the heart from the pistol of Herbert McMillan.

Photo courtesy *The Lebanon Democrat*

All the heartache, all the loss, all the sadness — launched, it was later reported, when Mrs. McMillan took some inexpensive jelly glasses the farmer claimed belonged to him. My mentor, Sheriff Harold Griffin, was dead because he was caught in the most dangerous place on earth — that tedious, unrelenting space between a feuding husband and wife. A photograph of the sheriff lying dead on the floor of that farmhouse was printed in the newspaper the next morning under the headline, "Death With Retirement Near." It's certainly not the type of photograph that would be seen in modern newspapers, sensibilities and sensitivities being what they are today, and that's a good thing. Seeing that photograph of my hero lying dead — his gun untouched in that old, brown, leather holster — really affected me as a child. Just realizing that he never had a chance to defend himself against his assassin hurt me deeply.

Sheriff Harold Griffin would never know what an impact he made in my life.

Before the funeral services for Sheriff Griffin were to begin at Round Lick Baptist Church that following Thursday, prisoners at the county jail expressed their wish to pay respects. With Mrs. Griffin's consent, the funeral home brought the casket to the jail where the tearful prisoners had a viewing and final tribute of their own.

Herbert McMillan was found to be insane and was never tried for his crime, but spent the rest of his life confined to Central State Mental Hospital in Nashville. Mary Jane McMillan never walked again; her husband's bullet had pierced her spine.

The sheriff's 35-year-old wife, Rosalind, expressed her desire to serve out the rest of her husband's unexpired term, and she was approved unanimously.

Since Sheriff Griffin was such a good friend to our family and a strong influence in my life, it was an honor for me that many years later, Rosalind publicly endorsed me in my first run for sheriff of Wilson County in 1982.

It was the strongest endorsement of the campaign for any candidate, and it meant more to me than anyone will ever know.

Dad

During WWII, my dad served with the First Marine Division near Guadalcanal. Like many men of his generation, he came home after serving his country to work in a factory, and he tried to supplement his meager paycheck with income from our small dairy farm.

He was not against taking a little drink now and then, and would stop on the way home after work to pick up a pint from a bootlegger along Bluebird Road. Wilson County was dry back in those days, so anyone who was selling booze of any kind was doing so illegally and making a killing. The counties around the area were also dry, so the out-of-town trade was substantial.

Whiskey was cheap, and suppliers would go either to Nashville or out of state to purchase the booze, then smuggle it to Bluebird Road to sell to working men. Some of those customers, like my dad, only wanted a little sip or two to relax after work. Others made an entire evening of the booze run and were almost never at home with their families. I was so fortunate that Dad was not among that group.

Dad worked at Vultee, an airplane manufacturing facility near the airport in Nashville, in the same building where AVCO is now located. In an effort to economize, as many commuters still do today, Dad would travel down Bluebird Road, park his car, and catch a ride with other workers going from Lebanon to Nashville.

There were no interstate highways back then, and travel to and from Nashville was by Highway 70 — a winding, two-lane, back road that was being widened to accommodate the heavy traffic.

One morning, road construction had the highway blocked and traffic was at a standstill, bumper to bumper, at the worst possible time of day — even for that era. Dad needed a restroom in the worst way and couldn't wait until he arrived at the factory, whenever that was going to be. He got out of the car and was just about to cross the road when he was struck by a vehicle passing the long line of traffic in the other lane.

He was rushed to General Hospital, where he was immediately pronounced dead on arrival and taken to the morgue. Hospital personnel scrambled to find his next of kin. My grandfather, PaPa Ashe, was the emergency contact the hospital called first, and he headed to Nashville before notifying my mother about what had happened.

When he ran into the hospital, PaPa was in shock and demanded to see the body before he could believe the news that his son had passed away. The doctors were reluctant to allow him in the morgue, which was strictly for medical personnel only, but this grief-stricken father was relentless in his quest until he got his way.

He stepped inside the grim room to spend a quiet moment and gather his thoughts; he would tell us later that, at that point, so many questions were running through his mind, but the most taxing of all was, how was he going to tell his daughter-in-law her husband had been killed? How would he break it to his two little grandsons that they would never see their father again?

As he looked down upon the sheet-draped gurney holding his son's body, PaPa whispered a prayer and reached out to grasp his boy's hand one last time.

The sheet *moved.*

He stood still and held his breath, trying to focus his eyes, not quite understanding what he was seeing in the dim light of the cold hospital morgue.

The sheet moved *again.*

PaPa ran out into the hall looking for a doctor — anyone he could find to confirm his findings — and within minutes, Dad was wheeled into a treatment room where nurses rushed in to hook him up to diagnostic equipment, I.V. fluids, and a respirator. My dad was now listed among the living.

For the next 122 days, Dad was in a coma as a result of his severe head injury, and I didn't think my brother and I would ever be allowed to visit him.

When Mom finally let us go to the hospital, it was so traumatic that I remember wishing I had not been allowed to see him like that. I was too young to handle it. That image of my dad, so helpless and lifeless, hooked up to all those machines and tubes, stayed locked in my mind for months after I got home.

We would go to visit him in the hospital every weekend after that, only to sit there and watch him sleep for hours. Mom drove to Nashville to see him every day, then rushed back home to feed us, help us feed the animals, take care of the farm, and try to make ends meet.

The woman who ran over Dad with her car had no insurance of any kind. We had nowhere to turn financially. It helped my mother to be near her husband, but it was a terribly painful time for my brother and me. We were used to seeing our young, strong, dad out working on the farm or laughing and playing with us on the lawn. It didn't make sense to us that he could now be so weak and so helpless, lying there in that hospital bed.

My Father, My Protector

If Dad had been there with us, I'm confident that I would have shared with him a secret I've had to carry around with me until the night before this book went to the publisher. Along with my admiration of Sheriff Harold Griffin, I believe a traumatic encounter on the town square when I was only ten years old served to cement my desire to become sheriff.

One summer afternoon, my mom brought me in to town and dropped me off at the barber shop which was at that time, located near the historic log cabin on the square in Lebanon. She gave me just enough change for a haircut and a soda and told me to meet her at a certain time at a store down the street. Back in those days, parents were more likely to leave their older children to their own devices in the city as they did their grocery shopping and ran their weekday errands. Feeling every bit the man of the house without Dad around, I climbed up in the chair and told the barber to give me a "Mohawk," as popular a haircut for teenagers back then – as it is for some of the more rebellious teens of today. Feeling on top of the world with my new look, I left the barber shop to walk around the square and treat myself to an ice cream soda while I waited for Mom to finish her shopping.

I was making my way around the square and crossing in front of the old pool hall, which was beside a vacant "stairwell to nowhere," from some store that had burned on an upper floor. As I passed the stairwell, a young man approached me; his cigarettes rolled up in his dirty tee-shirt, his hair greased back to a slick duck-tail.

"Come with me, kid, I wanna show you something," he said, as he motioned for me to come into the dark stairwell. In one motion, he pulled me toward him with one hand, while pulling a switch blade out of his pocket and holding it to my throat with the other.

"One word outta you and I'll slit your damn throat," he warned as he reached into the pocket of my jeans and pulled out the pitiful contents: thirty five cents and my prized pocket knife I had carried with me on the farm throughout my childhood.

"You tell anybody and I'll track you down and kill you and all your people. You got that?"

Numb and almost hyperventilating, I nodded in agreement. I had no intention of going to the police if it meant my mom or brother would be hurt. When he released me from his grip, I ran to the opposite side of the square to get as far away from him as possible. I couldn't decide whether to cry or throw up. I do remember being simply terrified, along with feeling violated and angry at the same time.

I was now a victim of an armed robbery –a label I would wear forever. But I was lucky. Sadly, in this day and time, a child in that situation would have been assaulted in other ways and probably wouldn't be alive to tell about it.

I had no intention of telling my mother what had happened to me. I just knew the guy would make good on his promise if I did, and it just wasn't worth the risk. I would have told my dad if he had been healthy and at home with us. He'd know what to do. He wouldn't have been afraid of that pimply-faced teenaged thug and he would have been there to protect us no matter what the consequences. But dad wasn't there. I was on my own.

Perhaps if I had told Mom about what happened, she would have felt sorry for me and taken pity on me when she stopped to pick me up at our appointed meeting place. Mom took one look at the Mohawk and had a fit. She snatched me up by one arm — I don't think my feet touched the ground — and marched me back to the barber shop to demand a G.I. haircut.

In less than an hour, I had been threatened with a deadly weapon, robbed, and then publicly humiliated at the barber shop, but that dreadful afternoon served a purpose in my life. Not only did it cement a law enforcement career in my mind, but today I can approach a victim of crime with the sensitivity and compassion of a person who has experienced that awful feeling of helplessness.

Thirty years later, wearing my sheriff's badge, a more normal haircut, and a big gun, I made an arrest in a brutal armed robbery. Before me in the booking room stood a meaner, tattooed, time-worn, old thug whose beady eyes I recognized from that afternoon in the abandoned stairwell.

The creep died in prison never knowing that the sheriff who arrested him for his last crime was also one of his victims.

Life had come full circle for both of us.

Our Changing World

Around 1957, as my father lingered in a vegetative state, it became apparent that my mother couldn't run the farm on sheer willpower alone. She tried, but it was too much — even for a strong, determined woman like her.

I was only a fifth grader, but even I could see we couldn't avoid the inevitable. There simply wasn't enough money coming in to keep us afloat, and we were going to lose our family farm. Everything we had worked for, everything we loved, would soon be gone with the crack of an auctioneer's gavel.

I remember Mom talking to someone on the old crank telephone one evening as we were at the table doing our homework. She was telling the person on the other end of the line that she didn't know what we were going to do — that her husband was unconscious in the hospital in Nashville, and she was trying to raise two little boys with no income. She had tears in her eyes. I knew our lives were about to change, but I had no idea how drastic those changes would be.

When we finally did have to put the house up for sale, my brother and I were farmed out to live with aunts, uncles and cousins as Mom tried to look for work and find us a decent place to live.

When I say "farmed out," I mean that term quite literally. All of our relatives had farms, and they took turns working my brother and me as though we were the strong new field hands. But that was a good thing. They paid us for our work, and that's how we bought our school clothes and supplies for the next three years.

I was in pain throughout the whole process. I missed the animals and the land and the smell of fresh cut hay. I missed the old red barn, and I longed to fish in the creek again. Most of all, I missed lying in my own cozy bed, listening to the frogs in the pond and the crickets outside the window at night. When we lived with relatives, my brother and I had to sleep on quilts on the living room floor. It wasn't that bad, because we knew we were with family who loved us and were sharing their lives and everything they had with us, so we dared not complain.

As the months passed and we were no closer to returning to our mother and our farm, we knew the storybook days of our childhood were gone forever.

The day we had to pack up our belongings at the farm and move into a 4-room rental house in the city was traumatic for all of us. There was quite an adjustment to be made to the close quarters. A tiny kitchen, living room, one bedroom, and one shower stall had to be home for the three of us for the time being.

I was able to bring my dog, Trigger, and that helped me make the difficult transition from country to city life. I only wish he had been given a chance to adjust.

As we were just beginning to settle in to city life ourselves, we had to keep Trigger chained outside — something he never had to endure and couldn't begin to understand. As he tried to make sense of what had become of his good life, his barking apparently became annoying to some of the neighbors. They poisoned Trigger.

On that day, I experienced a heartache that couldn't be named. I put all of my built-up sadness, anger and frustration into mourning the death of this innocent little creature, which had become a victim of circumstances just as I had been.

With him went the last vestige of life on the farm: hours of fetch and running through the corn field playing hide and seek, and sunny days of carefree freedom that I thought would never end.

It seemed so wrong as I sat on the back steps and cried; Trigger wasn't there to lick my tears away as he had been so many times before when I had skinned my knees or gotten a spanking, or any of the dozens of times I had cried over things which now seemed so unimportant.

I couldn't help but think he would still be alive if only we had been able to stay on the farm where we were all loved and accepted for who we were. This adjustment was going to be so difficult, on so many levels, and it had just been made more taxing for me now, since I had lost my best friend.

Someone taking one of the only good things I had left in this sadistic, thoughtless way, was just a small taste of what I would witness later in life: the limitless cruelty of the more unsavory and ignorant elements in society.

The Long Road Ahead

Times had changed in so many harsh ways for us. My brother and I had gone from playing in wide open spaces to sharing a tiny living room sofa at night. Once, there was plenty of farm fresh milk and all the eggs we could eat for breakfast. Now, we were pouring hot water on our cereal as Mom tried to stretch her meager income from paycheck to paycheck.

I was turning eleven and was old enough to realize that even if Dad regained consciousness and was moved into a nursing facility from the hospital, it was not necessarily a sign of progress for any of us. My dad would never be home again and there was nothing we could do about that.

One Saturday, we were at Dad's bedside with his favorite cousin, Ford, and some other members of the family. We were chatting among ourselves as we always did when, out of the blue, my dad spoke and said, "Is that you, Ford?"

My dad had come back to us — albeit in a very small way. He was soon moved to the Veterans' Administration Hospital where he would spend the next 31 years, partially paralyzed and with a limited ability to communicate.

He died in that place due to complications from Crohn's Disease.

Joe Ashe was a decorated war hero, a brave man who was wounded while fighting for his country in World War II, only to come home and suffer like this, cut down in the prime of his life.

I don't think I was ever able to completely process the unfairness of it all.

There's one thing I have processed, and that is, so much loss at one time changed me. Losing the family farm and everything we owned, then mourning my dad at such a young age made me more compassionate for those who lose people they love. It breaks my heart to hear about people losing homes they've worked hard for all their lives.

I've walked a mile in those shoes, and today, when I hear a story on the news about orphaned, homeless or hungry children, it strikes a chord deep within me and brings all those old feelings to the surface.

Sergeant Joe Ashe, United States Marine Corps, 1943

Sergeant Terry Ashe, United States Army, 1968

CHAPTER TWO

There was certainly no money for college when I graduated from high school.

Besides, there was still that thing called the draft that all 18-year-old boys had to think about in those days. With the escalation of the fighting in Vietnam, the writing was on the wall; I was going to follow in my father's footsteps and go to war.

I was sent to Southeast Asia on a hot day in August, 1967, aboard a TWA commercial jet which was contracted to carry troops in and out of the region, along with a handful of civilians who had business there for whatever reason. It was a twenty-hour flight, and we began our descent over the coastline of South Vietnam at four o'clock in the morning.

There were about 150 to 200 people on board, and as land came into view ahead, you could have heard a pin drop in the eerie quiet of the cabin. Those of us in uniform were too overwhelmed to say much, and the civilians were just too tired to stir around after the long flight. As we came closer to the coastline, the captain turned off all of the cabin lights to ensure that the approaching plane wouldn't be an easy target for the enemy. I remember exactly where I was sitting — over the left wing in the window seat.

Everything was dark, but as I pressed my forehead against the glass for a closer look, I was able to figure out which way was east.

The black of the sky was turning into a light gray, melting into an almost yellow glow as the sun was coming up. It looked like a postcard. Absolutely beautiful.

I didn't realize it at the time, but we were descending quite rapidly. I've been in a lot of planes, and I haven't seen a jet prepare to land quite like this since. As the clouds parted, it became apparent why the pilot was in such a hurry.

Hundreds of flashes of light glittered as we got closer to the runway, and it occurred to me that those flashes were from a full-out war that was going on below, and I was about to be a part of that war, like it or not.

For every little flash of light I saw, I had to squint because the bursts were very bright, like flashes from an old camera. It gave me a very strange feeling. As the plane got directly over the war-torn area, I remember thinking that from this distance, the flickering lights reminded me of the little fireflies I used to collect in a jar as a child. My brother and I would be thrilled to look outside after supper and see the "lightnin' bugs" flying all around our front yard in the summer.

Oh, to be in a time machine instead of this plane at this moment, to be able to travel back to those summer nights with my brother on the farm when we didn't have worries and when we were still just playful little boys. So many thoughts like that were drifting in and out of my mind as I sat there and gazed at the exploding landscape below — a sign that American soldiers and our allies were under fierce attack.

When we were just about fifty miles from the Bien Hoa airstrip, I was amazed at the size of the explosions from this angle. It was my first experience with war.

My mind drifted home again. The sky was lighting up with all this activity, just as it had on the June nights in Tennessee when the big thunderstorms would roll through.

A chill went over me and I came back to the present as I heard the wheel wells open and the pilot prepared to land. I was really frightened. All of my training, all of my talk, all of my courage would be tested from this moment forward.

I was in Vietnam, my home for the foreseeable future.

Before today, I couldn't have spelled one word in the Vietnamese language, to save my life. That was certainly about to change.

The pilot asked the flight attendant to prepare for landing, just as he would on any other flight. Other than his voice over the intercom, and the roar of the jet engines, there was not another sound — only a deafening silence as some of us stared out the window with mouths agape, while others looked at the ceiling as if in prayer.

Back in those days, cigarette smoking was allowed on board commercial jets and there were a lot of guys doing just that. The air was white with smoke until the "no smoking" sign went on, and we buckled our seat belts and prepared to land in a war zone. The pilot spoke through the intercom again, but this time, he was addressing those of us in uniform.

"Gentlemen, you are about to land in Vietnam. It's very hot here this morning, not only from the heat, but because this airstrip is under attack."

He informed us that we were being directed to circle the airfield until our troops could make it safe for us to land. His voice seemed very matter-of-fact, as if he were telling us that Hartsfield in Atlanta was experiencing heavy traffic or something.

All of a sudden, the reality of the situation hit me like a rock.

A choking sensation came over me. This is it. My mouth was dry. I was so thirsty. I had on a short sleeve khaki uniform, and I had sweated through and pitted out the shirt in just a few short minutes. I was having some kind of panic attack.

The pilot spoke to us over the intercom again in his calm, soothing voice. This time, he wanted to introduce himself. All I remember is that he was Captain ... such and such ... I don't recall. My mind was on other things. He told us he would be landing the jet in another 5 minutes. Another five *hours* of flight time would've been fine with me.

In an effort to assure us that this was going to eventually be a safe round trip for all of us, the captain related that his civilian crew had flown in and out of Vietnam safely many times, adding that he would be praying for us and our safe return to America.

The captain closed his remarks by saying, "God bless you all."

At that moment, flashing lights and flares could be seen from every window of the aircraft and practically lit up the interior of the cabin.

The plane's tires made that familiar screeching noise as we touched down on the airstrip with a thud. With that, the pilot was back on the intercom with the same calm voice, but with more disturbing news: air traffic controllers had warned that the airfield was under rocket attack, and passengers needed to exit the plane as quickly as possible and in an orderly fashion. To me, this begged the question, how does one exit a plane in an orderly fashion as a rocket is bearing down on one's head?

The plane stopped and the door flew open. The ground crew hurriedly pushed the stairway up to the door and we jammed the aisles to exit. The flight attendant had tears rolling down her cheeks as she touched each man on the arm and made eye contact with him as he reached the door.

I've often wondered what was on her mind. Did she have a boyfriend or husband already there in Vietnam fighting for our country? Was her sister a nurse in a M.A.S.H. unit here? Had she lost a brother in Vietnam? She was showing so much love and concern to each of us.

She would never see any of us again. She had never met any of us before this day, but her simple gesture reminded us of our mothers, our sisters, and our wives at home. She helped us remember all of our families, all of our loved ones for whom we were fighting.

When I stepped out of the air-conditioned plane onto the steep steps leading to the tarmac, the hot air hit me in the face and took my breath away. It was still very dark, very early in the morning, but I could just make out to the left of me a sea of green duffel bags which had been dumped from beneath the belly of the plane onto the runway.

As we all made our way down the steps, a sergeant on a bullhorn was screaming at us to *hurry the hell up* with every four letter word he could manage.

In the heartbeat that the last boot hit the tarmac, the jet engines roared and the 747 was ready to take off and fly out of harm's way. I watched as it taxied on the runway with its door still open. The door slowly began to close and the light inside the plane became smaller and smaller — a slit in the darkness. It was like a waning moon, symbolic of the last little bit of light and freedom, leaving us all behind.

Meanwhile, the screaming sergeant was sounding more nervous as the seconds passed: "Grab your duffel bags! Grab your duffel bags! Follow me!"

The first order we were being given upon arrival in Vietnam was easier said than done. The duffel bags were identical: olive drab green, our last names stenciled in small letters on the outside. As the irritated commander was barking, more than one hundred and fifty GI's were nervously scrambling and scratching around the pile in 112 degree heat, in the dark, looking for the one bag belonging to them.

In the middle of the duffel bag rush, we began to take rocket fire. Some of the guys attempted to seek cover under the pile of bags while the sergeant continued to bark into that damn bullhorn about what dumb asses we all were.

I was relieved to watch the safe take-off of the TWA jet that had left us in this place. For a minute, I thought of the tearful flight attendant and again wondered about the story behind her emotional goodbye.

The sun was finally making its appearance through all the haze as a big red ball in the sky. It lit the smoke clouds from where the rockets had struck on the horizon. Machine gun fire was all around us and getting closer and louder. Scrambling to the safety of the hangar, I glanced down at the duffel bag I had grabbed in all the confusion and, of course, it wasn't mine.

So this was my "Good Morning Vietnam," as the sun rose on a new chapter in my life. I was only one of one hundred fifty young men, scared to death, thousands of miles from home, running on the tarmac to escape machine gun fire while lugging a big, heavy bag belonging to a soldier whose name I couldn't pronounce.

Little did I know that my experiences here would shape my future and the way I would view living and dying for the rest of my life.

Tam Ky November 1967

Number Two

After what happened to me on my second day in Vietnam, I would no longer stare at a clock on the wall in some air-conditioned office cubicle, wishing for five o'clock. Twenty-four hours after landing in Vietnam, I had begun to question why the Army's adage had always been "hurry up and wait."

In my experience so far, there had been a lot of hurrying but no time — absolutely no time — to wait.

By now, we had sorted out the whole duffel bag thing, had shed our khaki uniforms, and donned our jungle fatigues and combat boots. This would be our fashion statement for the next year. All of our personal items had been taken from us and put in a locker at the airstrip. Our commanders did have the courtesy to remind us that our stuff would be safely stored for us until the day we left Vietnam — either on foot or in a metal box. This was our first taste of the gallows humor that permeated this atmosphere.

After very little sleep we apprehensively loaded up onto a couple of dirty, dusty, baking hot, old busses, not knowing where we were headed. Would we be going to the front lines this soon? Were we not going to be given at least a day or two to get used to the idea of being shot at?

The ride along the bumpy, country road took about an hour. Sad, poorly constructed, little shacks with rusty tin roofs lined the trail and reminded me of the poorest of the poor up in the mountains of East Tennessee.

As I sat crushed up against the bus window, I was watching this depressing scenery fly by and observing what kind of civilization this was. So poverty-ridden. So backward. These people had absolutely nothing.

We had chicken houses on our farm that were built better than some of these houses that large Vietnamese families shared.

Some children were pushing an old tin can around with a stick, and I wondered how many of them would live to see another birthday. These were just innocent kids playing in the street — babies who didn't understand this war or the politics behind it.

Perhaps the same thing could have been said about a few of us kids wearing the camouflage and the helmets.

We turned onto a road that took us to an army holding area about twenty miles from the airstrip. For a war zone, this place was hospital quiet. There were a few soldiers standing around dragging on their cigarettes and whispering conversations, but that was about it. Our bus pulled up alongside a high barbed-wire fence, and I looked over the hillside where rows of old wooden barracks were barely standing alongside deep trenches washed by heavy rains. I would later learn that those deep trenches made for good cover during a rocket or mortar attack.

These boys were going home. Some of them wore medals and ribbons on their chests, a proud testimony as to what they had accomplished on their tour of duty.

We pulled up in front of the barracks alongside a battle-weary group of fully uniformed soldiers, eagerly waiting to climb on board. The bus would be taking them to the Bien Hoa airstrip, the same field where we had landed the day before.

You could see the look of joy and relief on their faces as the bus came to a stop and we piled out.

As they climbed aboard, some of them began to look back and laugh and make fun of us, telling us the best troopers had already been killed and they were leaving our green asses alone out there. They called us *cherries*, and told us we weren't going to make it.

They were right; we were cherries. Some of us *weren't* going to make it.

I'll never forget the feeling I had in the pit of my stomach as I watched that busload of soldiers disappear around the curve in the dirt road, bound for the airstrip to reclaim that locker full of their personal belongings. They were healthy, on foot, and headed for freedom. It was like watching that TWA plane take off again — that lonely, homesick feeling that a child gets on his first day of school when momma waves goodbye.

Now that all of my worldly possessions could fit into one small duffel bag, I placed them in the barracks and began to settle in — for exactly what, I didn't know. Within a few minutes I would find out. There was not a lot of waiting around at this place.

The sergeant called out for a roster check, so we fell into formation and stood at attention.

"How many of you here are paratroopers?" The sergeant never took his eyes off his clipboard when he asked the question, as if he already knew the exact number.

Out of the two busloads of us arriving at this holding area, only about fifteen of us were actually airborne certified infantry. We proudly stepped forward like the elite group we were. Sarge had us take our place to one side, like star athletes being chosen to play for the big team or something.

While we were standing there at attention, all full of ourselves and imagining what special, high-flying, airborne assault assignment awaited the elite fifteen, our leader announced to the entire group that the 101st airborne division was getting the shit kicked out of it up North, and we would be the first to leave in the morning to help them.

The minute I heard this, you probably couldn't have driven a greasy nail up my ass with a sledgehammer. That's Tennessee lingo for, I was scared.

For the first time, it occurred to me that I might be shot at and might not survive the next twenty-four hours.

Bunker at Camp Evans, Vietnam, 1968

In the next breath, the sergeant ordered us to report to him in thirty minutes for a detail before chow. It was already chow time in my book. It was high noon, dry and hot, and I was starving. Some of my comrades were falling out as they succumbed to the heat; others might have passed out from fright — or from hunger if they felt as I did.

Our small group of paratroopers was loaded into a truck and dropped off near some tattered old outhouses scattered around the base. None of us had a clue as to what all this was about, but we were beginning to think that perhaps God didn't like paratroopers. Beside each outhouse stood a soldier ready to bark orders for the work detail that was about to ensue. Suddenly it occurred to me why the sergeant had asked for paratroopers instead of volunteers; one of the first things you learn in boot camp is, *never volunteer for anything.* Sergeants know we're on to them. They work around it.

Our assignment was to dispose of the human waste inside these rickety wooden buildings — evil ancestors to the outhouse I had grown up with. While we only had a two-holer outhouse on the farm, this facility was built to accommodate a brigade of butts. Under the holes, a 55-gallon drum had been cut in half and placed on its side to collect the waste. Once this container was full to overflowing, it had to be emptied, and this, the sergeant felt, was the perfect job for brave, highly trained and uniquely skilled paratroopers.

The containers had to be pulled from the outhouses, topped with diesel fuel, set on fire, stirred, and burned again. This disgusting ritual had to be repeated multiple times until every last bit of crap had disintegrated.

This detail, the first work detail I would ever experience as a paratrooper, served a good purpose (as it turned out). I knew as I stood there, watching this smelly shit burn, and burn, and burn, that this was my *guarantee* that nothing worse was going to happen to me the rest of the day. Not many people wake up in the morning with that kind of confidence.

Don't talk to me about shit jobs. I don't think I ate for a couple of days after that.

Tet Offensive, January 1968

I didn't get a wink of sleep that night. It's not that I wasn't totally exhausted from that awful work detail, but the explosions and machine gun fire in the distance were something I just couldn't tune out. The sounds of war raging in your ears when you're used to crickets and bullfrogs is not an easy adjustment. I could see the faraway flares in the darkness, and sometimes the explosions would be so intense that they would light up the inside of the barracks.

I learned later that the flares we had heard throughout the night were all around our compound as the Vietcong probed our defenses.

Before I knew it, it was time to roll out of bed and fall into formation so Sergeant could bark in our ears once again. He began to call our names from a list, putting us with the different units of the 101st Airborne Division we would be assigned to.

"Pfc. Henry T. Ashe, you're going to A-Troop, 2nd 17th Cav, 101st Airborne Division."

You might say that's the last thing I remember before a huge helicopter swooped in and picked up all of our equipment and our rifles. We climbed into the chopper, and in one mad rush we were flying north, up the coast of Vietnam.

I don't recall much of what happened after that, but I will say this: that day of battle lasted *all day*.

Yea, though I walk through the valley of the shadow of death I will fear no evil; for thou art with me. Thy rod and thy staff they comfort me.

Psalms 23:4

June 6, 1968

This is going to be a hard chapter to write, but I'm going to try to put June 6, 1968 into perspective.

In the previous ten months, I had seen and done so much killing, and so many of my friends had died right in front of me from August to June that it almost numbed me. We were all dealing with the oppressive heat in the jungle, carrying six canteens at a time just to make sure we had enough water. It's amazing what the human body can adjust to; sometimes the human mind takes longer.

Like every other soldier out there, letters from home were very important to me. I know it's hard for anyone under the age of thirty to imagine, but back then, there were no emails or text messages — only handwritten letters from loved ones back home, if you were lucky.

The letters from home helped bring me back to reality since I felt so far removed from the rest of the world out there in the jungle. It's easy to become hardened and cynical. In fact, cynicism becomes a way of life for the soldier in battle. *Kill or be killed* is the mantra.

When guys would get killed right in front of us, we would all bump fists and repeat the phrase, "don't mean nothing... don't mean nothing." But of course it *did* mean something. It meant everything. Our fraternity-like reaction to the deaths of our buddies was a way of masking the pain and devastation, and moving forward with the mission we had to accomplish at that moment.

At best, you can gain a great deal of faith going through something like this, but you can also lose your innocence and perspective as it relates to what is valuable and what is not.

The last few years or so, I've been in contact with the families of some of my buddies who were killed in Vietnam. These were guys who were killed in my presence, maybe even died in my arms. As I look back on these horrible days, I just don't understand how we took comfort, even temporarily, in saying it didn't mean anything. The phrase, "don't mean nothing," just doesn't ring true once you're away from the front lines.

With soldiers returning to the real world after their tour in Vietnam, and with so many being killed every day, there was turnover all the time. The "cherries," as we called them, were always showing up to replace someone who had been wounded or killed a day or two before, and that was a hard adjustment.

It got to the point, for me anyway, that I just didn't even want to be friendly with these new guys. If I did get to know them — learning personal things about them and their families back home — and then something happened to them, it hurt so much more. You tend to build a wall around yourself emotionally because you witness too much pain every single day.

I survived the first Tet Offensive and four other ambushes in which there were untold casualties. Song Be City was the scene of a horrible firefight near a remote place in the jungle. It was terrible. I lost so many friends in such a short period of time. Quang Tri, Dak To, Camp Evans, Camp Eagle. There were so many battles it seemed as though I was never going to get back, even to the rear of Vietnam. They just kept the 101st Airborne Division out there on the front line day in and day out. We were airmobile, so we could be transported anywhere to engage in a fight with any other Army or Marine Corps units in a moment's notice.

The 'A' Troop 17th Cavalry was a scout recon unit of the 101st Airborne Division. We could be running a convoy with gun Jeeps one day and be airborne and in a helicopter the next, landing in a hot zone doing reconnaissance or going in to relieve some other unit. This was an amazing strike force unit that I had been assigned to.

Forty-seven people were killed in our unit, and around 270 were wounded. I read recently that our unit certainly fought back successfully; it was responsible for killing more than 873 Vietcong. We saw a lot of combat.

But the date that stands out in my mind, more than any other, is the day my life was changed forever.

By June, 1968, I was a sergeant. At twenty years old, it was my job to lead men into combat. Actually, if I had been in my thirties, I would have been considered an old man by the troops, so I was a typical sergeant at twentyish. It certainly wasn't like the Afghan or Iraq wars, in which men and women in their forties and fifties are well into their second tour of duty. I was just another kid growing up too fast in a leadership position in hell.

Since the first of June, we had been running convoys around Monkey and Marble Mountain and all through the northern part of Vietnam where the fighting was so heavy. On a daily basis, our convoys were either ambushed from the jungle or blasted by land mines which lined the roads.

So many of our troops were either wounded or killed, or were being sent home at the end of their tour during that time, and replacements had to be brought in weekly to fill positions. In the scout gun vehicle that I commanded, I had to find a replacement for the gunner since the previous one had fulfilled his tour of duty. I also had to replace the driver because he was transferred to another unit.

I was quickly training these replacements so they would be ready for the next mission coming up in just days. These two guys had not been "in country" very long, but had already experienced a baptism by fire, so to speak. Their gun Jeep had been ambushed, their commander killed right in front of them.

Michael Bia (pronounced by-yah) was the new gunner — a shy, quiet young man of American Indian descent. He grew up on a reservation in Window Rock, Arizona, and was highly ranked in national bull riding competitions. Michael was married to the love of his life, and not a day went by that he didn't find time to write a letter to his young bride, Lula, or his beloved mother. His dark, sparkling eyes had a wide-open alertness and kindness to them. I never heard a foul word from his mouth the entire time we worked together.

My new driver was Samuel Boyd, a mild-mannered but wisecracking African-American from northern New Jersey. His great sense of humor and fun kept me laughing and boosted everyone's spirits. He didn't speak that much of his family, although from our conversations, I gathered he was raised by a single mom. Samuel had a good attitude about life and didn't wear the misfortunes of his childhood on his sleeve and, like Michael, was one of those rare soldiers who never uttered a curse word or used blue language.

The only complaints I ever heard from Samuel were when he groused about how tight his boots were and how his corns and calluses hurt. But even his griping was in the spirit of good humor, and I couldn't help but appreciate that.

As we shared stories of how we grew up, my world expanded. I had been shipped from the farm to the little city of Lebanon, Tennessee, then to the jungle, and didn't have a clue as to how people lived in New York or out West. I only knew what I had seen in the movies. But I had them at a disadvantage too; I'm sure neither of those boys had ever caught crawdads or cured country hams, so I held their interest as I regaled them with tales of life on the farm.

Bia and Boyd had only been with me a short time, but they looked up to me and hung on my every word when it came to the job we were doing. They trusted my judgment since I had already been through so much on my tour of duty.

On June fifth, our unit escorted a convoy and had some heavy contact with the enemy. We finally got out of that mess and were able to set up camp about eleven o'clock that night. We circled our gun Jeeps the way they used to circle the wagons in the cowboy days. We took turns staying up to keep watch, although I don't think those of us who were supposed to be sleeping caught one wink in that atmosphere.

The next day when we rolled out of bed at three A.M., we were told that we were going to be taking a convoy of ammo, food, and other supplies deeper into enemy territory up North, where the heaviest fighting was still going on. The company commander called all of the sergeants together and told us that we would be taking this convoy beyond where any American troops had ventured — to an out-of-the-way base run by the Navy and the Marines.

It goes without saying, but I'll admit this in writing anyway: I was scared out of my wits at the thought of blazing the trail through VC territory. *Again.*

I had seen so much already that my mindset before convoys had become fatalistic: *if it's your time to go it's your time to go*; and the other cliché, *if there's a bullet out there with your name on it, there's nothing you can do about it.*

I thought I had become mercifully numb to the idea of walking around like a target, but feelings of apprehension were starting to come back to my brain with a rush.

Michael and Samuel were frightened — I sensed that — and I had to be strong for them. They respected me and they couldn't see me sweat if I was going to be effective as their commander. They had only been in country six weeks at the most, and when you're that green, you look up to your sergeant and take all of your cues from him. In their minds, if I was still here after so many dangerous missions, I must know something about survival. I didn't have the heart to tell them I was still alive by the grace of the Man upstairs and what I knew, or didn't know, had nothing to do with it.

We were loading the ammo and the supplies into the gun Jeeps to prepare for our journey when the captain's voice came over the radio. My radio call sign then was "Shadow Man One-Six," a moniker I had picked up from running night ambushes when I first got to Vietnam. The captain ordered me to report to the command center immediately to go over strategy for the mission.

The meeting started with the words no soldier wants to hear, especially from a captain who has been at war for so long: "This is going to be a dangerous operation today, Sergeant." The captain looked straight into my eyes as he said it.

It was as though he wanted to make damn sure I understood what the day held. It couldn't have been clearer to me — a convoy led by scouts, going deep into enemy territory, carrying ammo and food. We were going to be like lambs staked out for lion bait.

"Ashe, you're going to be the lead vehicle."

Just when I thought the news couldn't get any worse. I didn't feel good about this at all. Why would he choose us to lead the convoy?

"The reason you're going to be the lead vehicle is that you're the senior NCO and you've been north before." He answered my unspoken question as though he could read my mind.

"We'll be going through Hue-Phu Bai, which is still partially occupied by the North Vietnamese, and we're going to go all the way through to this isolated Navy Seabee compound. There's a certain speed we're going to have to keep up to get through there, because this could really be a bad time."

It seemed the captain was going out of his way to underscore the danger of this mission.

We ended our meeting and I headed back to the Jeep to "mount up," as we called it in cavalry terms. As we all took our positions and began our journey, not a word was spoken. Michael, Samuel and I were simply too nervous to carry on a conversation.

During this abnormally quiet ride, I had myriad things going on in my mind as we led a two-mile-long convoy of trucks up dusty old Highway One. I was wondering how I got back to this highway again. This was where I had led so many of the night raids as a machine gunner when I first got to Vietnam. It was hot, sticky, and dusty, but I preferred this to the darkness when the bugs would fly into my mouth as I fired off ammo rounds into the dense jungle. In the heat of battle, I didn't even have time to spit them out. I soon found myself comparing the different tastes of the insects as they collided with my tongue. It's funny that I would think of the bugs as being the most unpleasant part of those night raids.

After traveling all day and gripping our weapons until our fingers were numb in paralyzing fear of being attacked, we made it to Hue-Phu Bai without as much as a single shot being fired at us.

In the twelve hours we were on the road, we stopped only briefly for fuel along the way. There was no time to eat; we felt it was too dangerous to lower our guard long enough to take a bite.

Hue-Phu Bai is one of the oldest cities in that part of the world, so I was expecting it to look the way it did, with its crumbling structures blown out by the ongoing Tet offensive. As we got deeper into the city, we passed some Marine Corps units and rounded a sharp curve into an area dotted with ruins of buildings.

Then I saw them.

There they were, standing behind piles of debris stacked in the road — civilians alongside a group of AK-47-toting, black-pajama-wearing, VC. They were as surprised to see us as we were to see them, but they just stood there, doing nothing.

I ordered Michael to slowly turn his machine gun toward them as I got on the radio to the captain.

"Sabre Two-Six, this is Shadow Man One-Six. I think I got un-friendlies here, but we're not being fired upon." I had to whisper the transmission, fearing my talking would upset our audience.

All down the convoy, I could hear the radios as the word was passed down about what was ahead. Still, nothing happened and the un-friendlies didn't move a muscle, as our long, slow convoy safely passed by the VC as though we were in a holiday parade down Broadway.

Just before sundown, we reached the Seabee compound which was about the size of a football field, fortified with heavily guarded, barbed-wire fences. There were Navy Seabee engineers guarding a pipeline and doing highway construction work north of the compound as we made our way past a blown out bridge area, through a dry creek bed, and into something that was reminiscent of an old soccer field. The field was surrounded by concrete walls about six feet high. There was an eight-foot-wide stream running through this field with continuous water flow and, possibly, fish. This spot is where we would circle our wagons for the night and regroup.

I think all of us were praying that we weren't going to be sent on a mission for the night because we were exhausted from being under such stress and riding on brutal, bumpy roads all day in the heat. But just as we were trying to grab a bite and wash the trail dust off our bodies and out of our throats, the radio began to crackle again.

"Sabre Two-Six to Shadow Man One-Six." It was the lieutenant calling me to the command center, where it soon became obvious that we were not going to escape an assignment for that evening.

I was exhausted, I was hungry, and upon hearing about this mission, I became frustrated.

Here I am, on this dangerous job with this new lieutenant who had only been in country fewer than ninety days — a man I

considered to be an absolute dumb ass. My original impression of
him was about to be reconfirmed... *times ten.*

He ordered us to take three of our gun Jeeps — two M-60
machine gun Jeeps, one of which was under my command, and
one 106 Recoilless gun Jeep — and travel *back* to that Navy
Seabee compound because they had received information about
an impending attack and they needed more firepower there.

My walk from the command center to where Michael and
Samuel were waiting was a long one. I hated to be the one to tell
them that they wouldn't be able to unwind from the day's
relentless stress. I told them to check out the equipment, clean
and reload the machine gun, and make sure we had plenty of fuel
because we were headed back to the compound in a few hours
and once again, we would be the lead vehicle.

I admitted to them, almost as an apology for sharing this
unwelcome news, that I didn't have a good feeling about this
mission. As Michael, Samuel and I were making our preparations,
the nutty little lieutenant came over to share even more bad news.

"You guys are going to have to go back there with your
running lights on."

Why he felt the need to order this, I'm sure I'll never know.

"That's absolutely crazy!" It came out of my mouth before I
could think.

"When we came through there today, we came face to face
with North Vietnamese soldiers, and we were lucky they didn't
ambush us then!" I was raising my voice by now.

Our argument became more heated. I continued to question
his judgment, and he came right back at me with the confidence
of a man who knew he was going to get his way when the dust
settled anyway.

The lieutenant didn't walk away until I backed down and
acquiesced to a trip which headed us straight for the VC, the
enemy soldiers whose noses we had tweaked with our surprise
parade just a few hours before.

I was so discouraged, but there was little I could do.

I was so young I was still wearing my high school ring.

There was still an hour or two to kill before we could move out in complete darkness, so I took the radio antenna off the gun Jeep, fitted it with some string and a safety pin, and fashioned a makeshift fishing pole. It felt good to sit on the bank of that stream with Michael and fish, just as I had spent so many afternoons fishing with my brother back home. For about an hour, Michael and I were just two innocent little boys. It was a great escape and a little breather for me after my confrontation with the lieutenant.

When darkness fell, it was time to mount up and head out. Michael and I were nervously making small talk, because something about silence made us even more uneasy. Samuel grabbed the big transistor radio and attempted to tune in to a Red Sox-Yankees game on Armed Forces Radio. He joked about the irony of an Indian from Window Rock, Arizona, and a black man from Jersey taking care of this honky, hillbilly sergeant from Tennessee.

It was the first time we had all belly-laughed at one of Samuel's jokes in days. It felt great. Michael started talking about his wife and how excited he was that she was expecting their child. He was wondering if he would be home in time for the birth.

As we got closer to the compound, flares were going up from where other units were in contact. We passed the old blown up bridge again and drove through the dry creek bed, down one steep embankment and up the other side. My stomach was in knots.

Our Jeep was the lead vehicle again, but this time a much smaller convoy made up of mostly gun Jeeps and other firepower fell in behind us. To the enemy, we would look *much* smaller and much more vulnerable than we did during our earlier pass-through.

The moment we crested the creek embankment to get back onto the highway, all hell broke loose.

A loud explosion rocked the earth beneath us, and our Jeep was hurled into the air by the force of the blast. It landed on its wheels and kept moving forward, but that was a small consolation. We were in the middle of a violent ambush. Michael immediately returned fire with the machine gun as Samuel and I blasted at our attackers with our M-16's.

Samuel was too busy fighting to steer the Jeep, which was rolling down the road due to the momentum from the blast. The gunfight persisted as the front wheels bumped against the highway's retaining wall and the rear wheels continued to spin, throwing dirt behind us.

Tracers, bullets, and explosions from grenades lit the sky and fell all around us like hail in a bad storm. I had a concussion and was bleeding badly from my ear, but I continued returning fire with strength from pure adrenaline and total fright.

Suddenly, the machine gun fell silent as Michael slumped over and landed on top of me. Shot in the neck, he had died instantly.

In the next heartbeat, another explosion rocked the driver's side of the Jeep where Samuel was sitting, thrusting his body into the air and blowing him to pieces, his body parts raining down on me as I continued to fire.

Both Samuel and Michael were wearing steel pots and flak jackets that day. I was only wearing my boonie hat and combat fatigues. Somehow, I was still alive.

There was no one left in the Jeep to back me up — no one to help me get out of this mess.

My friends had been killed, and this attack was never going to end until every one of us on the mission was dead. I was going into shock and was returning fire by rote. This was far from over, and I had to keep fighting back as long as I could hold out.

I heard machine gun fire from the Seabee compound ahead of us, which meant I was now officially in the crossfire. In my peripheral vision, I saw about a dozen North Vietnamese soldiers running toward my Jeep to finish me off and pick the vehicle clean of supplies.

I closed my eyes, prayed, slumped over and held my breath, pretending to be dead. I was literally covered from head to toe in Samuel's blood and brain matter, and the carnage served to convince my enemies that they had indeed hit their mark and killed all of us.

In a sense, Samuel saved my life.

They took my empty M-16 from my hands and then tried, in vain, to get the machine gun loose from the tripod. The bullets flying from the compound began to hinder their efforts, as they stripped the Jeep of ammo and grenades. I heard them chatter and run back into the jungle with their loot as the explosions continued all around. Everything sounded muffled, and what really took only a minute or two seemed like hours.

I knew I had to get out of there somehow, or I was going to die.

I reached over and, ever so slightly, turned the steering wheel to the right in hopes of freeing the Jeep from the retaining wall. It worked. The Jeep veered from the wall and began to roll down the road toward the compound, making its way out of the crossfire.

Suddenly, what was left of Samuel's torso fell from the seat and onto the road as the Jeep rolled down the hill. It was more than I could take. I snapped.

All I could think about was going back to get Samuel's body, as the bullets continued to fly. The Jeep finally got close enough to the compound for a group of Navy Seabees to run out and bring me to safety and retrieve Michael's body, which was still stretched out on top of me.

As I was loaded onto a stretcher, I remember begging the medics to go back with me to get Samuel. They didn't say a word. It was still too dangerous out there to risk more lives, retrieving the dead. I felt I had abandoned my friend, and continued talking about going back until I passed out from the concussion.

Later, I would learn the Jeep that had rolled me to safety had 79 large bullet holes in it. I only suffered severe bruising, a concussion, and a busted eardrum. The next morning a trip to the ambush site to retrieve Samuel's body revealed the bodies of five North Vietnamese soldiers, but of all the bullets and shrapnel flying in every direction, nothing had hit me. I knew a miracle had occurred and that it had occurred for a reason.

My life changed forever in just *minutes*, and it took me a long time to adjust. Survivor's guilt engulfed me, just as I had witnessed it taking hold of so many Vietnam soldiers who watched their buddies die on the battlefield. That ambush is as clear in my memory today as it was weeks after it happened. It still haunts me and on occasion, 43 years later, I wake up in a cold sweat as the mental video of my friend being blown to bits replays over and over — a recurring nightmare.

How I think of everything today is colored by all of the emotions I felt on June 6, 1968. For instance, any preconceived notion I might have had about life being fair was shot to hell. I came home with a couple of medals. My brave buddies came home in a box.

My beliefs about everlasting friendship between people of different backgrounds were strengthened: Michael Bia, the bull-riding American Indian and Samuel Boyd, the shy, humorous African-American from New Jersey, were raised as differently from me as any men could possibly be, yet the three of us connected as human beings in brotherhood and fellowship when it came to defending our country.

My belief and faith in God's purpose for me was all brought to the forefront of my life after that experience. I truly believe I was spared because there's another task in store for me — another plan. For the rest of my life, I will remain in awe of God's forgiveness and will forever be grateful for his protection on that day and every day I climb into my patrol car to face the unknown.

Deputy Sergeant Terry Ashe, 1974

CHAPTER THREE

It was early in 1969 when I was released from the army. I was lucky to find temporary work to pay bills at a factory in Lebanon, but I knew I wanted to pursue a career in law enforcement. Old dreams die hard, and I had never lost the dream that Sheriff Howard Griffin had inadvertently planted in my heart so many years ago. I went by after my shift one day to see Sheriff Cecil Bryan to ask him for a deputy's commission — a popular thing to have back in those days, but mighty hard to come by.

Sheriff Cecil Bryan gave me my first job in law enforcement when I returned home from Vietnam.

I told Sheriff Bryan about my military background as a recon scout and about my work with the military police and my experiences in Vietnam. He let me ride with him a few times before he brought me officially on board as a part-time deputy, but we never ran up on anything really big going down, as I had imagined we would from day one. I was so excited when the sheriff finally told me I could outfit my own car with a radio, at my expense of course, and that I could make arrests under the "fee" system.

It's funny how the world turns; later in life, Sheriff Bryan served under me as jail administrator. For fifteen years, he was a trusted friend who was more like a big brother to me, and I'll never forget how he gave me my first chance to work in law enforcement. When he died in 2000, he left a legacy as one of the finest sheriffs Wilson County voters ever elected. His kindness and professionalism certainly will always be legendary to me.

Three of the five candidates for Wilson County sheriff, former Wilson County Chief Deputy Al Cook (left), incumbent Sheriff Gwin King (center) and former Lebanon city detective Terry Ashe (right) chat together before taking their separate turns on stage appealing for votes at the Mt. Juliet Kiwanis Club political rally last Friday night. Also seeking votes for their sheriff campaigns at the rally were former private security officer Paul Murray and Mt. Juliet police chief Charles McCrary. (DEMOCRAT photo by Bill Cook)

In 1974, I went to work full-time for another sheriff, Gwin King. Tennessee had three consecutive term limits for sheriff back then. I ran against him in 1982 and won, and I won again when he ran against me in 1986.

King worked for me on the drug task force and later in the Mount Juliet Police Department, until he retired in early 2012, and he did an excellent job. Even after those hard-fought political contests, we've remained good friends, and in the last six elections, Gwin and his entire family have come out to support me. His son, Chris, works for me now as my training officer, giving new meaning to the old saying, "politics makes strange bedfellows."

Little Chicago

Throughout the seventies, the efforts of law enforcement to clean up Bluebird Road were unsuccessful.

I left my job as deputy in 1976 and joined the police department where I rose to the rank of chief detective. It was during this time that I learned how and why Lebanon, Tennessee had earned the nickname, "Little Chicago."

Before I-40 was built, the only way to get south from up north was straight through Lebanon via Highway 231. There was a lot of business, a lot of traffic, and a heap of money to be made in the tourism industry. As the years went by, Bluebird Road's national reputation didn't change much, and word of mouth just meant more business.

Each sheriff, mayor, and police chief vowed to clean it up if given the chance, but it seemed to be an empty promise because nothing ever changed. Nothing ever could. Something was stopping the progress along the way, but no one ever tried to find the "clog in the pipe," so to speak.

The criminals were certainly seeing progress all around them. Taxpayer dollars were used to pave Bluebird Road, and those making the trip to buy whores and illegal booze had a smooth and speedy drive. Word of this improvement meant more illegal establishments.

On and on it went.

Stills like this were common.
This is the last one in the county that we seized in the early eighties.

Mr. Chief of Detectives

I worked two murders within hours of each other one Sunday in the winter of 1979. I had been appointed Chief of Detectives after my brief stint of working with Sheriff King, and it was quite a learning experience.

I got a call that a man had been found dead — where else — on Bluebird Road. When I arrived at the house, the Lebanon Police already had a woman in the back seat of the car, ready to take her to the station for questioning. The middle-aged, black woman looked familiar to me for some reason, but I didn't stop to think about it as I stepped up on the old wooden front porch of the decaying house, only four doors down from Les' Lounge.

Gwin King was still the Wilson County sheriff back then, and the honky-tonks on that famous stretch of road were at their peak.

When I walked into the tiny living room, the heat from the old wood stove hit me in the face; it was so baking hot, I was suffocating.

I saw the man's body, spread out near the stove, an empty whiskey bottle lying nearby.

"Honey" Britton, as he was known, was in his early fifties. Honey's family was well known to us down at the station, because his son, whom we had nicknamed "Honey Bun," had a penchant for taking things that didn't belong to him.

I fingerprinted the whiskey bottle and prepared to take the photographs of Honey's body, but I needed more details on the possible cause of death. I stepped outside to talk to the officer who had the apparent suspect in the back of his car.

The officer told me that the woman was drunk, which meant she couldn't be interviewed. Any statement made by an intoxicated person could be thrown out in court, so we had to wait until she was completely coherent to question her.

I had the officer take the woman to the police department, and I went back inside to continue my part of the crime scene workup which, in those days, meant doing the entire investigation. Fingerprints, photographs, diagrams. It was up to me to gather all the evidence back in those days, but I wouldn't take anything for the learning experience it gave me.

Dr. R.C. Kash was our medical examiner for the county. A prominent physician in Lebanon for years, he had taken the examiner's job because no one else wanted it. The position gave him a sense of importance, and he felt his practice benefitted from this additional work. He carried a number two lead pencil with him at all times. In all the years I had been on a homicide or even a natural death scene with him, I never saw him touch a black person with anything but that pencil.

On this day I called for Dr. Kash because we needed to determine the cause of death.

I knew what to expect long before he arrived, however.

It took him about an hour to get there. He came in, wearing his tattered fedora and an old faded and wrinkled overcoat that gave him a kind of unkempt, unclean, Columbo look. He always carried a worn leather bag containing his pistol and several badges. I think every sheriff he had ever known had given him a badge as a courtesy.

Dr. Kash wasted no time as he kneeled down beside Honey's body and, as I fully expected, began poking around on it with that pencil.

As always, he looked totally disinterested and distracted as he went about his work. I always felt I needed to be standing over him as he rushed through his routine, because I was afraid he would miss something.

I pointed to a suspicious lesion I had found on the body; I thought it looked like an entry wound of some kind under the arm, but it had not bled. He glanced at the wound, but didn't seem to really *see* it.

"Nah. That's where he fell over on this hot stove. I think he died of a heart attack. My diagnosis is a heart attack." Dr. Kash was emphatic.

He told me to note on my papers his official ruling: *"Death by heart attack."*

Dr. Kash quickly finished his paperwork without any further inspection of the body and without any further discussion with me. When he left, I called for an ambulance to pick up Honey's body to take it to the hospital. I wasn't satisfied with the medical examiner's findings, and I knew I wasn't going to rest until I had that body x-rayed.

The x-ray backed up my suspicions. Not only had Honey been shot, he had been shot *twice* — by two guns of *different* calibers. Both bullets were still in the body.

While Honey's body was being x-rayed and I was trying to deal with the media in the lobby, *another* murder went down — this time, in the hospital parking lot! I had to shift gears quickly and get out there to begin yet another investigation before the first one had even been wrapped up. I arrested a man for killing his son-in-law in what was, by comparison to Honey's murder, a cut and dried case.

The son-in-law had come to the hospital to visit his wife after he had beaten her up a few days before. He had no idea that his wife's 65-year-old daddy would be waiting for him with a .22 caliber automatic rifle. "Daddy" had decided that he was going to be trial, judge and jury and make darn sure that this guy wouldn't live to raise a hand to his daughter again. He shot his son-in-law, apparently not realizing several detectives and patrol officers were steps away, working on another case.

A nurse rushed in to tell me a man had been shot outside, and that the shooter was still standing over him. We both rushed out to the back of the hospital, and the first thing I noticed was the victim, lying on his back, blood everywhere. He was still barely alive, and I'll never forget the look in his eyes as I knelt over him to check his pulse. He was fading and suddenly stopped breathing. The nurse and I began CPR.

I looked up during all of this to see the father-in-law standing nearby, holding the rifle and smoking a cigarette as though nothing had happened.

You would think my first instinct would have been to disarm the gunman before attending to the victim, but I was too focused on the dying man. Maybe it was because I ran out of a hospital with a nurse and I was in a mindset of saving lives, not catching criminals at that point.

It wasn't but a minute or two after I noticed the guy, that Lebanon police officers arrived to disarm, handcuff, and arrest him. As we continued the CPR, the newspaper photographer who had followed me to the hospital to gather facts on the other murder snapped a photo of the two of us working to save the man. The next day, in today's digital vernacular, the photo went "viral." Newspapers across the country featured the Chief of Detectives of Lebanon, Tennessee and a nurse in the parking lot of a hospital, trying to save the life of this shooting victim.

The man didn't survive in spite of our best efforts, so I had to begin the investigation of my second murder of the day, and the day was still young. An outsider would have thought we lived in the old Wild West.

This had turned out to be one heck of a Sunday afternoon.

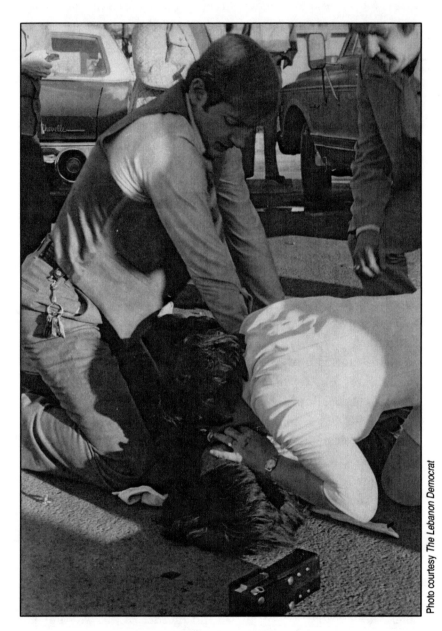

The photograph of the nurse and me performing CPR on a gunshot victim was printed in newspapers across the country.

When I got back to the police department a few hours later, I was eager to see if the woman we had taken into custody in connection with Honey Britton's murder was sober enough to answer a few questions.

Apparently, she had sobered up enough to call one of the best criminal defense attorneys in the nation, Jack Lowery. Jack was on the phone to me as soon as I walked into my office, advising me that I was not allowed to question the suspect, since she was now officially his client.

Just a Corner, Your Honor

Jack Lowery is good at what he does. So good, in fact, that you forget he's an attorney and find yourself getting lost in an intricate tale that's so cleverly crafted that it's ten times better than anything you've ever seen on the Lifetime Network or read in a New York Times bestseller.

I've watched many a spellbound juror, mouth agape, as Jack artfully weaves a story of the hardships and troubles his victimized clients allegedly experienced at the hands of the now deceased.

The trial of the woman accused of killing Honey Britton has to be listed among Jack Lowery's finest hours, in my book. And since it *is* my book, I can say this.

Jack's opening statements in the murder trial outlined the beatings and verbal abuse this woman suffered at Honey Britton's hands for as long as she had known him.

On the day Honey was killed, the woman admitted she had shot him, but claimed it was in self-defense.

I thought the prosecution had an air-tight case. I thought we had all the evidence we needed to send this woman to jail for at least manslaughter.

We were never able to find the two different-caliber guns, however, and that fact bothered me. Other than that, I thought we had all our bases covered.

I was called to the witness stand to offer up all the evidence that I had found in my investigation. We were getting into the preliminary details; District Attorney Tommy Thompson and attorney Guy Yelton were asking the questions about what I found, and I presented the photographs, fingerprints, and other findings I had gathered at the crime scene.

The jury was getting rather restless, and since it was getting close to noon, the judge recessed for lunch.

An hour later, when it was almost time to re-convene, a few of us were standing around talking in the hallway. Tommy Thompson, Guy Yelton, and Jack Lowery, stood there with me, along with Frank Evetts, an agent with the Tennessee Bureau of Investigation, whose office was there in the courthouse. We were just carrying on a conversation about the weather or politics — something totally unrelated.

Frank was standing next to me, leaning against the wall, casually cleaning from underneath his nails with a pink, twelve-inch long, knitting needle. Frank was a big man, and you couldn't miss that snow white hair and hearty laugh if you tried. He was always joking with us about something and putting in his snide two cents worth. We gave it back as well as he dished it out, for the most part.

Jack asked Frank if he knew anything about this case we were all there for today.

"Ya see this knittin' needle? This is the *real* murder weapon!"

Frank announced this with his poker face, usually reserved for his best pranks and went back to cleaning his nails.

We all laughed and rolled our eyes and didn't think any more of Frank's joke.   Everyone filed back into the courtroom to resume where we had left off. I got on the stand and was prepared to get back to the business of grinding through the more tedious details of the investigation.

When Attorney General Thompson finished his line of questioning, Jack Lowery stood up to begin his cross examination. He approached the jury box and gave a nod to the men and women who had already sat through hours of grueling, mundane testimony that had many twists, turns, and conflicting stories. Then, he looked at me.

"I told the jury that this was a complicated case, and indeed, we just learned more about this case a few minutes ago. Let me ask you something, Mr. Chief of Detectives for the City of Lebanon. And remember, sir, you are still under oath. Is it not true that a member of the Tennessee Bureau of Investigation, Agent Frank Evetts, admitted just moments ago, that the puncture wounds in the deceased man's body were caused by a knitting needle? Yes or no?"

I opened my mouth to try to explain that Frank was only making a joke.

"But he ..." I stuttered.

Jack stopped me before I could get another word in.

"Did that conversation take place right out there in the hallway just a few minutes ago, yes or no?"

"Yes ... but ... your honor ... Mr. Evetts ... was only ..."

"Yes or no, Mr. Ashe?" Jack interrupted again before I could explain.

I sat there in stunned silence as I felt the tone of the trial reverse before my very eyes; it completely changed all because of a little comment, made in jest, by Frank Evetts.

"No more questions, your honor," Jack knew he had us all by the shorthairs.

Jack then called the defendant to the stand. Frail and unkempt, this woman looked pitiful. I knew exactly where he would go with his line of questioning. He asked her about the number of times she had been beaten by the deceased — about the countless times she had been hurt and abused. Then, he asked her if she was drunk on the day Honey Britton died.

"No, Mr. Lowery, I was not drunk."

Jack then pulled out the whisky bottle I had found at the crime scene with her fingerprints on it.

"Does this look like the brand of whiskey that you and the deceased were drinking that day?"

"Yes, it does. That's it, that's the bottle," she answered.

"Just how much did you have to drink that day?" Jack pressed.

The woman looked up at the judge to answer this question.

"Just a corner, your honor!"

The judge looked at her as though she were speaking another language.

"Would you repeat that, please?" The judge asked.

"A corner, you know, like a *corner.*" She tried to explain, but all she was managing to do was confuse everyone even more.

With that, Jack handed her the whisky bottle for a little show and tell.

"Could you show the jury exactly what a *'corner'* is?"

The woman took the bottle, turned it to a 45-degree angle and pointed to the bottom, where the last few drops of whisky would settle if the bottle were tilted that way.

"Just a corner, *here!*" She asserted, as if we would all now be perfectly clear on this new unit of measurement.

The jury roared with laughter. It was funny. I had to chuckle even though I knew we were going to lose this case just as sure as I was sitting there — one of those laugh-to-keep-from-crying deals. An entire murder trial had come down to a knitting needle and something called a corner.

As expected, the jury deliberated for less than two hours and came back with a verdict of not guilty. It was just another murder on Bluebird Road, and it meant nothing, since that area was the setting of so much deadly activity at the time. The way the public saw it, if you hung out to party and drink on Bluebird Road and something happened to you, you got no less than you deserved.

For a man who grew up on the road — a law enforcement officer trying to clean up the area for future generations — it was so frustrating to have a case like this slip through my fingers.

After that, all I wanted was a *corner* ... to sit in and brood for a while.

The Blue Tank

I was assigned a robin-egg blue patrol car in 1981. It was a Ford Fairlane shaped like the tanks we had in Vietnam, and was by far the ugliest damn car I ever saw. It was like driving a blue baby bootie around town. Try looking tough in that. But it's what the city ordered, and I was stuck with it. Walking out the door to go to work on that warm April morning, I took one look at this parade-float-looking thing, and winced at the thought of getting behind the wheel. *Maybe I should take the back roads.*

When I got to the police station, I walked into the coffee room, which was full of the brass and some of the other boys putting off their paperwork as long as they could and trying to wake up. Lt. Teddy Owens was telling jokes, and everybody else was looking at the newspaper, drinking coffee and gossiping. It was obviously a slow morning.

Chief L.R. Jones wasn't wearing his usual uniform. He was all dressed up in a bright pink shirt that was blinding us. We began to make fun of it, until he informed us that his wife had made it for him. That shut us up, and quick. It was one thing to make fun of a man's shirt, but to make fun of something his wife had made? Well, I certainly knew better than to go there.

I did smile at the thought of how much it would resemble a traveling baby shower if he drove my blue car around town while wearing that pink shirt.

He told us he was going to a chiefs' luncheon meeting at noon in Nashville. As he left the room, he ordered us not to let the town burn down, and we promised to do our best.

On my desk was a stack of paper two inches thick left over from a homicide I had worked that week, and that was the first thing I tackled.

Three grueling hours of filling out forms later, I was ready to stretch my legs, uncross my eyes, and grab some lunch. While I was out, maybe I'd try to look up those people I wanted to interview about a robbery I was working on.

As I sat in my macho patrol car and ate my glamour lunch — a burger, delivered curbside — I marveled at how quiet the radio was at this hour of the day compared to how annoying it was at night. No wonder the brass liked the day shift. This was a piece of cake.

I had no sooner driven up in front of the station to park after lunch, that Sgt. Tyree came running out. The armed robbery alarm had gone off again at Joe Riggan's grocery store. The alarm had sounded several times by accident in the last few weeks, and I told Sgt. Tyree that I'd take the call for him since we were only two blocks away and I was already in my car. I figured the alarm had malfunctioned again. No biggie.

As I was leaving, however, the dispatcher called for all cars to respond to that alarm, since they had tried to telephone the store and weren't getting an answer — a sure sign of trouble.

By now, I was only a block away with the lights and siren off. I spotted a greenish-brown Chevy Nova speeding toward me from the rear of the store with two men in it. The driver waved at me as the car passed. I looked in my rear view mirror and noticed the car had Nevada plates — probably stolen. Bet those two weren't in Joe's store asking for directions.

Joe Riggan ran out of the store and toward my car. He was mad as hell and yelling into my passenger side window.

"Those bastards robbed me with a shotgun!"

Before I could respond, Joe jumped in the car with me. I took off and turned around to head in the direction of the puke-green Chevy Nova. And I thought *my* car was ugly.

I caught up with the men on Market Street, but there was heavy lunch hour traffic around Lebanon to contend with — bumper to bumper around the city square. I managed to maneuver until I got in behind the getaway car. I turned on my blue lights and siren, hoping the guys would realize they were caught and couldn't go far.

"Be careful, they've got a sawed-off shotgun!" Joe wanted to make sure I knew about the weapon that had been shoved in his face just a few minutes before.

I could see the driver's beady eyes looking right at me through his rear view mirror as he made his move, pulling out of traffic and heading south on Maple Street in the Northbound lane. He was running other cars off the road and gunning it. I managed to stay right behind him in my baby blue tank car. When we got to the intersection of Maple and West Main Street, he ran the red light in a big intersection and cars were braking, tires were squealing, and people were running off the road to avoid hitting the cars in front of them.

He drove toward Spring Street, doing about eighty miles per hour, right in the middle of town, and I was on his bumper. We crossed the railroad tracks with a green light, but when we got to the top of the hill on Spring Street, traffic was at a standstill.

I stopped, jumped out of the car, and crouched behind the door of the cruiser. As I was making my move, the suspect put his car in reverse and gunned it. He was coming right toward us with his tires screeching and his sawed-off shotgun pointed at me out the driver's side window.

Joe let out a scream and I told him to bail out. I pulled out my .38 caliber Smith and Wesson Special and fired one shot. The driver didn't stop, and the backup lights of that Nova were getting closer and closer.

I could see by the look in his eyes that the "sumbitch" behind the wheel had every intention of running over me. He got about twenty feet from the front of my car, and I fired another shot which knocked a hole the size of a basketball in his rear glass. I fired again, and the entire rear glass cratered into the backseat of the Nova.

The accomplice went down, and I couldn't tell if I had hit him or not.

The driver immediately put the car in drive and headed into ongoing traffic, south on Highway 231, bound for the interstate. I quickly climbed back into the car with Joe, who was as white as a ghost, speechless, and by now, *very* sorry that he had decided to accompany me on this little joy ride.

Off we went to resume this high-speed chase with the blue tank's engine roaring along at a little over one hundred mph. A lead patrol car was in front of our convoy, clearing a path for us and trying to get traffic out of the way in case there was another shootout down the road.

The trouble with that was, the shooting never stopped the entire time.

The driver was shooting at me with his sawed-off shotgun out the back window as he was steering. Darnedest thing I ever saw.

Shards of what was left of his rear glass and all that buckshot was slamming into my car. I don't know how I looked since I had almost crapped in my pants, but all the color had drained out of Joe's face, and he was crouching in the floorboard in a little ball.

My fellow officers were trying to set up a road block between 231 and I-40 as all this was going down.

As we approached the area, I saw something that was glowing in the middle of the road like a traffic cone. It was the bright pink shirt of the police chief. He was standing there on the center line holding a shotgun across his chest and as we blew past him, he almost spun around in the road.

It was a brave thing for him to do, and I was thankful for his help, but I can't think of a more dangerous place to be during a high speed chase — unless, perhaps, it's in the floorboard with Joe Riggan.

Two patrol cars were trying to block the entrance to the interstate, but they weren't parked closely enough to be effective. The suspect didn't hit either patrol car, but simply drove between them. He was headed west toward Nashville, and the race continued.

My windshield was full of cracks and dings from the buckshot, but I could still see well enough to notice that the driver was raising his shotgun again and aiming it directly at me as we sped down the interstate. He fired through the rear of his car, and the buckshot coming toward me looked like a swarm of bees as it struck the hood, the top, and the windshield.

I only had three bullets left in my gun. I rested the revolver on the huge side mirror to steady my shot, and I squeezed off my remaining rounds. I had five bullets in the right pocket of my trousers, mixed in with spare change, keys, and who knows what else. I reached in and dumped the contents into the front seat. I asked my now zombie-like travel buddy to load my pistol as another shotgun blast struck the patrol car.

"Duck, damn it!" Joe was yelling at me over the loud roar of the blue tank, which I feared was going to overheat at any minute.

"I can't duck! I'm trying to drive this damn thing!" We were starting to sound like an old married couple who had gotten lost on a road trip.

Joe fumbled with the gun as he tried to load it with trembling hands, and I thought for a minute he was going to lose my last five *precious* bullets in the seats. Finally, the gun was loaded and back in my hands. I lined up and fired two more shots at this asshole in the car ahead of me.

Less than two miles from the Highway 109 exit on I-40 West, I put the "pedal to the metal" so to speak, and was gaining on the Chevy Nova.

I was starting to appreciate the blue tank. Its baby-like, girly-car appearance belied its stock car performance.

We took another blast from the shotgun and I returned fire once more.

Two Wilson County deputies had used their patrol cars to block the entrance to 109, and the former chief deputy, Al Cook, was running interference to my right. I steadied my revolver on the side mirror again and fired my last two rounds at the suspects. I was now out of ammo. The serious arsenal that I kept for such occasions was stored in my trunk.

Note to self: not a convenient place for it at a time like this.

Deputies squeezed off a round or two, but didn't hit pay dirt. As we approached the exit to 109, we took the ramp doing a little over eighty miles per hour. Shots rang out from every side, and from every deputy out there trying to help. As we took the turn, I noticed the Nova was starting to slow down. Smoke was pouring out of its engine, and one of the tires had been shot and was deflating fast.

The suspect turned his crippled car into the parking lot of a historic landmark in Wilson County, the first Cracker Barrel Restaurant ever built.

The driver's door flew open, and out came the robber with the sawed-off shotgun in one hand and the bag containing the money in the other. He took off running into a wooded area behind the parking lot as a crowd of thrill seekers ran from the restaurant to see what all the commotion was about.

A former police officer-turned gun dealer, Donnie Keaton, just happened to be eating in Cracker Barrel that day, and when he saw what was happening, he ran to his trunk, pulled out a .30 caliber carbine, and handed it to me.

Some of the deputies were running after the robber in the woods, and the rest of us were approaching the smoking car where his apparent accomplice was still hunkered in the floorboard.

I thought I might have wounded him when we first started the shootout since I hadn't seen him during the chase, but like my frightened passenger, he had decided to lay low. A good call as it turned out. The Nova had ten of my bullet holes in it and looked like a colander. The rearview mirror had been shot clean away. There were two holes in the passenger head rest, several holes in the back seat, and one in the dash.

The terrified guy uncoiling from the floorboard didn't have a scratch on him.

A few minutes later, the deputies emerged from the woods with the suspect — a dangerous man who, we later found out, was on the FBI's Ten Most Wanted List.

Peter Bennett Reeves gave us the alias of Steven Cochran for several days as he cooled his heels in our jail and we worked the case. We soon learned he had escaped from San Quentin Prison and was wanted for armed robberies in Nevada, Arkansas, and Texas, but it was his detour through little Lebanon, Tennessee, that would eventually land him back in the pen — this time for thirty years.

Peter Bennett Reeves was on the FBI's Ten Most Wanted List

The 22-year-old man assumed to be his accomplice turned out to be a hitchhiker from Ireland, an innocent tourist that Reeves had picked up a few hours before the grocery store heist.

Poor James Carroll had no idea who he had climbed in the car with, and was just a victim of circumstances. We held him in jail until his story checked out. I don't know where he is now, but he certainly has a cautionary tale for his grandchildren about hitchhiking in a foreign country.

Left to right: Now-Major Dan Hamblen, Sheriff Ashe,
and Hitchhiker James Carroll, a tourist from Ireland, who got quite a
lesson about climbing into cars with strangers.

During the trial, Reeves never let up with his intimidation tactics, even in front of a courtroom full of witnesses. This guy was as hardened as they get.

"I'll be back to see you!" He stared a hole through me as he made his threat.

I just learned a few weeks ago, as I'm writing this book, that Peter Bennett Reeves has been released from prison. I haven't seen him yet, so maybe he's forgotten about our little date with destiny. We'll see.

After that day, I never had another unkind thought about the "Blue Tank." After all, appearances aren't everything. That tough old car probably saved me and Joe Riggan from getting our butts shot off.

The Public Works Department got my reliable hand-me-down a year or two after that, and I would smile when I saw those guys driving it around town. It still ran like a top.

It was no worse for the wear. Neither was I.

As for Joe Riggan, he sold his store not long after that adventure. He said being in the grocery business was just too dangerous.

Photo courtesy *The Lebanon Democrat*

Joe Riggan and I are interviewed by WKRN-TV's Larry Emsweller after the high speed chase.

Photo courtesy *The Lebanon Democrat*

Mayor Maddox reviews the map of where the rapes committed by
The Southside Rapist occurred.

Left to right, Detective Mike Barbee, Chief of Detectives Terry Ashe,
Mayor Tex Maddox, and Detective Gary Mack Foster

CHAPTER FOUR

The Southside Rapist

The biggest case I ever worked is one people around here still talk about to this day here in Lebanon. The term, "Southside Rapist," is one that brings chills to anyone who was around to read the papers or watch the news in those days.

In the fall of 1979, and then in early 1980, there were a couple of rapes which occurred on the South side of Lebanon that were eerily similar. Both of the victims were elderly white women who lived alone, both were beaten, and their attacker threatened to come back and kill them if they went to the police. These incidents didn't occur close together, but there were so many similarities that I couldn't help but surmise they were committed by the same person — a young, black man who would enter the victim's home through an open window or unlocked door before dawn. If the victim normally left a porch light or other outside light on at night, the man would observe this during the day and slightly unscrew the bulb in preparation for his attack. Most of the time, the elderly victims wouldn't realize the bulb had been tampered with, simply assuming it had burned out, and they would replace it the next morning.

Once the man entered the home unnoticed in the darkness, he then removed his shoes and tip-toed through the victim's house wearing only his socks. He didn't make a sound, and by the time the victim awoke, he was already standing over them, holding a knife, ready to attack.

The newspaper reported that both rapes were on the South side of Lebanon, which had a predominately African-American population.

Long before the term "racial profiling" was used, everyone in the law enforcement community was cautious about picking up every black male anywhere from 5'8-5'10 with short hair and a mustache. We did have one characteristic to go by, and each victim commented on it: the rapist was extremely well spoken. He was violent, but he could communicate very intelligently. Trouble with that description was, it fit so many good, law-abiding citizens that it wasn't much help.

During the investigation of one of the early sexual assaults, we took with us as evidence a yellow light bulb from the back porch of one of the victim's homes — a bulb which had been disabled by the rapist before he entered the home. It turned out to be one of the best forensic moves we could have made at the time. This was in the day before elaborate fingerprinting systems, computer technology, and other forensic instruments we rely on today. The old fashioned way was all we had: shoe leather, interviews, and countless reviews of evidence gathered at the scene. When I sent the bulb to the Tennessee Bureau of Investigation, they lifted a perfect fingerprint, but it would be another 18 months before we would be able to match that print to a suspect. I kept the bulb in an evidence bag on my desk. I couldn't take my eyes off of it.

In that 18 months, there was a third elderly victim, then a forth. The heat was on law enforcement, and women in the community were terrified of the man the media dubbed "The Southside Rapist" in all the headlines regarding this case. Every victim lived on the Southside, and he had not changed his M.O. He had warned each victim against going to the police about the rape, which led me to believe there were more victims who were just too intimidated to come forward. The Lebanon Democrat ran a story asking, "Are there any more rape victims out there?" The article urged the victims to come forward as a "Jane Doe" and help police capture the man who was terrorizing the community. Once that article ran, I received two telephone calls — one from a very dear friend of mine whose husband had died a few years before.

She had been afraid to come forward, even to a friend, about her beating and rape a few weeks before. What she had to tell me about her attack gave me chills. The details were identical to those given by the other rape victims. This lady was a former teacher. She immediately got the sense that her attacker was well educated — perhaps even college educated — and well informed, noting that his grammar and even his accent were distinctive for this part of the south. She observed his mannerisms and his voice, and she shared every detail with me, urging me to find this animal and bring him to justice.

The cliché "weeks turned into months" comes into play here. I thought we would never catch this guy. He was on my mind constantly as the clues and details of each attack churned around in my head. Det. Gary Foster and Det. Mike Barbee were assigned to this case, and I was so fortunate to have these two hardworking pros there to help. Every patrol officer was on edge, not knowing when or where the rapist was going strike again. It seemed we could never second guess him.

Soon seven women had been raped — that we knew about — and we were no closer to catching this guy than we were the first time he attacked. We began to patrol the area in golf carts late at night, up and down the miles of interior roads around Cumberland University. We rode around the many dark side streets in the freezing cold weather, just watching and waiting. Our work wasn't in vain. We felt that we were achieving something if we just kept moving and just kept him guessing where we would be next.

Some officers thought that the rapist might be a jogger, an opportunist who chose victims at random. Others disagreed, arguing his attacks were well-planned and organized in advance, and that law enforcement was being taunted. We agreed on one thing: we were chasing a monster.

We used a big map to plot the area of the attacks; many were only a few blocks apart, but all were around Cumberland University, which sits squarely in the middle of Southside

Lebanon. We continued to send fingerprints of every assault suspect we arrested to the crime lab, but there was never a match.

Early in 1981, we got the report of our first extremely violent physical assault on a victim of the Southside Rapist. This woman was severely beaten because she fought and struggled so desperately with her attacker. I feared after that night, our rapist was becoming more like a wild dog that had gotten the taste of blood and would continue to beat women, or perhaps even kill after he raped. If we didn't catch him soon, we could be working our first Southside Rapist murder.

This thing was escalating, and the public was becoming impatient with us. Our department had an excellent reputation of solving crimes very quickly and getting things done, but this case had all the twists and turns of film noir. Chief L.R. Jones' phone was lit up like a Christmas tree day and night, with people calling for action and complaining that taxpayers weren't being protected. I was feeling the heat physically and mentally as I had to work other assaults, burglaries, robberies and murders. The Southside Rapist was not the only criminal on the streets of Lebanon, but he did seem to be the only criminal catching a break. This guy was slipping through our fingers like mercury.

Another Night, Another Call

There was *another* victim — this time, at a trailer park barely inside the city, but still on the South Side. The rapist entered the home by cutting a screen door with a knife. During the rape, a strange twist of fate almost caused a tragedy. Two Wilson County deputies arrived at the trailer park to deliver a death message to a family, but they didn't know which of the ten trailers the family lived in. They started at the first trailer in line and began to knock on doors, working their way down.

The rapist, meanwhile, was brutalizing the woman who lived in the last trailer in that row, bending her over a chair, holding a knife to her throat, and raping her.

The family who got the death message lived *next door* to the victim, and the deputies delivered their message and left, never realizing the most wanted man in Middle Tennessee was only steps away in the last trailer. This victim gave us a clue we had not heard from the other women; she said she heard him start a car and leave after the attack. She could only tell us that the car was a big sedan. In the late 70's and early 80's, all cars were "big sedans." Her information did help us figure out this guy was mobile.

The trailer park was four miles from Cumberland University, where we had been working this case all along, thinking our rapist was a jogger who might live or work near campus.

As weeks passed, the victim count jumped to nine. The patrol division, detective division, and the county deputies were all extremely focused on putting an end to this menace's reign of terror, but to no avail. We were getting nowhere.

Late one night, patrol officer Andy Woodall ran a routine tag number on a suspicious car parked at the little league ball field on the South side around midnight. The dispatcher logged the tag number down, as he always did. Around 4:30 A.M., we got a call from yet another victim of the Southside Rapist. Victim number ten was an elderly lady I had known for many years who was almost beaten to death. She lived just down the street from the ball field where the suspicious car had been reported by officer Woodall a few hours before.

The routine of the attacker had not changed. He had loosened the light bulb on the victim's back porch and made his way in as she slept, silently creeping in sock-feet down the hall and into her bedroom. When she woke up, he was standing over her with a knife.

With his socks over his hands to disguise his fingerprints, he picked up the telephone and began beating her in the head with it. He raped her several times and left her there, almost lifeless, on the floor.

When I got to the scene, there was blood everywhere. We looked all around the room, and then, silently at each other. We were all exhausted and frustrated, and we needed a break in this case. Something. Anything. While the detectives worked the crime scene, I gathered evidence and went back to the office to pore over the details and take a look at the patrol log from the night before. I sat at my desk with my head in my hands in an attempt to keep my aching head from falling off my shoulders. I was spent and felt totally helpless. As I sat there with my head bowed and my eyes closed at my desk, I whispered a prayer that the Lord would give us wisdom and help us get this dangerous man off the streets before he killed someone.

As all human beings tend to do, we try it our way until the only way out is to *look up*. It's a good thing I looked up that day, because within minutes of my silent prayer, the heaven-sent wheels began to turn.

Officer Woodall was still there and wanted to show me that tag he had logged after midnight down in dispatch. It was on an older, yellow Cadillac parked two blocks from where the victim lived. That's all I needed to see. It clicked. We had to move quickly. Every available patrol unit was sent to comb the streets around the South side of Lebanon. Up and down the small alleys and streets, back and forth, not missing a single driveway or hedgerow, we checked every house looking for that car and that tag.

Bingo. On South Maple Street, not three blocks from Cumberland University, the Cadillac was sitting in a driveway around some houses which had been turned into duplexes. My gut feeling was that this just might be the break that we needed.

We researched the license plate through courthouse records, and the plate didn't belong on that car. I ordered constant surveillance on our discovery until I was able to rouse the Assistant District Attorney out of bed and into my office to obtain a search warrant. It was now around 8:30 A.M. Our search team of patrol officers and detectives converged on that old house like termites swarming in for a meal. My heart was pounding. We could actually have the Southside Rapist in custody within the hour!

Officers took up a safe vantage point all around the house as I walked up and knocked on the front door. There was no answer. I knocked again, no answer. I then called out, "Police!" I heard footsteps coming toward the door. When the door opened, I was taken aback. An attractive, young, well dressed white woman stood there with two small children. One of them, still in diapers, had his tiny arms around her neck while the other, barely walking, was tugging at her dress below. I told her why we were there and that we were looking for the driver of the car parked in the yard. She told me the car wasn't theirs, but her husband had been driving it for a while as their car was in the shop. "May I talk to your husband?" I asked her above the loud whining and protests of the little ones who were still tugging at their mother as she held the door open.

"No, not right now, he's asleep. He's been working all night." I could tell, somehow, that she really believed she was telling me the truth. I showed her my search warrant and stepped through the door, past her and past her restless babies. I had walked just a few steps down the hall when her husband, a 5'10 black man with a mustache and short hair, fitting the *exact* description of the Southside Rapist, stepped out of the bedroom wearing only his underwear.

I had never seen this man before, and I thought I knew just about everybody in town. You're not a detective for long before you're introduced to every citizen one way or another.

"I'm Chief of Detectives, Terry Ashe. What's your name, please?"

"I'm Ronnie Johnson." He was well spoken and his voice was smooth and educated as he answered each of my questions intelligently and politely. He was fitting the description to a "T" right now. He was bit taller than the victims described, but in sock feet, everyone is shorter. All the victims told me we should be looking for a well-educated, well-spoken man. It was a small detail we left out of media accounts. It was our "ace in the hole," so to speak.

I advised him of his rights and told him we needed to sit down and talk, if possible. He whispered that he wanted to talk in private, that he and his wife had just moved back here from Germany where he had been in the U.S. Army, and he didn't want her to think he was in any kind of trouble. As we stepped into the bedroom to begin our discussion, he asked me if he could get dressed. It seemed to me he was obviously embarrassed to be standing there in his tighty-whiteys talking to the cops.

My mental wheels were turning as he talked. He said he had been out with a woman friend the night before and he didn't want his wife to find out. I asked him to show me the clothes he had worn on his date. I knew there would have to be some blood on them because, at the crime scene, there was blood everywhere after the cruel beating of the last victim. He picked up some worn out, old, badly wrinkled pants and told me he had worn them and then tossed them in the floor when he got home. I didn't believe him. He was too neat and took too much pride in his appearance to wear something like this on an alleged date with a mistress.

As the other detectives began to question him, I went into the bathroom to look for clues. Everything in there was neat and buttoned-down military style, but something told me to look in the clothes hamper in the corner. With those babies in the house, there were certainly a lot of dirty clothes. When I dumped the overloaded hamper's contents on the bathroom floor, a pair of bloody socks fell to the floor from the bottom of the basket. He came into the tiny bathroom and stood beside me as I picked up my discovery.

"Are these your socks?" He was the only man living there, so they certainly had to be his, I was thinking.

"Yes, they belong to me."

The minute he said that, I knew without a doubt we had our man. I looked at his face in the mirror and then I looked back down at the bloody socks I had in my right hand. Socks would now go to the crime lab to join that yellow light bulb I had gathered at the scene of one of the first rapes. These everyday items might give us all the information we need to put this guy away for a long, long time.

"Whose blood is this?" I asked him as I looked at his eyes in the mirror.

"It's mine. I cut myself shaving," he answered, as he looked back at me without blinking. We were side by side talking through the mirror at each other. It made for an interesting dynamic.

"Show me. Show me where you cut yourself shaving." I had not seen a single scratch on his clear, black skin. "That's a lot of blood on socks just from a shaving accident!"

I didn't even wait for him to make up a ridiculous ruse this time. I advised him of his rights once again and arrested him on the spot. As we left for booking and all the paperwork I would have to finish, I didn't dread all the work ahead of me. I felt nothing but sheer relief and thankfulness to the Lord that we were led to this man before another innocent person was attacked or murdered. When I got back to my desk, the officers already had Johnson standing in my office where he had made his phone call and hired an attorney.

Within minutes, Bill Martin, the man who had earned the nickname "Wild Bill" back in the day, stepped into my office. Bill was one of those good old country lawyers — honest and straightforward. He called them as he saw them and expected everyone else to do the same.

After their private, attorney-client meeting, Johnson was led back to his cell, and Bill sat down to discuss the case we had against his client. Bill told me he had never met Ronnie Johnson, but that he did know the family of the young woman Johnson had married. He knew them very well. They were decent, respectable people, and they had called him in to represent their son-in-law. He asked me what I was going to do next.

"I'm going to get a court order and draw Johnson's blood so I can get a match with the socks, and I'm going to match his fingerprints with the prints we've pulled from a light bulb at one of the crime scenes," I said confidently, as I laid out my case.

He didn't flinch, but agreed to sign the waiver to allow Johnson's blood to be drawn. A few days later, the moment of *truth* came, as they say in the movies. The fingerprint from that light bulb that I had saved 18 months earlier — the bulb I had stared at for so long that every curve, every swirl of that perfect fingerprint became ingrained in my mind, the light bulb which had captured the perfect clue — was about to pay what it owed me.

I wanted to be the one to roll Johnson's prints. I didn't want there to be a single smudge. I wanted everything to be precise and on the mark. Besides, I had a photographic memory when it came to that print on the light bulb. I'd know it anywhere, even if I were to see it on a piece of paper in the next few minutes.

I took Johnson back to the booking room and placed him in front of the big ink pad on the fingerprint table. He began to sweat and fidget as I prepared the card, signed the documents and got ready for the procedure. As I picked up his hand to roll it across the ink pad, his palms were soaking wet with sweat. I had to dry his hands with a towel or the ink wouldn't work properly. I took his right hand index finger and rolled it across the ink pad, and then onto the white card.

Instantly, I could see the very same print that I had stared at for a year and a half – the print taken from that light bulb. There was no doubt in my mind; I knew we had our man. At the very least, we had the man responsible for rape number three, the house from which we had removed the bulb. My heart began to pound as I stared at the print.

I needed to calm down and finish this print job, or I was going to need a towel for my palms. *Finally*, we had the Southside Rapist. Better still, I had a firm grip on his hand and he wasn't going anywhere. Johnson probably wondered why I was so consumed with this one index fingerprint. I can only imagine what was going through his mind. His hands began to shake. I finished making the rest of the prints and gave him a towel to wipe off the ink. I studied the card once more, and looked him right in the eye.

"I've got you big boy!" I just had to say it. He needed to hear it.

He lowered his head and he never spoke another word to me. *Ever.*

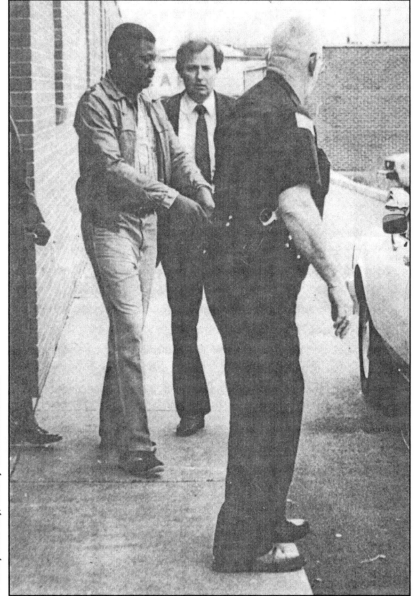

Rape suspect Ronnie L. Johnson, far left, being led to a waiting police car by Lebanon Chief Detective Terry Ashe and Police Chief L. R. Jones.

Detectives were standing by to lead him through the next step — having his blood drawn.

All we had to do was find one item — in our case, the socks — which had Johnson's blood stains and the victim's blood stains. If we could do that, and if his prints matched those taken from the light bulb, we had an airtight case. In those days, we didn't have DNA testing, but we were able to break down blood types, and all of that blood evidence was highly successful in court.

At Last

The blood on Johnson's sock turned out to be a perfect match with the blood of the last victim. Johnson's prints matched perfectly that print taken from the light bulb. We also had at least one brave, intelligent victim who was willing to testify in court to put this monster away for a long time.

Every victim I spoke with felt that their lives would never be the same. They felt violated and frightened to be in their homes alone after the attacks even though our suspect was in custody.

As I looked back at all the evidence in preparation for the trial, I thought about all of them. I thought of my friend, the sweet, 73-year-old lady who was his first victim, who had called me with terror in her voice. She almost died after being so brutally beaten. I drove past her house not long after the attack and noticed she had installed steel bars on every window. It's still that way to this day.

The Trial

Ronnie Johnson's trial was a media circus. Johnson's family was very vocal, ready to tell anyone within earshot that the police had the wrong man, but they failed to recognize that since their loved one had been arrested, the rapes had stopped. One of my biggest fears was a copycat rapist, and that's why I was careful to release only the bare minimum of details about the investigation to the media. A copycat would have been a double-nightmare, which would have made it almost impossible to convict Johnson.

The case of the Southside Rapist had to be the finest hour of the late Assistant District Attorney Guy Yelton. We were asking for the maximum: life in prison. The jury was chosen, and then came a long week of testimony. The most damaging to the defense came from a couple of our brave, elderly victims who did a superb job recalling every detail of the hellish night they were beaten and raped. One had to testify about the rapist's voice. Another had to endure harsh cross-examination. The last person we put on the stand was the rapist's last victim — a respectable lady who had been beaten beyond recognition. She had to relive that night for the jury to hear in brutal detail. She went public with her broken bones, black bruises, and bloodshot eyes to bring this man to justice, and she rose above her humiliation with dignity and grace.

You could have heard a pin drop as she told her story.

The judge charged the jury, which left the room to deliberate. Ronnie Johnson sat motionless in his chair as the men and women who would decide his fate filed out of the room. I sat at the prosecution table and felt him turn to glare at me. I didn't feel sorry for him. Not one bit. All I could think about were the victims and their tears, heartache, shame and embarrassment. I thought of the pain he had inflicted on so many women. He was about to get what he had coming to him.

I just glared back at him as if looks could kill.

We were summoned back to the courtroom after our lunch break with the news that the jury was back after only a few hours of deliberation. Not a good sign for Johnson. As the courtroom filled up with spectators, I noticed that almost all the victims were there. I was glad they were all alive and well enough to be present when justice was served on a platter, as it was about to be. The jury filed back in to the box, and the courtroom fell silent.

Photo by Jim Bond, Courtesy *The Lebanon Democrat*

**I sit in court with the man it took months to capture:
Southside Rapist Ronnie Johnson**

"Will the jury foreman please stand?" The judge addressed the men and women as they sat down. A man stood up and was holding some papers in his hand.

"Has the jury reached a verdict in this case?"

"Yes we have, Your Honor."

I held my breath as the jury foreman read the verdict: guilty on all three counts in the indictment.

We did it. Assistant District Attorney Guy Yelton, the detectives, the officers, and the victims who testified. It was a great moment — a moment made better when I watched the bailiffs handcuff Ronnie Johnson and accompany me as I escorted him to the Wilson County Jail. It's a jail I would soon be running. I didn't know that at the time, of course. Johnson would have crapped his pants if he had known it.

Ironically, as I began to dig further into Johnson's past, I found out he had been discharged dishonorably from the U.S. Army for an alleged sexual assault in Germany. Unfortunately, we weren't privy to that information here in the states because sex offender registries didn't exist back then. We had to find out the hard way.

Johnson filed appeal after appeal to try to get out of his life sentence, and he was always being brought back and forth from prison in the years that followed. Seems he had a problem with how we got a warrant, came to his home and grabbed his bloody socks out of his dirty clothes hamper. Dude. Get over it. We've got ya.

Live with it — just as the victims have to live with what you did to *them*.

Fade In, Fade Out

Twenty-five years had passed, and Ronnie Johnson was still in prison where he belonged.

It got my day off to a rotten start, however, when I received a notice one morning from the Pardons and Paroles Board, informing me that Johnson was eligible for parole and his hearing was coming up. Once word of this got to the victims and the victims' families, my phone began to ring. They were terrified. Two of the elderly witnesses who had testified were still alive, and they feared Johnson would make good on his promise to come back and kill them in their sleep if they went to the police.

The day of the parole hearing, I went to the penitentiary to testify on behalf of the victims with Assistant District Attorney Guy Yelton and Det. Mike Barbee.

Det. Barbee was an excellent investigator — the first African-American detective for the city, and one of my first hires when I became Chief of Detectives. He worked tirelessly to help put Johnson behind bars, and he didn't want to see him out on the street again anytime soon.

As they led Ronnie Johnson into the room, I hardly recognized him as the same man we had put away 25 years ago. He had pumped iron and worked out in the prison gym and was muscled up and built up beyond recognition. He had the same steely gaze, however, and he shot nasty looks at me throughout the hearing.

One by one, Johnson's family members pleaded with the board to release this son, brother, husband, and father of two. But the play of the day came from Johnson's diminutive grandmother. When she stepped to the front of the room, she appeared to be a stately, typical, sweet little old lady in her seventies, dressed in her starched, flowered cotton dress and her best Sunday hat. In a weak, cracking voice, she politely and kindly asked the board to consider the release of her grandson. She then turned toward Detective Barbee, and her face took on a scornful look.

"You've disappointed us all!" It wasn't difficult to see her implication; Barbee, in her opinion, had gone against the people of his race simply by doing his job. Did she *really* think that because he was black he would look the other way when a black person committed a crime? I must have shaken my head in disbelief, or rolled my eyes or something, because I got her attention somehow. She turned her eyes, and her ire toward me.

"I'm gonna pray for you Sheriff, b'cause you need prayin' for!"

Throughout the hearing, Det. Barbee and I had been the only investigators to testify, so it stood to reason that she would go for our jugular first. Guy Yelton was just sitting there, thinking he had escaped Grandma's wrath. Then it happened. Her demeanor changed for the worst. It was like something from an exorcism movie.

"Satan!" she screamed as she *got all up* in Guy's face. "You are SATAN!"

It was like Dana Carvey's church lady character on Saturday Night Live.

Guy sat there and looked right through her, nonplussed by her almost comical hissy-fit.

The board came back with the decision we were happy with: Johnson would go back to prison, and that's where he is as of this writing.

In the car on our way back from the parole hearing, Guy Yelton couldn't stop talking about Grandma's verbal attack on him. I think it gave us all a little comic relief after such a close call. The three of us had spent the last few weeks terrified that the board would vote to release this scourge on society, and we weren't rested up from his last reign yet.

Johnson may be released in a year or two, and if so, it'll be interesting to see if he still wants to make good on his threats toward me and others who testified against him.

The case of the Southside Rapist brought a lot of attention to Tennessee law enforcement and our ability to work big cases. As it stands today, it's one of the biggest cases I've ever worked.

I pray that nothing comes along to break that record.

Photo courtesy *The Lebanon Democrat*

TBI Agent Frank Evetts and I investigate one of the
murders on Melrose.

CHAPTER FIVE

Murders on Melrose

Melrose Avenue in Lebanon is one of the shortest streets in the state, about the length of a football field. Only three or four small, wooden frame houses still stand close to the street facing west at approximately where the fifty yard line would be. Back in the 30's and 40's, five rose-covered cottages stood along this tiny road which dead ends on a shallow waterway called "Town Creek." Melrose Avenue certainly sounds like a pretty street, and at one time, I'm sure it was all its name implies. But things change and not always for the better. Bluebird Road immediately comes to mind.

If you're trying to form a mental image of this and you're coming up with a Thomas Kinkade painting of picturesque little cottages by a bubbling brook, picture this instead: the creek is mostly a flat bed of solid rock that runs through the entire city and even under the town square, bending and curling like a snake. In the past, this nearly dry creek bed has served as a superhighway for those who wanted to walk undetected from one end of the city to another; mostly petty thieves, drug dealers and drunks. Melrose ends at this wide creek and re-connects with a busy secondary road on the other side, intersecting with Highway 231. When the water level is low, many drivers cross this to avoid downtown traffic — that is, if they're willing to test their vehicle on the rocky holes and offsets of the unpredictable creek bed. Occasionally, heavy spring rains can cause this dry creek to turn into a raging white-water spectacle, overflowing its banks and threatening the houses nearby. Hedges on Melrose are overgrown into tangled fence wire and what's left of a wooden gate or two. Unkempt, vacant lots remain where a couple of the houses have been torn down.

Adding to this lack of curb appeal, if there had been bleachers instead of weeds on the side of this street, spectators could have witnessed some of the most horrific murders on record.

In less than nine years, I worked three murders in the five homes on this street. All of these murders were as different as daylight and dark. There were different motives; one was about sex, one involved rage, and another was about robbery. In two of the murders, I was the primary investigator. In the other, the Sheriff's Office assisted the Lebanon Police in solving the crime.

The first murder was at 537 Melrose, and the call came into our office with a blood curdling scream from a woman who had stopped at the house to check on the welfare of her 72-year-old mother that morning. What she found when she stepped through the front door is certainly a crime scene I'll never forget. I can only imagine how it replays in the daughter's mind to this day. I rushed to Melrose Avenue as soon as I got the call from dispatch.

"I'll bet Tony did it! I'll bet you anything *Tony* did this!" The daughter, who was in her late 40's, was screaming and crying as she met me at the door.

I came in and walked through the house, across the old linoleum which crackled beneath my feet, and into the small bedroom in the back of the house. I've never seen so much blood in all my days as a detective. The floor in the hallway from the bedroom slanted downward in this old house, and the blood had made its way down the hall toward the kitchen. The body of the elderly lady, Mrs. Minnie Bennett, was lying face down in a pool of blood. I was sure her throat had been cut for there to be this much of a mess. She was still wearing her nightgown and several lights were still on throughout the house, indicating she was murdered the previous night as she was getting ready for bed. I had met Mrs. Bennett on a number of occasions, and it's always so difficult to work a murder scene when you know and like the victim. In this case, it was a sweet, gentle lady who always greeted me with a smile when I saw her in town.

My partner, Det. Gene Murray, took photographs of the body, and I lifted prints and asked questions while we waited for the arrival of the medical examiner, good ole' Dr. Kash. He would be able to move the body and determine the exact cause of death.

The daughter told me that her mother's car was missing and that her mother's step-grandson had been staying with her while her dad was in the hospital. She talked about how "different" this boy was — not only in his actions, but in his appearance. His name was Anthony Wayne "Tony" Kamahele, a native of Hawaii. The daughter looked around the house and noticed that her dad's gun collection was missing and that her mother's purse was turned upside down on the kitchen table.

I got a detailed description of Kamahele, the car, and the weapons from the victim's daughter, and I had dispatch place a nationwide alert on him. We learned that Mrs. Bennett had some relatives in Knoxville — 150 miles away — so we contacted that police department to be on the lookout because he might try to hide out there.

Dr. Kash finally arrived and we put the D.A.'s office on notice that we would probably order an autopsy immediately. As Dr. Kash and I slowly rolled the body over, the head fell backwards and almost came off. Mrs. Bennett's throat had been slashed almost all the way through, three to four inches from one end to the other. The vertebrae were exposed, and the cut was so clean, you could see down through her entire body. Dr. Kash determined that she probably lived a while longer after her throat was cut because her heart continued to pump all of her blood onto the floor. The doctor speculated that, according to the condition of the body, the woman had been dead for at least ten to twelve hours.

I had to find the murder weapon if it was still in or around this house. I went into the kitchen, where everything was neat and organized except for two things: the contents of the victim's purse were dumped on the table, and a large hunting knife — used to field dress deer — was left in the sink. It certainly didn't look like a tool this elderly lady would own. At the time, it didn't appear there was blood on the knife, but there was a folded, bloodstained cloth lying next to it. I put both the items in a plastic evidence bag.

The daughter told us that the doors were locked when she arrived. Whoever killed her mother took the keys and locked the door behind them when they left. Mrs. Bennett owned an old 1966 white station wagon, which would be easy to spot with a native Hawaiian behind the wheel headed east on I-40. But we couldn't concentrate solely on him and rule everyone else out. Not yet.

We knocked on the doors of the other four homes, interviewed, and fingerprinted the neighbors to see if anyone saw or heard anything. These residents had no way of knowing that, within a short period of time, their home would be also cordoned off with crime scene tape and someone in their family would become a murder victim.

It took us all day to complete our investigation at the crime scene, but as we were working there, other officers were on the lookout for the victim's stolen station wagon and Kamahele. No one had seen the car or the boy.

As Gene and I were on our way back to the department, the radio blared out, "Lebanon, 506, Knoxville PD needs you to call their office right away." Of course there were no cell phones in those days, so I rushed into the office in hopes of hearing some good news from Knoxville. Bingo. They had Kamahele in custody and had recovered the car and the weapons. Just as we had assumed, he had gone to hide with relatives and had hoped he could use that visit as his alibi. But the Knoxville family was so concerned about how he was acting around them that one of them slipped out of the house and called the police. The officers say when they got to the house, Kamahele ran out the back door, hid in the back seat of Mrs. Bennett's stolen car, and hunkered down in the floorboard alongside the stolen weapons.

I didn't say this guy was a genius.

Finally, it appeared that we had a break in the heartbreaking case of this elderly woman killed by her grandson while her husband, her partner and protector, was helpless in the hospital after an illness.

It was already dark when we headed to Knoxville to pick up Tony, our number one suspect in this gruesome murder. We made it up there in record time, but it took the rest of the evening just to sort through the paperwork, sign receipts for the weapons, and make arrangements with the family to get the stolen car back to Lebanon.

I was taken aback when I first laid eyes on the young man who had slaughtered his own grandmother. He looked like the typical gang member with a stocking cap pulled over a shaved head. He also had unusually long, slender arms. It was around midnight when we walked him to the car in handcuffs. He had a dazed look in his eyes and didn't utter a word. We did most of the talking, telling him that he was a suspect in his grandmother's murder and that we were taking him back to Lebanon for questioning.

Less than 24 hours after committing a heinous crime, he was in the back seat of our patrol car, headed to jail. Sometimes it all comes together like clockwork.

"Could I have a cigarette?" he finally spoke when we got almost to the city limits of Crossville.

I glared over at Gene, who looked back at him and said, "Yep, sure, but if you're going to talk to us, we need to advise you of your rights again." Gene advised him of his rights in hopes that once he started drawing on that cigarette, he'd be in the mood to give us a statement.

Gene lit the cigarette and Tony leaned back and puffed on it as we made our way toward Nashville. Gene and I were making small talk about the case in an effort to get him to say something. Then, out of the blue, like a Chatty Cathy doll, Tony blurted out his confession:

"I didn't mean to do it!" There was the opening we needed to begin our line of questioning.

As I was headed west, there was no traffic and I was running hammer down in that old gold Ford, flying low at more than 95 miles per hour.

But just as our suspect was beginning to sing like Polly Parrot, blue lights appeared in my rear view mirror. It was the Highway Patrol. I was thinking about how mad the chief was going to be if I got a ticket as I slowed down and stopped on the shoulder of the road. I saw through the mirror that the trooper was approaching our car with caution — a good idea since we had blind tags and tinted windows on the unmarked vehicle. He had no way of knowing that we were law enforcement officers breaking the law in the wee hours of the morning. He stood to the rear of the driver's door as he approached the car, just as he was trained, with his hand over his gun.

"Hey, hot rod! You know how fast you were going? Let me see your driver's license!" he demanded.

I began to explain our situation. I told him that we were law enforcement officers and that when I reached into my jacket for my license, he would see that I was wearing a gun.

"Just do it slowly, then."

I painstakingly reached into my pocket for my license and identification, and as I did, I explained we were headed back to the jail with a murder suspect.

"Is that the guy out of Lebanon you put the APB out on this morning?"

"Yes, it is," I answered, relieved that the trooper knew about the case and we were now on the same page, so to speak.

"Go ahead and give us a ticket and you can have him," I joked, gesturing to the back seat where our stocking-capped booby prize was still puffing away on his ciggy.

The trooper chuckled and stepped back from the car. Like a kid at a drag race, he put both hands over his head and then dropped them, as if starting the competition.

"GO!" he smiled as he gave us permission to get this jerk to jail as soon as possible. "But, drive carefully!" he advised.

Gene and I were both afraid that this little interruption would shut up our once chattering suspect, but, Tony wanted another cigarette and we saw this as another opportunity to get the conversation flowing again. That's back when I was still smoking and I think I even joined him in a puff or two after the stress of being stopped by the Highway Patrol.

Tony told us that he went to his grandmother's house to borrow her car late that night, but she refused to let him have her only vehicle — her only way to get to the hospital to visit her husband. After she went to bed, he got her purse and took the keys. He thought she was already asleep, but when he saw her bedroom light come on, he panicked, went into her room, and got into a fight with her about the car. He said she called him names and they got into a struggle over the keys.

He admitted carrying the hunting knife for protection because "he looked different," and he felt the need to defend himself.

As they struggled, he reached for the knife in his pocket. He said he didn't know why, but suddenly he grabbed her head and cut her throat. He said he didn't remember much after that because he was so scared. He claimed he took his grandfather's guns and headed toward Knoxville where he had some relatives.

I described to him the knife I had found in the kitchen sink at the murder scene. He admitted that was the knife he had used to kill his grandmother.

"I washed it off and left it there, 'cause I knew I was going to get caught," he admitted.

Tony didn't say another word for the rest of the trip, but continued to smoke Gene's entire pack of cigarettes. It was a small price to pay for the information to put this guy away for the rest of his life.

As with all murder cases, there was that good news/bad news situation. The good news was we caught the killer before he got out of state. The bad news was the family lost a great lady, wife, and loving mother. After a tearful and unexpected goodbye to their loved one, they would now have to go through the agony of a trial.

Mercifully, the trial was a short one, lasting only a day or two after we picked the jury. The confession and the overwhelming murder weapon evidence made it simple. Tony was caught with the stolen guns, hiding inside the stolen vehicle. You can't get more cut and dried than that.

Anthony "Tony" Kamahele got life in prison for the brutal murder of his grandmother. I heard a few years back that he was the leader of some Asian gang within the prison system. I used to keep in touch with the victim's family, but I haven't heard from them in years. I've often thought of Mrs. Bennett and what might have gone through her mind in those final moments as her step-grandson held that hunting knife to her throat and made that cut.

Here was a boy she had welcomed into her family and her home — a young man she wanted to mother and bring up as her own because he had nowhere else to go. This was how he repaid her kindness.

Photo courtesy *The Lebanon Democrat*

Anthony "Tony" Kamahele (center)
was captured within hours of killing his grandmother.

Mrs. Bennett never had a chance, and her death and the images we saw on the investigation that night still haunt me. Any time an elderly person is hurt or killed, it takes me a long time to come to grips with it. I know that it's part of my job, but it's the part I've never gotten used to since I've always had a tender spot in my heart for the elderly. In my view, a killer who attacks an elderly person would attack anyone not able to defend themselves, and that includes little children. These criminals deserve the maximum penalty the law allows for their crimes.

The Perry Jennings Murder

There are no two murders alike. The murder of Perry Jennings took some time to solve, and took many strange twists and turns before it was solved. It was September 26, 1981, when another murder was committed on the smallest street in town. I remember I was at home and it was about 8 P.M. when I got that call to go to Melrose Avenue. I asked dispatch, "Which house on Melrose?" I don't know why I wasted my time with that, since there were only the five little houses at the time and no one had moved into Ms. Bennett's house after she was killed. Dispatch told me it was 513 Melrose, and I knew immediately that it was Perry Jennings' place. I had known him for years. My patrol division had found Perry's body after his wife had called and said she returned home and found her husband dead.

Mr. Jennings was a well-liked, long-time city employee who worked at the Public Works department and had formerly worked as a deputy, serving in a volunteer capacity. He was a big man with a big heart who was always smiling and telling stories about the olden days. His hobby was rabbit hunting, and he kept his dogs in a pen he had built behind the old wooden-frame home.

The Jennings' house was the closest to Town Creek, and whenever the spring rains came, his house would barely escape being flooded. He told me many times he would watch as the rain fell and the water rose to his doorstep. He stayed up all night long watching it rain one evening. He had packed up a car with all their belongings and was ready to get his family out when the water began to threaten. His family had lived there so long, they had a pretty good idea how much rain it took to get to that point, and since he worked for Public Works, Perry knew how much water that creek could hold before it started spilling over into the little neighborhood like a raging river. The city had a water gauge in that part of town that would calculate how high the water would be in downtown Lebanon within one hour if it continued to rain at a certain pace.

Living in a house that was so close to danger every time a heavy rain came meant that Mr. Jennings was constantly on the job.

When I arrived at the Jennings home, there were several patrol cars out front and my colleagues had already secured the crime scene for me. Getting out of my car, I felt a cold chill in the moist air from the creek as I saw Jennings' wife, Virginia, standing with officers in the front yard. Several officers on the force knew her, since she was a crossing guard at one of the elementary schools. She seemed to be extremely upset and was crying. When I walked up and introduced myself, I told her I wanted to speak with her after I viewed the crime scene.

I could already tell that this was going to be a long night. I would need some help on this one, so I called dispatch requesting Detectives Barbee and Foster to assist me. We had so many cases we were all working at once and were mentally and physically exhausted, but we had to persevere.

In small town America, there are well-trained detectives with the skills that those in many big city departments simply don't have, but we're spread thin. We've been fortunate to have good detectives in Lebanon, but the small staff had to do it all, from photographs, to fingerprints, to crime scene reconstruction and evidence gathering. There's something to be said for the skills that come with working a crime scene from beginning to end and seeing every single detail firsthand. Perhaps that's what makes the small town detectives so good at what they do.

As I stepped in the front door, I began to look around and take it all in. The front door opened into a bedroom as it did in many older homes back in those days, since the only source of heat was usually in the center of the home and living rooms had to double as bedrooms.

I walked up to a recliner chair and caught my first glimpse of the body. From behind the chair, I could see Perry Jennings' bald head. His skull had caved in on the top from a hard blow, and there was a crease in his head the shape of a large, round pipe of some kind. Blood was everywhere. Obviously, someone had surprised Mr. Jennings from behind, because he was still sitting in his chair and apparently never knew what or who hit him. As I stepped to the front of the chair, I could see he was reclined all the way in the chair, lying back in his t-shirt and underwear. The rest of his clothes were on the floor, and the old black and white television set with a rabbit ear antenna was blaring in front of him as if he were still watching.

It was obvious to me that whoever killed this active, alert, older man apparently had to sneak up from behind him while he was taking a nap after a long day at work. I reached over and turned off the TV, wondering about the last program Perry ever saw. It was an odd thought at a time like this, but when you know the victim, these little details race through your mind.

Detectives Barbee and Foster had joined me at this point with the fingerprinting kit and the camera equipment we needed to get started. We were all wondering what the hell had happened in this room and if Perry knew his killer. I called District Attorney Tommy Thompson to tell him about the murder and discuss arranging an autopsy in Nashville the next morning, getting the proper paperwork signed, and all of those other details that only he could help us with. We wouldn't need a medical examiner right away because we would be gathering this evidence a while longer, but when the time was right, we knew we would have to call Dr. R.C. Kash to come over and do his thing. Try as he might, he was going to have a helluva time convincing me that Perry Jennings died of natural causes.

It always took Dr. Kash so long to get to the crime scenes, but he only lived six blocks away from downtown, so we wouldn't have to wait around for him this time, right? You would think not. But we did.

He finally arrived in his rumpled, dirty khaki raincoat and looked as if he had slept in his clothes. He had on that old brown hat as usual. After his examination, we moved the body to begin our search for clues. This murder just didn't look right to any of us. Someone could have broken in on him and robbed him while his wife was gone — that was our first impression, of course. We searched through his clothing and saw that his billfold was missing. His wife Virginia said Perry had gone out back to feed his hunting dogs, but then came in to watch TV, which is where he was when she left for the evening to go visit some friends. She said he kept his billfold in his pants beside the recliner when he relaxed at night, and he usually carried a great deal of money around with him since he was always buying, selling, or trading hunting dogs.

We did our routine interviews with the neighbors, but we couldn't keep our eyes off the creek. Since the Jennings' home was at the end of the street, and that dry creek bed was a place where thugs walked up and down like some kind of boardwalk at all hours, it was possible that someone could have walked up and seen an easy target — a sleeping man. I've arrested a lot of people through the years on that creek after they broke into houses, smoked dope, hung out under the bridges, and generally were nuisances to everyone.

Back then, Larry Bowman, who is now Chief Detective, was a patrolman helping us with this investigation. He came up to the back door of the kitchen and knocked.

"We've found some of Mr. Jennings' personal papers in the yard that backs up to the creek," he said as he held up a plastic evidence bag.

We were speaking through the aluminum storm door, and as I reached to open it and go outside, I noticed it was hooked with one of those old screen door hooks. No one had sneaked in this way. If someone came up from the creek, they had to come in and go out the front door and then run around to the back yard. I stepped out back to see what I could find.

Photo courtesy *The Lebanon Democrat*

It was a veritable junk yard out there, with old five-gallon buckets stacked around the perimeter of the house. The dog pen was attached to a separate garage, and rusty containers of rainwater and other debris were scattered everywhere.

The beagles were barking the entire time at all of this police activity. If only those dogs could talk, we could wrap this up and call it a night.

Larry took us to where he found the personal papers, which led us to a trail of Mr. Jennings' personal belongings leading into the weeds toward the creek. There, on the ground in plain view, we found his driver's license. It was just as I thought; we were on the trail of a killer who uses this creek to travel throughout the city undetected. We needed some tracking dogs, so I called dispatch to see if we could get the Metropolitan Police Department in Nashville to send me a K-9 unit to help in this investigation. If we could track this evidence, it would lead us to the killer. I was certain of that.

It was our lucky night, apparently. Metro had two dogs — an attack dog and a tracking dog — that were located on the Wilson/Davidson County line and were available to help us.

Within twenty minutes, the K-9 unit was on Melrose ready to go to work. We held everyone off the trail so the scent would be fresh. With a little luck and a very big dog's nose, we could be led right to the killer's door. All of this took place just as the ambulance was arriving for the most unbearable event for the family, the removal of the body. Mrs. Jennings was visibly upset, and other family members were trying to console her as her husband left the house for the last time — feet first, on a gurney, and covered with a sheet.

"Lebanon 506!" My call sign was being yelled out over the radio. "We've found more property belonging to the victim out here," the officer said.

This was just too good to be true. A robber and murderer as careless as all this would be a cinch to catch. He'd slip up somewhere and that would be soon if this continues. More than an hour went by, and the trail was leading us to East Adams Street until the dogs lost the scent there. That was very disappointing news. We were able to find the victim's billfold and other personal belongings, so perhaps we could get some fingerprints from that. Since there was no money left in the wallet, we gathered that the motive was most definitely robbery.

The Nose Knows

The Metro officers brought their dogs back to the car for a much-needed rest and some cool water. As the officers were loading up the K-9s to head back home, I gathered the family together to advise them I was doing everything I could and tapping every possible resource available to me. I asked Mrs. Jennings to walk with me to the end of the driveway to thank the officers and their dogs for helping us. As the two of us walked past one of the cars, the dog went *crazy* trying to jump through the glass at us. It was really frightening and easy to see why K-9 officers are so effective at getting criminals to surrender.

The dog was jumping around in the back seat with the window rolled half way down, and I thought for a minute he would come through that little crack in the window and eat us alive. I introduced Mrs. Jennings to the dog handlers, and she and her family thanked them for being there for them. The entire time we talked, the dogs didn't stop their wailing. I didn't think about what had just happened until much later.

As we walked back to the house, Mrs. Jennings told me that she was too scared and upset to stay in that house alone tonight. It was already after midnight, so I told her to go home to be with her family, and we would contact her in the morning to get her statement.

We needed to put our ears to the ground and work very hard on this difficult case. Perry Jennings had a lot of friends, and we needed to find out where he had been going and who he had contact with in these past few days. He dealt with strangers when he worked with those dogs, so anyone could have seen him pull a roll of money out of his pocket. But who could have wanted to bash his head in like *that?* What kind of weapon did they use? I've seen a lot of skull licks in my time, but none more vicious than this one.

It was getting very dark and we needed flashlights to see two feet in front of us, since there were no streetlights out there near the creek. If the murder weapon were lying in the yard or scattered among the debris in Mr. Jennings' yard, we'd have to wait until morning to locate it. I placed crime scene tape around the house and put a patrolman on the residence to secure the area for the night. I was exhausted and went home to get some shut-eye. I wanted to be fresh and approach this puzzle with a clear head first thing in the morning.

The next morning, I arrived early to relieve the patrolman who had watched the house all night, and I noticed just how much junk was around that house that we couldn't begin to see with flashlights the night before. Old buckets, barrels, piled up wood, fence posts, and fence wire Jennings used to make his dog pens were scattered around. The dogs looked hungry, so I found the dog kibble in the kitchen and gave them a generous portion. They also needed water. My search for that took me to these 55-gallon drums Jennings had placed under the eaves of the building to catch rainwater running off the garage roof. Each barrel was full. I dipped water out with one of the small buckets and gave it to the thirsty dogs. They would be fine until I came back later to look around more and check on them, but for now, I would go back to the office and pore over the evidence we had collected in hopes that something would jump out at me.

I stared at the photographs of the victim's head. What could bash his head in and leave a mark like that? It wasn't a sledge hammer. The object, whatever it was, had left a strange, canal-like imprint in his skull. Maybe the autopsy would tell us more, but I'd have to wait for those results.

Meanwhile, I called the first officer on the scene, the one who was talking to Mrs. Jennings when I arrived. He said he thought it odd that Mrs. Jennings told him she had called from a *neighbor's* house to report the murder. She claimed that she didn't even go inside her home. How did she know her husband was dead if she didn't enter the house? When I stood at the front door of the house and looked in, I certainly couldn't see the recliner from that angle, and there were curtains in the way. Perhaps the officer misunderstood what Mrs. Jennings said. I wanted to get a statement from her within the hour and clear up some of this confusion, but when I called the family, they told me a doctor had given their mother a sedative to help her sleep. An interview wouldn't be possible today.

That afternoon, the detectives returned from the autopsy. One of them looked a little green around the gills after the experience, but that was expected sometimes. The medical examiner confirmed our speculation that the skull was completely crushed with a long, heavy object — a big steel pipe with an edge on it. I decided that I needed to take another look at all that rusty junk out in the back yard of the house to see if I could find anything like a big steel pipe out there.

Searching For Clues

Lebanon Police Detectives (left-to-right) Mike Barbee, Terry Ashe and Gary Mac Foster, examine a possible piece of evidence in the homicide case of Perry Jennings who was found dead at his home Saturday night. Robbery has been determined by police as the motive behind the slaying. (DEMOCRAT photo By Bill Thorup)

The three of us went back to Melrose Avenue and scoured the front and back yards looking for anything that we thought could have caused that kind of damage to a human skull. We walked around for a couple of hours in the tall weeds along the creek and even in the creek, but came up with nothing. There were plenty of small pipes and some fence posts lying around near the house, but nothing with the same circumference of the U-shaped gash left by the murder weapon.

It was getting late, so I fed and watered the dogs again and went back to the office to decide on our strategy for the next day. Det. Barbee was planning to question the city employees who worked with Perry Jennings, and Det. Gary Foster would gather up the physical evidence to take to the crime lab for examination. I would try, yet again, to talk to the widow Jennings. Before I left for the evening, Virginia Jennings called and apologized for being out of reach for the past couple of days. She promised we could talk first thing in the morning. Tomorrow was going to be a very busy day for interviews.

As I walked into my office early the next morning, I got another phone call from Mrs. Jennings. She said she would be at the Melrose house later in the morning, and that's where we would do our interview. Her family was still with her, and they were all standing outside when I arrived, so I took her aside and began my line of questioning.

She Was the Dancing Queen

Virginia Jennings told me she had left the house that night to meet her friends and go square dancing at Cedar Forest State Park in the early evening, but that they didn't get to dance because they arrived after it started. She said she left early because she wanted to come home to fix supper for Perry, but when she returned to the house around 8:30 P.M., she found her husband dead.

"How did you know your husband was dead if you didn't enter the house?" I asked her the question that had been hanging out there for all of us.

"I could see through the front door, and I could see Perry in the chair," she answered without skipping a beat. Her answer didn't satisfy me. Not in the least.

When we finished our interview, Mrs. Jennings went into the house to gather some belongings, and I walked up to peer into the living room to see what I could see. I was able to see Perry's recliner from that vantage point, but it would have been difficult to discern if someone were dead or just asleep from that distance. It would be hard to tell if someone was even sitting in that enormous chair. I had to walk right up to the recliner before I could see the top of his head when I first arrived to investigate that night.

Her story had holes in it and, like those K-9s from the night before, I was hot on the trail of suspect number one — the wife. What was really going on with her? She seemed like such a sweet, older lady. Why was she going to the square dance with her girlfriend instead of her husband?

After I had time to mull over our conversation at the office that afternoon, I wanted to ask her a few more questions. Her family told me I could find her at the Melrose house, where she had gone to pick up another load of her belongings. When I drove up, her car was parked out back and she was feeding and watering the dogs. She was kind and cooperative and gave us permission to search the house again by signing a waiver. Back in the day, the owner of the home could do that, which saved us from having to take the time to get a search warrant.

As I was just about to leave, I turned around to ask her the important question I came to ask:

"I need to know the name of the girlfriend that you went square dancing with. I'll need to talk to her."

"Oh, the name ... the name of the person ... well ... that would be ... Bob," she stuttered. "Bob Likens. We go dancing all the time together. Perry wouldn't dance."

Okay, I was thinking to myself, I have suspect number two — the boyfriend. Now all I needed to find was the motive.

Det. Barbee had gleaned some information from one of Perry Jennings' coworkers that perhaps Mr. and Mrs. Jennings weren't getting along. The coworker said that Perry was concerned that his wife was spending too much time square dancing and running around with her dance partner, but had admitted that it at least gave him time to spend on his hobbies — hunting and working with the dogs. To me, it sounded like the typical story of a troubled marriage; she was going her way and he was going his, and the two never had time together.

Perry Jennings' funeral was attended by several former sheriffs, judges, deputies, and city workers. Virginia wore black, playing the part of the grieving widow. I figured Bob Likens would show up, so I went to the guest register after the funeral to look at all the signatures of those who had come to pay their respects. If he was there, he signed another name. Maybe Virginia told him to stay away.

We couldn't question anyone in the family today, so I focused once again on looking over the evidence. My mind went back to that old aluminum door in the kitchen and how it was hooked when we arrived on the scene that night.

No one could have sneaked up on Perry Jennings. Not with all those dogs out there. Even if the door had not been latched, it made such a noise when it was opened that it would probably wake the neighbors if not every dog in the area. The killer or killers had to use the front door and they probably entered holding the murder weapon. It would have been a lot more convenient for the robber to come through the door with a handgun than with a murder weapon weighing fifteen or twenty pounds. Whatever that thing was, he or she or *they* probably took the object with them when they left, because we had yet to find anything as "heavy as a sledgehammer but shaped like a large pipe," as the medical examiner described for us.

Det. Barbee, Det. Foster, and I went back to the house the next day to get a better look at that back door. Maybe there was something we were missing. I was hoping we could find something to counter what was going through my mind: that Mrs. Jennings and her boyfriend had planned this and that they had waited until Perry was his most vulnerable, fast asleep in his easy chair, before they hit him over the head with … whatever it was.

And that was the sixty-four thousand dollar question. Where and what was the murder weapon? We had to find an answer on this day, before the crime scene was compromised and before the trail went cold. Searching the same ground we had covered time and time again, we soon grew tired of hearing the poor dogs wail, and I'm sure they were tired of our poking around their territory. They were hungry and thirsty, so I decided to give them an early supper and shut them up with a little kibble before they drove us nuts. I took a bucket and scooped up some fresh water for them from one of those 55-gallon barrels Perry had placed near the house under a rain gutter — not realizing that at the very moment I was doing this chore, the murder weapon was right under my nose.

Call it divine intervention, cop's intuition, or having a vision, but something told me to look inside the rain barrel. I pushed it over with my foot, and as gallons of water flooded the high grass and debris at my feet, Barbee and Foster looked at me as though I had lost my temper if not my mind.

Finally. What I sought was at the bottom of the barrel. You always find something in the last place you look, as Grandpa used to say.

A long, heavy, iron pipe rolled out onto the ground. The three of us looked at each other. Found it. When I reached down to pick it up, I realized what it was: an old window weight.

Photo courtesy *The Lebanon Democrat*

No one under forty is going to know what I'm talking about here, so I'll explain: double-hung windows in vintage houses had a rope and pulley system that helped them easily slide up and down. The ten to twenty-pound window weight that held the rope taut and kept the pulley working properly was a long, iron cylinder that was hidden deep inside the walls.

Normally you wouldn't even see one of these weights until an old house is demolished or the windows are torn out and replaced. Our particular specimen weighed in at about twelve pounds, was twenty inches long, and was a doozy. It had a rough edge on it and that edge had, what appeared to be, a bit of flesh stuck to it. In my mind, I was picturing how that edge matched the indentation in the top of Perry Jennings' head. I was confident the coroner would agree that the shape of the weapon matched the wound. We would know for sure when our "find" got to the crime lab.

Now we were in search of a motive. We kept the news of finding the murder weapon secret, hoping it would help us nab the one who had placed it in that rain barrel. Was it sweet little

ole' Virginia, the long-suffering, crossing guard widow? Or was it
her square-dancing boyfriend Bobby?

Det. Barbee and Det. Foster went to the next square dance at
Cedar Forest State Park looking for answers. Did anyone see
Virginia or Bob at the dance the night Perry Jennings was killed?
Not one person recalled seeing either one of them on the night in
question. The plot thickened, but it was going to have to get
thicker before I could pick up Bob for questioning. Still, even
though we knew we had our prime suspects, we hadn't reached
that final point where we could rule everyone else out, so we
continued to track down more leads.

Out of the blue, I got a call from a waitress at one of the chain
restaurants on Highway 231. She wanted to meet me and talk
some place privately, because she couldn't be seen talking to me.
This waitress knew Perry Jennings and his wife very well and had
served them many times at that restaurant, which is why she was
particularly puzzled at what she saw one evening. She couldn't get
it out of her mind, especially after reading the accounts of Perry's
murder in the newspaper. The newspaper had reported that
Virginia Jennings had returned home from square dancing to find
her husband's body the night he was murdered. This waitress had
a different story to tell.

I met her late at night after she got off work near the old rock
quarry on Four Mile Hill. She was terrified of losing her job and
getting her name in the paper somehow, so I assured her that I
would protect her privacy.

She said Bob Likens came into the restaurant alone, around six
o'clock the night Perry Jennings was murdered. He sat and sipped
on cup after cup of coffee for nearly an hour. Then Virginia
showed up, as she had so many evenings after square dancing with
Bob, and they moved to another table. She said they were both
acting very strangely after Virginia arrived, and when she went over
to take their food order, only Bob ate. Virginia said she wasn't
hungry. The waitress described Bob as "not the typical square
dancing guy." She said he was — as the former California governor

would say — a *girly-man*. Not masculine and muscular like the other square dancers who came in there. I asked her if she could remember what time Bob and Virginia left the restaurant, because that was the key. She said the couple left around eight o'clock.

As she opened the door to get out of my car, she looked back at me and almost as an aside, said "Oh, by the way, after I heard that Mr. Jennings was killed the same night Bob and Virginia were together, I went back through my records and found the ticket where they had paid for their coffee and food. I thought it might be important, so I kept it. Let me know if you need it."

"I'll take that now if you don't mind," I said. She gave me the ticket, got in her car and drove away. I wanted to pump my fist in the air and yell, "YES!" but I sat there a minute in silence — probably grinning from ear to ear — and thought about my next move. It was time to start asking some tougher questions even as I cooled my heels waiting for the evidence results to come back from the Washington D.C. crime lab. None of our informants on the street knew of anyone else involved in this crime, and everywhere we looked beyond Virginia and Bob, we were hitting dead ends. In my thought processes, Bob had graduated from being simply her "dance partner" to being her "lover." He had to be more than a friend, or she wouldn't be spending so much time with him. In this day and time she would have been known as a "cougar" since she was a much older woman seeing a younger man.

I had seen it all at my ripe age of 33, and I was going to see even more if I was lucky. My mind was bouncing from one odd scenario to another as I walked through the crime over and over, trying to figure out Bob's role, Virginia's role, and whether they were together when the murder was committed. All the dots were there. I just had to connect them.

After talking to the waitress and getting this extremely valuable information, I was very coy when I talked to Virginia on the phone. I never divulged that I had found the murder weapon in the rain barrel, and I never let her know we had sent any evidence to the crime lab in D.C. In a very polite way, I tried to pin her down on what time she left home to meet Bob Likens, what time they arrived at the square dance, and what time they left. I never told her I had a witness, nor did I let her know we had tangible evidence that she was at a restaurant with Bob for more than two hours instead of at the square dance as she claimed. Finally, in one of our phone conversations, she volunteered Bob's address, telling me exactly where and what time I could find him if I needed to question him. I knew they had already tied up loose ends and talked about getting their story straight, but I had them dead-to-right so I didn't care what they did at this point.

A Perfect Performance

The next morning, I went to visit with Bob. When he answered the door, I knew immediately what the waitress was talking about. He was a small-framed man, around forty, and looked like a fragile bird. Not the kind of brut who could crown someone with a twelve-pound window weight. He was a girly man, alright, but girly or not, he was ready for me and my questions as he sat in his tiny two-room apartment on the second floor of a run-down old building he called home. When I asked Bob about the night he met Virginia at the square dance, his story matched hers to the letter: they arrived at the dance too late to participate, and Virginia left about 7:30 or 7:45 because she wanted to get home to fix supper for Perry. I gave him my card and told him if he thought of anything else he wanted to tell me, he could give me a call any time. Bob told me that he "thought a lot of old Perry," and that he had been friends with both of them for a long time.

Weeks later, I was still waiting on the results from the crime lab. I knew these guys were busy, but please! I just wanted the lab to tell me what I already knew. There were no texts or emails back then. We had to wait on the U.S. Mail for our results, and it was slower then than it is now. Just as I had given up one morning, the letter postmarked "Sender: FBI Crime Lab, Washington, D.C." arrived and I tore into it like a child on Christmas morning. The summary confirmed what I thought:

"Human skin, hair and blood samples identified as matching that of victim."

"Blunt instrument caused damage to skull."

"Window weight was the murder weapon,"

Damn. Now I'm working a murder case and I'm full-throttle. I've got the body, the murder weapon, and two suspects. I also have a possible motive with this affair between Bob and Virginia. All that was left to figure out was how I was going to spring the trap.

Two days later, we planned to pick them both up at the same time and question them separately in hopes of turning them loose on each other. I didn't know if she had let Bob in the house and he had done the killing. I didn't know how someone could have entered the house without Perry knowing. I didn't know a lot at this point.

What I needed was a good, old fashioned confession. Or at least I needed one of these turkeys to totally rat on the other. I had to have this. Interviewing these suspects would be like the one-eyed dog in a butcher shop; he knew he was going to get a bite of steak, he just didn't know where it would be coming from.

Their stories matched, but their alibi didn't add up. They weren't at the square dance and they still insisted they were. A dual questioning session would put an end to the "Virginia Reel" the two of them were making us dance.

I called Virginia and asked her to come by my office at two o'clock to go over some evidence I had found. She agreed to meet with me. I figured she would warn Bob of my phone call, so we had her followed and had his apartment staked out so we could nab him if he wanted to make himself scarce. Just as expected, she drove straight to his apartment and went in to talk to him.

The minute she left, we moved in to bring in scrawny little Bob. She never knew he was in the building as she was being questioned by Det. Barbee and me in my office, and he was being questioned by Det. Foster in an office down the hall.

As the Worm Turns

I started out with the basics, thanking her for coming in, and generally bringing her up to date on the criminal investigation. Then I told her I had learned something disturbing about her relationship with Bob Likens. She looked me right in the eye with a blank stare and claimed nothing had ever taken place between the two of them. Then I dropped the bomb.

"We have witnesses who are telling us that you and Bob didn't go to the square dance at all that night. But before I ask you any more questions, Virginia, I need to advise you of your rights." I went through the rights waiver with her. She signed the paper acknowledging that I had read the rights to her.

"As I was saying, Virginia," I continued, "It's our understanding that you and Perry were having some marital problems."

"Yes, but everyone does," she answered.

"Yes, and I understand that, but not everyone goes around killing their husband." I quipped.

"I'm offended by your statement!" she blurted out before I finished my best line.

"So who's Bob?"

"Just a friend."

"Just so you know, I've got ole' Bob next door right now and we're gonna see what Bob tells us today. The stories the two of you have been telling are just straight up and down and match perfectly, and that concerns me," I said.

She stared at the floor for about a minute and said nothing. Then she looked up at me with the coldest expression I've ever seen.

"I want to call a lawyer," she said. "I'm not gonna say anything to you or anybody else."

As she was being escorted from my office that day, I got in the last word.

"Virginia, you had better get a damn good lawyer, cause you're gonna need one!"

I walked down the hall where Bob Likens was being put through the wringer. Or maybe he just felt like it. He was sticking to his story about going dancing. But he did admit that he didn't know what happened before Virginia left home that night. When I walked in to the interview room, he became nervous as hell. I told him Virginia had just confessed and that she told me that he had killed Perry Jennings. I told him that she explained how she had let him into the home and that it was he who had hit Perry on the head with some heavy object.

Bob was ghostly white when I finished my tall tales. His eyes filled with tears.

"I've never been to their house," he cried, "That's a big lie because I went by the restaurant to have coffee!"

That's the most truth I had heard out of Bob since we had met.

"Cut him loose," I said, "We'll just try both of these SOB's for the murder of Perry Jennings!"

As I let him go, I thought I would give him some time to absorb what I had just said in hopes that his memory of what happened that night would "come back" in a few days.

Meanwhile, I paid another visit to the waitress who had served Bob and Virginia that night in the restaurant. I really didn't want to drag her into this, but I needed some additional witnesses who might have seen the two together at the table. I asked her if she remembered other customers who might have been sitting nearby.

"I thought you might want to talk to more people, so I wrote down some names of customers who were in here for dinner at the same time. They might remember something," she said. "These folks are regulars in here and we know them real well, but please don't tell them you got their names from me."

Pulling my own teeth would have been easier. This woman was a sweetheart to come forward and help me, but to sit on a list of witnesses and bring it up as an afterthought? I asked her why she was only giving me tidbits of information at a time. She explained that her husband had been laid off from his job and she was the sole breadwinner in the family. She was terrified of losing their only income and didn't want her bosses to find out she was getting customers involved in a murder investigation. I assured her I would protect her in any way possible.

This was golden information. Now I had two more witnesses, people I knew and trusted who would testify that Virginia and Bob were not at the square dance, but were sitting in a corner booth at this restaurant for two hours. We interviewed this man and his wife, both of whom knew Virginia but didn't know Bob Likens very well. The couple said there was nothing unusual about the way the suspects acted that night, but they thought it was odd when they read in the paper the next morning that Virginia's husband had been killed.

It was time for me to take the findings to D.A. Tommy Thompson to see if he wanted to pursue this case. His reaction was what I expected; we needed even more evidence if we were going to make a strong case against these suspects. He suggested we continue to interview witnesses and hinted that we could probably get Bob Likens for accessory to murder after the fact. This was certainly a good little tidbit of information that might get ole' Bob to talking for sure.

This case was a tough assignment, since we had so many other cases we were working and didn't have the luxury of putting full-time manpower on it, but I was determined to solve the Perry Jennings murder case. We were so close. Neither of them knew we had the murder weapon, although I had wondered if Virginia even noticed the 55-gallon barrel had been turned over and the window weight was missing. If she noticed, she was keeping quiet.

After a few days went by, we picked up Bob Likens again to see if he had changed his story. He had not. Loyal to a fault, this guy.

He did tell us that he and Virginia were not seeing each other as much as they had before. That turned out to be another lie. We kept close surveillance on the murder scene-turned-love-nest, to see if they would screw up and show their hand on their own. Christmas was right around the corner, and in the front window of the room where Perry Jennings was murdered, a fully decorated tree adorned the space. Bob and Virginia were seen coming and going from the house and living together as though they were married.

It appears the two had moved in together and were "setting up housekeeping," as we say here in the South.

There was more going on here than square dancing, and that only made the murder motive stronger. Also, the more we watched the two of them, the more convinced we were that she was the boss of him. She was tougher, meaner, and more likely to have planned and carried out the murder than passive little Bob. She was using him as an alibi (And he probably thought all along she wanted him for his body!).

One of Perry's relatives, who didn't care for Virginia at all, called me one day to tell me he had visited in their home — sometimes on a weekly basis — and noticed that Virginia spoke harshly and disrespectfully to Perry. I felt this person was someone I could trust, so I cultivated this source and asked him more questions. I asked him if he had known what Perry did with the old window weights that he took out of the house when he got storm windows installed.

"Yes, Perry kept three or four of them. He thought he might use them as boat anchors someday. One of those weights was used as a door stop between the living room and the bedroom," he said. Man, did I ever need *that* piece of information.

Funny Thing About Criminals

They'll lie when it's more convenient to tell the truth. If these two had told us about their time at the restaurant, it would have been tough to pin them down. But they stuck with the square dancing story for whatever reason, and that is what was going to take them down in the end.

Bob Likens had a wreck of an old car, and one day when he left the driveway of the Melrose house, Det. Gary Foster was sitting at the end of the road and pulled him over. Bob told Det. Foster that he had nothing to say to him.

"Looks like you've moved in with the widow Jennings," Gary observed. "You'd better watch out, or she'll be doing away with you next!"

Bob drove away and, according to Gary, he had a very sick look on his face.

We had learned early in the investigation that Perry Jennings had a modest life insurance policy and that Virginia had already collected the money. From what we saw, she was spending more on Bob and her new lifestyle than she spent on the casket and funeral for Perry.

When school started back up again after Christmas, Virginia was right there as crossing guard at the elementary school as though nothing had happened. I made a point of going by there every few days as she was helping the children across and standing in the middle of the street directing traffic. I knew I was driving her crazy as I drove through there. Gary Foster and Mike Barbee did the same thing. We wanted to mess with her head and show her that *we knew* she killed her husband.

Life Goes On

Winter had come and gone, and it was time to begin the campaign for sheriff of Wilson County. My mind was consumed with all the details of the political race, but I was determined to concentrate on my daily job and all the cases we were working at once. I had some loose ends that needed to be tied up in the Jennings case, and I needed to bring Virginia Jennings to justice. This murder may still be unsolved as far as criminal court proceedings went, but it was not an unsolved murder in my mind. I needed to reconcile these two notions and find some peace.

Spring came, and Bob Likens left Virginia's life. As far as we could tell, Virginia had cultivated another love interest and kicked Bob to the curb. I can only imagine the sense of achievement she felt; her husband was out of the picture, she was confident she had conned this little ole' country boy right out of arresting her for murder, she had a little money and a new boyfriend. Life was good.

But God doesn't let things like this go unpunished for long.

I was in the middle of a campaign, fighting for my political life, and I didn't know if I would even have a job after Election Day. I had been told that if I ran for sheriff, I would have to take a leave of absence effective immediately. I wasn't about to give up a run for the job I had always wanted, so I took the chance with the faith that everything would work out the way it was supposed to work out according to the plan for my life.

I was out on the campaign trail in my old pickup truck and trying to make my savings account stretch when, finally, Bob Likens decided to call me. We arranged to meet in private the next morning at his apartment because he wanted to give me a "statement." Even though I wasn't on the police payroll, I still had paid vacation time. I was *determined* to see this case to the end.

I knocked on the door and he answered it, looking more girly and sickly than ever. He led me to a dinette table that was just a few feet from his bed in this tiny apartment. When we sat down, he told me was very ill and he didn't want to leave this world without explaining what he knew about the death of Perry Jennings. He begged me not to divulge where I got the information. He told me he was very afraid of Virginia.

It had not taken him very long to find out she wasn't exactly the most charming woman on the planet. Very shortly after moving in with her, Bob got into a small argument with her and she threatened him with "the same thing Perry got if he didn't shut up." Everyone in town viewed her as a cold-hearted murderer who walked around with her head up in the air as if she knew she had gotten away with clubbing her husband to death.

According to Bob, Virginia was supposed to have met him at the restaurant at six o'clock so they could make it to the square dance in time. He said he waited and waited and waited and drank several cups of coffee before she arrived.

I knew this was true. It matched perfectly with what the waitress had told me.

Bob went on to describe how nervous and jumpy Virginia appeared when she got to the restaurant and how she wanted to change tables to a more private area. She began whispering and telling him about getting into a heated argument with Perry. Perry had told her the square dancing was over and she would no longer be allowed to go because she needed to stay there and take care of him and the house. She apparently told Perry she wasn't about to give up square dancing, and that's when she said the argument got heated.

According to what Virginia told Bob that night at the restaurant, she just "had enough of Perry." She said there was cursing back and forth and that he sat down in his easy chair in his underwear and was watching television, all the while telling her she wasn't going square dancing.

Virginia never admitted to Bob that she had killed Perry, but after Bob moved in to the house with her, several things occurred that convinced him she had murdered her husband.

Then Bob went on to confirm that all the evidence I had in my possession. I never told him about the murder weapon, but I asked him if he knew what a window weight was. He told me that he knew what they were because there were a few lying around the Melrose house where Perry had remodeled and put in new windows. Virginia used them as door stops throughout the house. I didn't tell him that's not all she used them for. It was all fitting together and it all pointed to the truth.

Bob put his statement in writing for me as we sat there at the kitchen table.

That's all we needed, and that's all the D.A. needed to put Virginia Jennings away for a very long time. Now, it was a race against the clock as we all wondered if Bob Likens would live long enough to testify. We went to great lengths in the next few weeks to get his statement recorded just in case his health got worse, but long before this went to trial, he became even sicker and we had to take his dying declaration in lieu of his testimony on the witness stand.

Waiting for this case to move forward seemed like the longest wait in history to me. All I could focus on was how this cold-blooded murderer was still out there, free as a bird, helping our children cross the street after school.

Stress and Adrenaline

Looking back at all this, I don't know how we got it all done, but we did. Not only was I in the fight for my life on the campaign trail during the last and most important part of this case, but my friend and colleague District Attorney Tommy Thompson was up for re-election. Neither of us skipped a beat. We did our jobs and we worked to get elected and re-elected, respectively.

When the newly re-elected D.A. finally let us present all of the evidence in the Jennings case to the grand jury, I was relieved because I had found peace in two areas: I had become the sheriff of Wilson County at long last, and with the help of two fine detectives, we were going to put the person who killed Perry Jennings in prison.

What a year it had been.

A special grand jury convened to hear all the evidence and all the interviews presented in this case: Bob Likens' statement, the window weight matching the indentions in the skull, the human tissue which matched Perry Jennings' blood type found on the window weight, and the clear motive of a love triangle that I had suspected early in the case. It was all there and it was air tight.

Later that afternoon, the D.A. called me and said, "We have a True Bill." The grand jury had decided we had probable cause to proceed with the trial, and Virginia Jennings' indictment was at the courthouse ready for me to pick up.

I was so relieved. Detectives Barbee and Foster were as well. I called them, and they came by my new digs — the Sheriff's Office — and planned how we would take Virginia Jennings into custody. I notified the media and told them we were about to make an arrest in the Perry Jennings murder case.

There was lots of speculation in town that it might be Bob who killed Perry, and I'm sure she was hoping we would believe that too. Virginia had no idea we called that special grand jury in session to nail it down and nail her to the wall.

Det. Barbee went out to the house on Melrose to see if her car was there, and after passing her house, he told us she was at home. We got a search warrant and headed to Melrose. There was so much anticipation about this arrest. We wondered if she would go willingly without a word or if she would be defiant and fight us all the way. We were ready for either possibility.

The three of us walked up on the same front porch where we had watched Perry Jennings' body wheeled out to the coroner's van so many months ago. I knocked on the old wooden door of the house. When she opened it, she didn't look surprised to see me.

"Whadda y'all want?"

"Virginia, I have a sealed indictment from the grand jury charging you with the murder of Perry Jennings," I said.

"Whut?"

She was noticeably calm as she stared at the three of us, asking this mostly rhetorical question. She heard me loud and clear.

"We're taking you into custody," I said.

Det. Barbee pulled the handcuffs from his belt and put them on her wrists. Bob was not there, of course. He had wisely moved out months before when he determined he was indeed living with a cold-blooded killer. He was our key witness. Without his testimony we would have a very difficult time putting her at the scene and killing her husband.

She asked us if she could have her purse and put on some makeup before she went to jail. We checked the contents of her purse before handing it to her. I knew exactly what she was thinking. She was worried about how she would look on all those TV cameras waiting at the police station.

Photo by Bill Cook, Courtesy *The Lebanon Democrat*

Virginia Jennings on her way to jail.

Her bond was high dollar for that time, but we knew there was a chance she would post. We had searched the house and uncovered some insurance papers, proving she had received a sizable amount of money from a death policy, and we found an old revolver under the bed and a few other miscellaneous items that we felt could be presented to back up our case. As we left that home for the final time that afternoon, I couldn't help but feel Perry was looking down upon us. This poor guy was simply resting in his easy chair after a hard day's work and was murdered as he slept by a woman he thought was his loving, lifelong mate.

Throughout the trial, the sentencing, and her transport to the penitentiary, I never once saw her show an ounce of remorse. She never broke down and cried. She never had an expression from those shark-like eyes. A 66-year-old woman, who should have been a grandmother enjoying retirement and life with her husband, would soon be making her home within four gray walls for the next twenty-five plus years. She was released from prison a few years ago, and I almost didn't recognize her. She looked haggard, rough and hardened. What had been eating on her insides for years was now showing on her face for the entire community to see.

Was murder a choice she made because of love, greed, or boredom? Or was it all about simply wanting to go square dancing so much that she was willing to give up her freedom for it? In the end, it was a choice she made because she wanted it all.

A good man's life was taken and another senseless murder was put on the books on Melrose, a short but deadly street.

The Murder of a Prince

The third murder on Melrose caught the media's attention more than the first two. From this day forward, this little cul-de-sac was a street with five houses and three murders, which made for one heck of a headline and one hell of a bad reputation.

This time, the victim was 62-year-old Prince Barrett — a well-liked gem of a guy who everybody knew from his days as a barber. He was a war veteran and a widower, living modestly in retirement on his military pension and social security checks. He was rumored to have a great deal of cash around at all times. Mr. Barrett lived in the first house on the right at 533 Melrose, facing Adams Lane.

Mike Barbee had become the chief of detectives for the City of Lebanon and worked this case for several weeks. He would come by my office regularly to fill me in on the grisly details and to see if I had any thoughts or impressions about this homicide. It didn't take him long to put the pieces together. Barbee is an excellent investigator who knew exactly how to get results.

The Plot

The savage robbery murder plot was contrived by a young, attractive store clerk named Stephanie Collins. Mr. Barrett often visited the little market where she worked to purchase his only vice, chewing tobacco. Stephanie always helped Mr. Barrett and made him feel as though he was her favorite customer. Many times, he would go in the market just to see her and flirt with her, as older men sometimes do with waitresses and other young women they encounter. She was married, but reportedly had a lot of male "friends."

Prince Barrett was visiting the store one morning while Stephanie's brother, Gary Collins, and his friend Michael Hooper were in there hanging around. When Mr. Barrett opened his wallet on the counter to pay for his tobacco, Stephanie noticed that he was carrying a large amount of cash.

As Mr. Barrett left and walked to his car, she called her brother and his friend to the window and told them that this man was their chance to score a huge amount of money. She told them where Prince lived, and the two men staked out the house a couple of days to hatch their robbery plan.

Late one night, Collins and Hooper pulled up in front of the house and knocked on Mr. Barrett's door, claiming their car was broken down. They asked if they could come in and use his telephone. They were surprised when he told them he didn't have one.

Hooper and Collins didn't know what to do at this point, so they left with a plan to come back and break into the house later in the week.

Before dawn on March 21, 1991, the two slipped into Barrett's house through a back window as he slept. As they were going through drawers of a desk looking for money, Barrett woke up and confronted the intruders. One of the robbers hit him over the head with the butt of a gun and knocked him out cold.

It was merciful in light of what happened next.

This is where the two men have different versions of their story. Collins claims Hooper pulled out his large hunting knife and began stabbing Barrett as he lay on the floor. The autopsy showed he was stabbed a total of *forty-three times*. Hooper claims Collins asked for the knife and stabbed the victim.

Either way, I've never understood why the murder of this gentle, harmless man was so violent. It's the type of murder detectives see when there are emotional ties to the victim — the kind of brutal slaughter that occurs when someone is trying to settle a score. This just didn't make any sense. I've always hoped the blow to the head took this poor gentleman's life, and he didn't feel the knife repeatedly slicing into his body.

Mr. Barrett was found on the floor of his bedroom by his family that morning around nine. He was missing only eighteen dollars in cash and a checkbook. It's all he had since he deposited his cash and pension checks in the bank the day before. Eventually, the blank checks that were taken from Prince Barrett's home were being passed in the community. Since the account had been closed, those checks bounced and led investigators straight to the killers. Some of the check returns came from a western store in Nashville where a cowboy hat and bolo tie were bought by Hooper and Collins. Stephanie went to Walmart with her share of the take and bought some Venetian blinds on sale.

The investigation first narrowed the field down to two suspects, Hooper and Collins, who then proceeded to throw Stephanie under the bus as the mastermind of the crime.

What always pissed me off about this case was that for a measly sum of money and a few checks which were worthless, this fine citizen was killed just as he was about to enjoy his retirement.

A grand jury handed down the indictment of the two men for the murder of Prince Barrett, and Stephanie was charged as an accessory. Since she had the lesser charge, her bond was lower than the other two. She talked her mom and dad into mortgaging their home to bail her out of jail. Stephanie was married to some ne'er-do-well guy, and wouldn't you know it? They both left town, skipping bail, hanging her mom and dad out to dry, and leaving her brother and his friend to rot in jail.

Leads on her whereabouts soon grew slim, and it didn't look as though she would ever be found. Meanwhile, the two murderers conjured up a scenario wherein Stephanie came to the Melrose house with some other guy and the *two of them* killed Prince Barrett.

One day, a letter came to Mr. and Mrs. Collins' house from the Florida Department of Safety. Stephanie had gotten a traffic ticket in Florida and failed to pay it. It was mailed back to her old driver's license address — her parents' home.

Mike Barbee was hot on her trail now. Mike contacted the nationally syndicated program, "America's Most Wanted," and they ran an excellent dramatization of the story, urging anyone with information on Stephanie's whereabouts to call the Lebanon Police Department. That was a good move. Gary Collins was interviewed in prison for the show, begging his sister to come home and face the charges. The mother begged her daughter to come back and face the charges before they lost their home and everything they owned due to the forfeiture of the bond. Of course Stephanie didn't turn herself in.

The TV show, as it usually does, paid off in a matter of days. Dozens of callers to the show's tip line told authorities where Stephanie Collins and her husband were hiding in Florida. The police department swooped in one night and took her into custody.

Detectives learned later that there was a fourth person who was at the scene the night of the murder, but he did not participate in the killing. I can't mention his name, but the state offered him immunity to testify against the other three. By now, all the suspects were telling different versions of the same story, but it was of no consequence. They were found guilty and all slapped in prison for their crime.

Eighteen dollars and a few blank checks bought these slimes a cowboy hat, a bolo tie, some Venetian blinds, and life in prison.

Three murders in five houses on one tiny street. All solved.

I think Prince Barrett's killers should have gotten the death penalty since the murder was obviously premeditated — planned and plotted over several days. Virginia Jennings should have died for what she did to her sleeping husband with a window weight. As for the step-grandson? He had every opportunity to let his grandmother live, but he chose to slit her throat.

He deserved to walk down Electric Avenue more than any of them.

Melrose Avenue was a short little road of horrors with a sweet sounding name. But ask law enforcement officers anywhere in this country the name of the most violent street in their community and you might be surprised at the names they give you. It may sound as innocent and picturesque as Bluebird Road, Tulip Street, or even Hummingbird Lane. In my experience, the best advice is this: if you get lost as you travel through a strange city late at night, look at the name of the street you're on.

If the name sounds like heaven, avoid it like hell.

I was in the middle of solving the second of the three
murders on Melrose when I ran for Sheriff.

CHAPTER SIX

There was certainly divine intervention in all my years leading up to the Sheriff's election of 1982. I stuck my political toe in the water by defeating the incumbent constable in the 14th Civil District back in 1976, so I had a small taste of what I was getting into, but the race for sheriff is what I had spent my entire life preparing for.

Depending upon how you looked at it, I was either fortunate or unfortunate enough to be in the middle of some very high profile criminal investigations as Chief of Detectives. I had worked so many murders in a period of eight years and had helped crack down on illegal gambling, bootleggers, and drug dealers that the resulting publicity got my name and face out there. That didn't hurt.

By 1981, I was already well known in the community, especially within the law enforcement ranks, and it was all due to the sheer quantity and quality of the cases I was able to work in the detective division. Back then, the Nashville television stations would interview me when I made big arrests, solved crimes, or headed up civic programs like the DARE anti-drug initiative in the school system.

The Civitan Club honored me with the law enforcement officer of the year award following that legendary chase and shootout with the prison escapee. I was making headlines and running on a fast track, but I was so busy that I didn't realize it at the time.

Indeed, small, consistent efforts are the bricks from which a political platform is built.

I've always thought that luck appears when preparation meets opportunity. I was prepared, I was given the opportunity, and now, if luck didn't show up, I was ready to make my own. But never could I have orchestrated my career moves to work like an intricate puzzle as they did. The pieces eventually fell into place for a perfect fit, forming the big picture.

When I was working for the former sheriff after coming home from Vietnam, I thought I was on the right career path to achieve my goal. Then Jack Lowery, the mayor during that time, asked me if I would be interested in coming to the police department to head up the detective division. I hesitated, thinking I would be getting off track, but then I said yes.

Jack went back to practicing law, and I continued on a career path contrary to the one I had planned for myself. I didn't know that the successes I would enjoy as a detective would lay the groundwork for me to achieve my ultimate goal: to become the sheriff of Wilson County.

It was my childhood dream. There's a picture of me working a crime scene that almost mirrors a photo I have of my hero, Sheriff Howard Griffin. I realize just how much the political process has changed since Sheriff Griffin was elected, but I don't think the reason a citizen votes for one person over another has changed one bit. It all comes down to trust. People like to vote for someone they know and someone who knows them.

If I had to shake every single hand in the county, I was determined that everyone would see or hear the name Terry Ashe before they walked into that booth on Election Day in 1982.

The Leap of Faith

I started out my campaign for Wilson County Sheriff as nervous as a cat. I was working as Chief Detective for the city of Lebanon and was in the middle of solving the second of the three murders on Melrose when the city mayor, Tex Maddox, told me I would be without a job if I ran for the office. He was certainly putting a lot of pressure on me NOT to run, but, I felt called to do it. I took a leave of absence to pursue my goal of a lifetime. It was something I entered into with prayer and the support of family and close friends.

The single most important endorsement in my campaign
came from Sheriff Harold Griffin's widow, Rosalind,
who served out his term after his death.

Photo courtesy Neal Blackburn

The similarities between these two photographs are chilling; I'm shown here, crouched down, looking for evidence at a bloody murder scene.

In this photograph, taken decades earlier, Sheriff Harold Griffin is eerily in the same position as he looks for evidence. Sheriff Griffin was my hero and my inspiration to run for office.

I had to move forward because there was no going back.

I was extremely fortunate to have the backing of my old high school buddies, the support of my former bosses at places I'd worked as a boy, and business backing from the places where I had solved burglaries as a detective.

Everything had to be dealt with delicately. The incumbent sheriff had a lot of bad publicity with some personal issues and financial pressures, and the media constantly hounded him. Worst of all, he was frustrated with dealing with the political side of the county commission. He couldn't get funding for the resources to run his department at the proper level. He was the high sheriff, but he had just given up on getting anything done. That certainly made it easier for me to run when I saw him throw up his hands at the whole process. You would think I would've run the other way.

That first campaign was brutal. Not only was I running against the incumbent, but the sheriff's chief deputy was running against his boss and seemed to be in the lead in some polls. The police chief of Mt. Juliet had thrown his hat in the ring as well. They were all tough opponents, and I had to work harder than I've ever worked in my life.

My closest friends dedicated their energy, their entire summer, their initiative, and even their money to help get the word out about my campaign. If not for their support, I wouldn't have known where to begin. Jerry McFarland worked tirelessly to get the votes.

There were threats to contend with from the beginning. I had to make a speech on the square in Lebanon, and on that single day of campaigning there were a number of calls threatening my life. A charity wanted me to sit in the dunking booth at a fund raiser one weekend and my supporters didn't want me to risk my life to participate. They feared my enemies would make good on the death threats if I were, quite literally, a sitting duck.

The criminal element kept an ear to the ground about my promises to clean up Bluebird Road and rid the county of organized crime and everything that came with it — dog fighting, illegal gambling, bootleggers, and drug dealers. I'm pretty sure they knew I was serious. Their livelihood was about to sprout wings if I became sheriff. That was a guarantee I had up my sleeve for them.

The rhetoric grew progressively heated. It got ugly. Money was low, so I had to get creative and do new things that no one else had done before.

My first campaign speech was made at Cumberland University, and I was terrified. But I gained confidence with each speaking engagement as the campaign steamed toward the finish line. I knew I had the right people on my side. All these friends and supporters who follow a candidate no matter what; I can't stress how important — how vital they are — to victory.

We'd travel to these rallies in Statesville, Noreen, and Crossroads in huge motorcades. With more than a hundred cars traveling in a convoy, it was like a big circus coming to town. People who ran these little community centers and organized these rallies were all about getting as many people as they could at these events to raise political awareness and get out the vote.

This sheriff's race had gotten so hotly contested that they were putting all of us at the bottom of the program in an effort to keep the rally going for as long as possible. My supporters would get the crowd started with a little pep rally with shouts of "Teh-Ree, Teh-Ree, Teh-Ree," which would always signal my turn at the microphone.

It was interesting to see that the caliber of the people cheering me on matched that of the voters backing Police Chief Charles McCrary — citizens of quality who were demanding change, voters who were looking for a candidate they could believe in. Everyone was talking the talk of change, but only one of us would be allowed to walk the walk.

I was relentless. I would see a McCrary sign in the yard of one of his supporters and I would knock on the door and tell them I would appreciate them thinking of me when they went to the polls, even if I had to be their second choice. I knew no shame. McCrary heard that I was doing this and told me I was killing him out there. I was encouraged by that.

The Sheriff and Don Knotts, who played everyone's favorite deputy, Barney Fife.

Mayor Maddox had fired me from my job. No surprise, since he supported the incumbent. My future was on the line, and when you're that committed to something you just don't let up. You can't.

You also can't afford to let your political enemies intimidate you.

During the campaign, I had a beautiful old Irish Setter who was playing in my front yard in broad daylight, and somebody drove by and shot him. He survived that attack, only to be shot again during the 1986 campaign. Luckily, like me, the dog was a tough old bird and survived the second shooting as well.

It's a damn dirty race when you think you have to shoot a man's dog to distract him.

Cake Walk

This election was playing out like a Hollywood drama — good against evil. There was no gray area.

The excitement and tension were building over the months until every rally took on more of a carnival atmosphere. At the Gladeville Rally, as the campaign was in its final weeks, it looked as though the race was between me and Al Cook. This was Al's home district. He had to look good here, and he was certainly pulling out all the stops to make sure he did.

At this particular rally, the sponsors held a cake auction with proceeds going to charity. There was nothing special about the cakes, but to the candidates, and those in the audience egging us on, the baked goods became symbolic of the bigger prize that was up for grabs. Within minutes, one cake had already gotten up to about five hundred dollars. People were watching all of us politicians bid against each other. Then, as the price went up, up and up, on what had to be the world's most expensive cake, it got down to just me and Al.

None of us had made our speeches yet, and Al was trying to get the momentum going before he stepped on stage. He was trying to outbid his opponents and buy all the cakes, thinking that by doing so he could somehow buy a victory. Then it occurred to me that I should lose the cake and win the war. I bid seventeen hundred and fifty dollars for it. I certainly didn't have that kind of money on me, but I knew I could collect it from several hundred supporters I had there with me. The auctioneer looked at Al Cook and, as I hoped he would, Al topped me by bidding eighteen hundred.

I let him have his cake. Now he could eat it too.

I let my opponent pay eighteen hundred dollars for a cake, which was more fun than if I had hit him in the face with a cream pie. I think the audience got a kick out of it too. We still joke about it to this day.

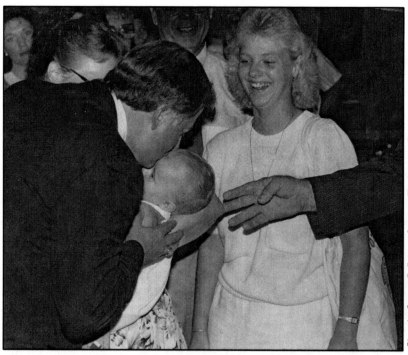

Photo by George R. Bouton, Courtesy *The Lebanon Democrat*

**The quintessential campaigner:
kissing babies and clowning around at a fundraiser.**

The Valley

The physical toll of going door to door in the hot sun, losing ten or fifteen pounds the hard way, and not getting any sleep was hard to deal with. But for me it was all about survival. I was not going to have a job if I was not successful in this campaign. There was too much on the line for me to give up now.

The threats soon went from threats on my life to threats of harm coming to my supporters. It got so bad at one point that some of the folks — especially my African-American supporters — were afraid to go to the gathering in Norene, which was to be the last and most important rally before the election.

Personal safety issues loomed for all of us. It's one thing to be in the political crosshairs and be a target of criticism from your opponent. That's expected. It's quite another to be a target of someone determined to get rid of you before you can destroy their criminal way of life. I guess I'm supposed to be flattered that the bad guys wanted to wipe me out before I could be elected. I don't take compliments very well if that's the case.

One of the most heartbreaking things that happened during the campaign turned out to be a tragic coincidence. When we had a rally on the square, I talked about cleaning up the gambling and the prostitution in the old hotel there. This was the historic hotel where Gen. George Patton set up his living quarters during the maneuvers of WWII.

I was the only person to successfully raid the notorious gambling operation on the top floor of the old building as Chief of Detectives, and I used that as an example of how I could clean up Bluebird Road if I were elected sheriff.

Late that night, the hotel burned. Our fire chief was killed as he tried to battle the blaze.

The speculation was running rampant; some were saying there was a lot of animosity because I brought up the topic of the hotel gambling raid in my speech. Political enemies put the blame of the deadly fire squarely on my shoulders.

I was vindicated later, but it was a bittersweet victory. I arrested two boys who burned that abandoned hotel because they were smoking dope. They knew nothing of the politics of the whole thing. They were just in there getting high and they set the building on fire.

Photo by Bill Cook, Courtesy *The Lebanon Democrat*

Job One

My philosophy from day one is the same as it is today: I'm going to run the office for four years. I'm going to run it the right way — the way I think it ought to be run — and I'm not going to worry about being re-elected. I entered into the job with that philosophy and never waned. I had a window of opportunity to do what I could do, and I couldn't worry about the politics of it.

What comes from that is, when a candidate continues to win time after time, there is a *perception* of power. But I have no real power. The power is with the people. They hold all the keys. They just allow me to use their keys to unlock doors for them.

The people have continually shown that they trust me to be the guy they depend on when their families are in trouble or they have a crisis in their lives. They have complete confidence that I'll come to their homes or their businesses and help resolve their issues.

I think that's the way they felt about me when they went to the polls in 1982, and thankfully, that's what they've remembered time after time when they stepped into the booth to cast their vote.

My campaign manager was also my close friend, the late Jerry McPeak. He and his wife were always there, heart and soul, during this race. His wife, and mine at the time, were teachers who made sure I had the support of the educators and the backing of labor. Anyone in Wilson County who wanted change was getting the message that they needed to vote for me and back my campaign.

I was in the right place at the right time, with the right message. If I didn't win, it wasn't going to be for lack of trying.

Photo by George R. Bouton, Courtesy *The Lebanon Democrat*

Huge crowds came to our fundraisers.
This was the 1990 campaign party at Cumberland University.

You've Got to Roy Up

You can't put your intentions into motion, of course, until you do everything you can to be elected. In those days, it was customary to "hire" people to get the word out about your campaign — to put up your signs, put in a good word for you, and drive people to the polls if they couldn't get there. You rewarded them in some way, whether it was with a little gas money or a half pint of whisky. Thirty years ago, the game of politics was certainly played on a different field. Was it *ever!*

There was an elderly black gentleman who lived on Bluebird Road, "Mr. Roy" Carson. His grandson had been in a bit of trouble at one point, and a judge asked me to help the young man get on the right track. I did, and Mr. Roy never forgot it. He told me that if I ever decided to run for sheriff, he would help me because of what I had done for his family.

Mr. Roy served in his church, worked in his community, and lived in the heart of the seedy underside of Bluebird Road. He had many friends and lots of influence in the black community. In fact, it was made crystal clear to me that if I had any designs on pinning a badge on my jacket, I would have to go see old Mr. Roy at some point. Two weeks before Election Day, I was reminded that I had not yet made that trip to see Mr. Roy.

My funds were depleted. I had fifty bucks in my pocket, and that was it. I bought a few bottles of the old fellow's favorite whiskey, and off I went to Bluebird Road to shake hands with Mr. Roy and get him on my side before the big day. It was a sultry, hot July night, and as I walked up the sidewalk to the screen door, I could see Mr. Roy and some of his friends sitting around the kitchen table playing cards.

I walked in and shook hands with each of the men and asked them for their votes. I got Mr. Roy aside and told him that I would really appreciate any help he could give me, whispering that I had a few bottles of whiskey for him out in the car.

Mr. Roy nodded for me to follow him and led me through the kitchen to a back room of his little house. I couldn't believe what was in front of me; entire cases of whisky were stacked to the ceiling against all four walls like a liquor warehouse. He then pulled a big wad of money out of his pocket that would have choked a mule and looked up at me with a mischievous grin. My opponents had obviously gotten there before me. I certainly couldn't compete with that. I admitted to Mr. Roy that this game was too rich for my blood.

Mr. Roy's grin morphed into a pensive expression as he put the roll of money back in his pocket.

"Terry, I can get some votes for you. I told you I was going to help you, and I will. How much money you got?"

"Fifty dollars," I answered, in an embarrassed, barely audible tone.

I pulled my little stash of wadded up bills from my front pocket. You know a man is broke when all the money he has is in his front pocket. Mr. Roy took it from my hand and shoved it into his bowling shirt. Maybe it was enough cash for him to finish that hand of poker I had interrupted. At least I would be making some memorable contribution to the evening.

As he walked me to the door, he assured me he would do everything he could because he thought a lot of me and what I stood for. He said he would never forget how I helped his grandson.

I didn't carry Mr. Roy's precinct on election night, but I got more votes than I ever imagined from that area. According to those who make those predictions, I wasn't supposed to come anywhere *close* to a respectable number over there.

Apparently, Mr. Roy put in a good word for me. I exceeded all expectations and it only cost *me* fifty bucks. It was another Al Cook "cake moment."

A Nail Biter

Coach Tribble, who used to be my football coach in high school, hosted my election party at his house on Murfreesboro Road that night. There was a terrible thunderstorm as we all gathered around the television set in the living room to watch the returns. The power went out just as the election coverage began, which was unnerving.

We had poll watchers scattered throughout the county and were waiting to hear from them as each precinct closed. I remember telling one of my campaign workers that if I could just carry *one district* in Mt. Juliet, I had a chance to win. Not long after I said that, a poll watcher announced that I had carried Mt. Juliet Elementary School by one vote.

After hearing that, I just had a feeling I was going to be the next sheriff.

As the night dragged by and the returns slowly trickled in, however, my emotions hopped on a roller coaster.

In the western and southern part of the county, Chief Deputy Al Cook seemed to be doing well at the big polls. Hearing the numbers was excruciating: 525 votes for Al Cook, 127 for Terry Ashe, 98 for the incumbent. My heart sank.

The returns from the city of Lebanon would tell a different story. This is where I had worked so many crimes and had enjoyed so much success with the high profile cases: the Southside rapist, the interstate shootouts, the infamous "Ten Most Wanted," and countless murders.

When the first box came in from Byers-Dowdy school, the results were encouraging: 630 votes for me, 102 for Al Cook, and 71 for the incumbent sheriff. An overwhelming block of voters were supporting me in Lebanon as the night wore on. It made all the difference. The final tally was a beautiful sight as I looked at the television screen: Al Cook 5,778 votes, Terry Ashe, 6,825 votes. Sheriff King came in last.

It was one of the most joyous, jubilant moments of my life.

Two weeks before, I was behind 14%, and none of the newspapers were predicting a win for the Terry Ashe campaign. My supporters didn't listen to any of that. They continued to work with their eyes on the goal.

I didn't get elected by myself that night. My friends, supporters, those who believed in me — *they* got me elected. Of course, God's hands were on my shoulders, as they've always been, leading, guiding and directing me every step of the way. I had prepared myself mentally in case I lost, but there was just something inside of me that said I was going to do this. I had to do this for the community.

The morning after I was elected, I got a phone call from someone who told me that nearly everyone on Bluebird Road had one of my bumper stickers on their car. I found out later, a clever entrepreneur was selling the stickers for five dollars each. The owners of these illegal businesses knew change was coming, and they thought I would look the other way if they were my supporters.

"It's a different day, guys. You just wasted five bucks," was my initial reaction upon hearing that. As bad as Bluebird Road was, it wasn't the only place illegal activity could be found. There was a lot of cocaine and marijuana in this county, and tackling the drug problem was going to be a massive undertaking. I promised the people I would do it, and I had to begin immediately. In all these years, I've never lost the passion for what I do. I've always felt that this was my calling, almost in the same way a person would be called into the ministry. I was called to make a difference.

Pursuing my passion for this duty has meant that I've butchered my personal life in many respects, but I look at it as the price I had to pay to follow a dream. It all worked out for the best. More on that later.

Our first campaign victory laid the groundwork for all we were able to accomplish in the following years. We didn't clean up Bluebird Road in the first four years, but it was obvious that there was real change taking place in the county.

When I ran for re-election, I ran against the former incumbent sheriff once again.

My victory margin was astronomical — a whopping eighty percent.

The Newly Elected Sheriff Ashe.

CHAPTER SEVEN

Mama Said There'd Be Days Like This

When I was a kid, we always came into town on Saturdays, which was pretty special, but the best memories of all were when our entire family made the trip to see the Lebanon Christmas parade. Back then, the Christmas parades were at night and were beautiful; the lights around the square, the soft snowfall, the reds and greens of the tinsel, and the decorations in all the shop windows were the perfect backdrop for the festivities. The square looked like those little porcelain Christmas villages people put on their mantels.

There was nothing like feeling that cold, crisp air and the snowflakes on my face as Dad would hoist me up on his shoulders to give me the best vantage point of the floats and the bands marching by. My brother and I would be almost frantic with the anticipation of seeing Santa, who rode on the fire truck at the very end of the parade. It was magic time, and the whole concept of Santa and his helpers seemed so very real to me. I was intimidated by this rotund old fella with the booming voice and the long white beard. After all, he was the one with the ability to know when I was sleeping, when I was awake, etc. Scary stuff. I was thrilled when he waved at me. It was as if he knew me personally and was going over my Christmas list in his head.

Fast-forward to just a little while after I was elected sheriff.

The Santa who always appeared in the Christmas parade died suddenly, and the Chamber of Commerce was in a bind. A parade with no Santa was just not a Christmas parade and I, for one, could not let that happen. When the Chamber's director told me of her plight, I volunteered to don the beard and become the jolly old elf himself. For the next seven years, when little children would wave at old St. Nick on the fire truck, they were actually waving at the sheriff. I could tell by the look on some of the parents' faces that they were trying to figure out where they had seen those eyes before. Some of them never figured it out, which was part of the fun for me. A number of Mrs. Clauses who rode on the float with me never knew my true identity until years later (don't read anything into that).

I really got into the role of Santa. Method acting, I believe it's called in Hollywood. I would put on the padding, the beard, the hair, the hat and the red velvet suit, and I was good to go. Once I was in that persona, the sheriff was out of town until further notice.

I would say I "had a ball," but then that would make this next story seem even more ridiculous.

Santa's Two "Acres"

Each year, the Watertown and Lebanon Chambers of Commerce join forces to sponsor a "Santa Train" for children and their parents. It's a brilliant concept that includes all the cool things kids enjoy — trains, Santa, candy, and gifts — and it's a great time for parents to go along and shop a charming little square that's decorated like a town in a Dickens play. The Chamber usually provides its own Santa for the train trip, but on this particular year, the guy who was supposed to help them came down with the flu the night before. Once again, the Chamber director called with a desperate plea for me to fill in. It would mean an entire day of being in costume and being jolly and charming, and frankly, I didn't think I had the energy for it, but I reluctantly agreed.

At nine o'clock sharp the next morning, there I was, at the train station near Fakes and Hooker Lumber Company on Maple Street, waving and ho ho ho-ing and getting everyone on the train and in the Christmas spirit. Once the children and their parents were all aboard, we chugged our way down the tracks, headed to Watertown.

Everyone certainly had plenty of snacks. I walked up and down the aisles throwing goodies from a giant bag of candy, and the area behind the passenger car was a concession stand where parents were buying hot chocolate for the kids. There was a pretty good sugar high going all the way around.

The train had an upper deck, and I made my way up there to pass out candy and talk to the children who were waiting patiently for their turn. In spite of my initial fear that the whole Santa act would be exhausting on such an extended trip, I began to get into character and play off the comments from the kids and the parents, asking the kids if their parents had been good this year and vice versa.

We were about fifteen minutes away from Watertown, and everyone had gone over their Santa list and had moved on to singing Christmas carols. It was the perfect time for me to take a break. I made my way back to the concession stand car where I thought I would catch my breath and have a cup of coffee before we reached the depot.

The man running the concession stand recognized me, and we began to talk about government, politics, law enforcement, and the usual things guys talk about when they have a few minutes to kill.

I stopped talking and got back into my Santa character, however, when I noticed a little boy coming down the aisle toward me.

He was about nine years old and had on one of those Elmer Fudd hats with the flaps pulled down over his ears. His fire engine red hair, curling out from underneath the white shearling on the cap gave him that look straight from the cover of "Mad Magazine." He was wearing some large, probably size ten, orange, lace-up work boots, a heavy, insulated jacket, rolled up jeans and a red plaid shirt. Maybe he was planning to go logging instead of Christmas shopping when we arrived in Watertown. He was so funny-looking he was cute. I gave him a jolly greeting as he entered the concession car and stood at my feet, staring up at me.

"Well, hello son, and how are you today?" I projected this with the best Santa voice ever — or so I thought.

"THERE'S NO SUCH THING AS SANTA CLAUS!" he screamed back at me so loudly I was afraid all the other children would hear. Then, with all his might, he kicked me in the groin with those size ten work boots.

Before I could say ho ho HOOGGHH, the fruit had indeed been knocked out of the loom.

I doubled over in pain and saw stars. I couldn't catch my breath. I almost fell to my knees as this little monster ran back to his seat, giggling and snorting.

The concession stand guy must have thought it was funny too, or perhaps he was reacting from embarrassment, but he stopped laughing when he saw the look on my face. As I used his countertop to pull myself up from the crouching position, all I could manage was a whisper: "I'm gonna get that damn kid!"

I meant it with every fiber of my being.

We were about five minutes from our destination and I had to get my act together for one last trip down the aisle to get everyone in the spirit as we arrived.

This was going to be tough, but I was on a mission to eventually exact revenge on my assailant; or at the very least, tell his mama what he did.

Santa's voice was a little on the soprano side as I welcomed the group to Watertown. My testicles were aching like the devil, but the show must go on, as the man said — blah, blah, blah — bet *he* never got kicked in the nuts! Down the aisle I shuffled and, very carefully and painfully, climbed the steps leading to the upper level.

Then I spotted him. He was sitting with his dainty, red-haired, four-year-old sister and his beautiful, red-haired mother. I looked over his head as I walked by him with my best "ho, ho, ho," wanting him to think he had failed in his effort to ruin my day.

The train stopped at the station in Watertown and everyone clamored off to begin their day-long shopping excursion.

Meanwhile, the conductor had the best idea yet. He suggested that I put my feet up, get out of my Santa disguise, and have a sip of Jack Daniels. In light of what had happened, I agreed that a little Jack in the Black was exactly what the doctor ordered.

He told me he would be sounding the whistle on the train fifteen minutes before time to load up in the afternoon, and that would be my cue to wake up and slip into the Santa attire to prepare for Act Two.

Oh No, He Didn't!

I had plenty of time to recoup with a combat nap before the whistle sounded, and I woke up with new resolve to end the day and leave this train with at least some modicum of dignity.

As the parents and children boarded, I stood on the platform and welcomed back each family, asking them if they had a good time, helping them up the steps, and making sure everyone was accounted for.

All the while, I had my eyes peeled for that little red-headed turd. Finally, against all my hope to the contrary, the errant child, his mother, and little sister showed up to board for the trip home. I gave him the evil eye and he quickly looked away. I was beginning to feel like W.C. Fields.

The ride back to Lebanon was comparatively subdued. The kids were all tuckered out from their big day and perhaps the blood sugar was crashing from all the candy they were given on the way to Watertown. Most of them were fast asleep in their parents' laps, and the parents who were still awake were quietly talking so they wouldn't disturb the napping children.

With everyone sacked out and the concession car closed, there wasn't much for me to do except burn up in that darned red velvet Santa suit. I was roasting alive, and to top it all off, I was walking like a chicken. Could this day be *any* more unpleasant?

I opened the back door of the train to catch a bit of a breeze in my fake whiskers and watch the tracks go by. I was drifting off to a very nice place there for a minute, but then, I heard the clump, clumping of those deadly boots coming toward me.

It was him again.

"I TOLD YA THERE WADN'T NO SUCH THING AS SANTA!" With that, the midget menace reared back to give me another kick in the crotch. I grabbed his leg in midair and pulled him toward me in one swift move.

The shock and dismay on his face couldn't compare to the anger I wish he could have seen under my white flowing beard. I grabbed him by the scruff of the neck and I led him to the open door of the train.

"I'm gonna throw your damn ass off this train right now and tell everybody you fell off!"

I know... I still can't believe I said it.

He began to squall like a little girl. "Naw, don't do it! Please don't throw me out! Nobody's gonna believe I fell off!"

"They'll certainly believe it if Santa Claus tells them it's so," I assured him.

His eyes got as big as golf balls as he realized I might be right. I swung him around and laid him in the aisle by the door; my fist had a tight grip on his shirt collar under his chin.

"If you ever do anything like that to me again, I'm ... gonna ... come ... get ... you!" I shook his entire body to emphasize each word. I let go, and he jumped up and took off down the aisle, running back to his mama.

Immediately, as I watched the back of that goofy Elmer Fudd hat disappear into the upper deck, I was thinking, "lawsuit."

I'm going to get the crap sued out of me. A perfect ending to a perfect day.

I went back to watching the tracks go by as I waited for the inevitable: an angry visit from the hot, red-haired mama. Much to my surprise and relief, it never happened.

I breathed a sigh of relief that just this once, luck must have had my back when my temper got away from me. But then again, what parent would believe that Santa Claus would threaten to throw a child off a train? I mean, *who does that?* It's just too bizarre.

He was too frightened for his own skin to get into the whole story with his mother. He would have to explain that he kicked Santa in the gift bag and that's why Santa threatened him.

Even Santa's motives would have to be proven in a court of law.

Later That Decade…

Nine or ten years later, I was in a department store looking for the perfect birthday card for my daughter when a very nice looking, mountain of a young man came up and introduced himself to me.

He was about 6 foot 2, had a head full of shocking red hair, and quite a substantial grip when we shook hands. He wanted to know if we were hiring at the Sheriff's Office.

I told him we were indeed hiring for some key positions, and we could use a few good men. I was impressed, so I encouraged him to come to the office and put in an application as soon as possible.

You know where this is going…

He thanked me for my time and then, with a mischievous grin, he said, "You don't remember me, do you?" I looked him up and down as I tried to think about it. Perhaps this was the child of one of my old high school buddies? Did my daughter date him? Did I arrest him at some point?

"You and I took a train ride to Watertown one time." My train of thought derailed when he said it.

Now, I don't believe *I* would have told that, but remember, here was one brave young man.

The memories came flooding back; there's the curly red hair of the little guy who had the gumption to kick ole' Santy's package up around his earlobes and then had the courage to come back and try it again.

I hired him on the spot. Don't ask me why. It was just the right thing to do.

He's still with us in the Sheriff's Office to this day, and I count him among some of the most trustworthy and loyal employees in the office. He's dependable and as fine a young man as you would ever want on your team.

I'll just never ride on another train with him as long as I live. I know how he gets.

Photo by Dallus Whitfield, Courtesy *The Lebanon Democrat*

The jolly old elf with the high pitched voice.

CHAPTER EIGHT

It was the fall of 1988, and I had been sheriff for six years when I strolled through the old dispatch office and noticed an aluminum baseball bat leaning up in the corner. I asked the dispatcher who the bat belonged to, and she told me one of the officers had brought it in after he picked it up at an assault scene. The bat was not the weapon used in the assault, and no one at the crime scene would admit to owning it, so the officer brought it in and left it with her.

I thought it was a bit dangerous to have something that could be used as a weapon so close to where people entered and exited the jail, so I took it with me and tossed it in the back of my patrol car. I vowed to give it to the first group of little kids I saw playing baseball or softball that day. Apparently that charitable opportunity never presented itself, because the bat shifted around in my floorboard for weeks. Every time I'd stop at a red light, that thing would roll under the seat, driving me nuts.

October 18th, 1988

A few weeks later, I overheard the dispatcher call for all cars to head to I-40 because an officer was down between mile markers 237 and 238. When an officer needs help, everything stops and everyone responds to those calls. The Sheriff's Office was behind the old courthouse at the time, right off 231, and since I was closest to the interstate, I got in my patrol car, blue lights flashing, and headed to the scene of whatever the highway patrol was facing. As I darted through the traffic, my mind went back to the high speed chase with Peter Bennett Reeves, eight years earlier.

He was firing shots at me around these same mile markers — an area usually congested with traffic this time of day — which made it imperative that I get there to help before an innocent person was hurt or killed. When I got to the entry ramp of I-40, I could see that traffic was already backed up way past the Lebanon exit. I was going west through the traffic, but for three miles to the east, cars were standing bumper to bumper. I pulled over into the median and could see the flashing lights from all the highway patrol cars that stretched about a mile in front of where I was parking.

Our radios were blaring with transmission from all the cars responding to the stranded trooper's calls for help. I kept wondering what could be happening down there. Had he been shot? We never got a confirmation on exactly what the situation was, so I was going into this blindly. It wouldn't be long before I would have my eyes opened. And how.

As I pulled to the head of the line, I was relieved to see that tractor trailer drivers were helping officers block westbound traffic, as they kindly do for us sometimes when we're in need. I pulled over to drive along the grass in the median and came upon a trooper who was keeping pedestrians as far away from the action as possible. He warned me about what I was about to encounter.

"Be careful, Sheriff, that's one crazy son of a bitch out there!" He nodded his head toward the west.

I assumed he was referring to the man I saw about a half-mile in the distance, walking in the middle of traffic, waving his arms and heading toward Nashville. I would say crazy was a pretty safe assumption. The guy had to be either drunk, on drugs, or just out of his mind to pull a stunt like this.

The trooper continued to bring me up to speed: "Trooper Farmer is just ahead of you, and he's hurt. He's had to shoot that guy." That's all he needed to say. I spun out of the grass, making my way to the injured lawman. As I drove, I called for an ambulance and anyone I could get from our department to come down here to help stop this guy before someone else was hurt. He had been shot and continued to sashay down the road as if he had just encountered a water pistol. None of us had any idea what we were up against.

When I got to Trooper Farmer, who was leaning up against his car in the middle of the interstate, I could see he had been through the mill with the suspect and was still trying to catch his breath from the scuffle.

He told me he found the man walking down the middle of the interstate, and when he tried to get him out of the road, the man charged him, fighting, kicking, hitting, and pinning him up against his patrol car. Farmer grabbed his night stick, but before he could use it to defend himself, the guy grabbed it, pressed it to his throat, and began to choke him with it. As Farmer began to lose consciousness, he reached down to his revolver, tilted his holster forward, and fired a single shot into center mass — the center of the guy's body. The man was blown back from the trooper by the sheer force of the hit, and landed in the roadside ditch.

The trooper's nose was broken and his mouth was bleeding from the fight; he was coughing from being choked and was barely able to stand. As he made his way into his car to call for help, he watched in disbelief as his attacker sprang up from the ditch, looked him right in the eye and said, "Shoot me again, mutha@!#*#!"

The man then continued his walk down the interstate with a .357 magnum slug in him, as though he was taking a leisurely Sunday stroll. It was the most amazing thing any of us could ever imagine.

I was next up. I was going to be the poor fool trying to stop the unstoppable. I got in my patrol car and slowly crept down the interstate in the center lane to get a closer look at our unwelcome guest. As I pulled up behind him, I was shaking my head in disbelief at the size of this dude. He was a hulk of a human being — over six and a half feet tall — and muscled up like a body builder. Me? I'm the sheriff. I may be short and I may not lift weights, but what God didn't give me in muscle mass, he gave me in communication skills. I can talk this guy down from the ledge if anybody can. I began to feel confident in my ability to disarm the situation and bring this awful work day to a peaceful conclusion. Yeah. Right. I stopped the car and got out to approach him with my kindest, most concerned voice.

"I know you're hurt, and I'm here to help you. You need to step to the side of the interstate right now because I have an ambulance coming to check on you."

I could tell he was hurt and was losing a lot of blood, but he didn't respond to my voice. He continued to walk and look straight ahead.

"Hey, did you hear what I said?" I tried to get his attention with a loud voice and stern tactic as I was walking in his very large shadow.

He turned around on a dime, a perfect about-face in the army. I found myself face to ... well ... *navel* ... with a giant who didn't know or care if I was the sheriff or the Easter bunny. I looked up at him as he threw both arms up in the air like a bear and charged toward me, growling. And that's just how he looked — like a big, angry grizzly which was going to flatten me with one fist.

I didn't realize I could run backward, but I did. Fast. I knew if I could get to my patrol car, I'd be safe. There was no help nearby because troopers were dealing with the traffic, and two of them had already been injured dealing with this man. For now, it was just the two of us. Not the lunch date I had in mind.

As I reached the open door of my patrol car, I had only a second to grab my thirty-eight-caliber revolver, cock it, and point it straight at him as he approached me. Just as he was about to pounce on me, I tried my art of persuasion one last time.

"Okay, buddy, if you don't back off, the funeral director is gonna be packing cotton in your ass tonight," I said, as I held the gun steady on the car door. I thought the mental video of this threat would at least slow him down. He wasn't amused.

"F!@# you!" was all he said as he turned and began to walk westward again as if nothing had happened.

There was no help in sight, and I was running out of ideas. This guy could ring my neck and not even flinch. I looked around in the patrol car and the old aluminum bat I had been carrying around for months seemed to jump out at me. This could be the very thing to get him to listen to me and get the hell out of the road.

It seemed like a perfect plan at the time.

As I re-holstered my gun, grabbed my bat, and approached him again, I was nervous. Kind of like those awful nerves you get before a first kiss, except I could be kissing my own ass goodbye after this encounter. I was determined to put an end to it because I was the *sheriff*, dammit. Who else was going to get out here and do this?

When I got close to him this time, I had made up my mind that there would be no more Mr. Nice Guy.

"Get the hell out of the road and that means NOW!" I screamed at him in my best "angry sheriff" voice.

He turned and lunged at me. I took a swing with the baseball bat, aiming at this Goliath's knees. Considering they were almost at my eye level, it was an easy target. He didn't feel a thing. My next blow was to his shoulder. Big, bad, mistake.

His ham-like right hand grabbed the fat end of the bat and the playground game of "choke-up" began. I grabbed, he grabbed, I grabbed, and he grabbed, and on and on it went toward the handle of the bat.

I knew if he got his hand on the handle and wrestled the bat from me, I was going to be in a fight for my life.

He did, and I was.

I pulled my gun on him again, and he turned toward Nashville and started walking. This time, I had armed this *crazy mofo* with a bat. As he walked, he was swinging the bat around and around above his head like the blades of a helicopter, and it looked like he was doing some sort of victory dance in the end zone. While all this had taken place, you would think the Cavalry would have had time to mount up and join me in my troubles.

There was not a soul to be found for miles. I was alone and had to get this jerk out of the middle of the road somehow. I was now about fifty yards from my patrol car and had no walkie-talkie, no radio communication, and no way to tell anyone what was happening to me in the middle of I-40. Just as I was beginning to feel sorry for myself, two of my correctional officers showed up and, although I was glad to see them, I knew they wouldn't be well armed.

The guy was moving more quickly down the road, and we were running out of time before he would come upon the traffic stopped in the eastbound lane up ahead. I ordered the officers to try to get around him and try to distract him in some way. Now, I had written the policy about firing warning shots, and I knew all about the consequences of such actions, but when I wrote the policy I never fathomed I would find myself in a situation where I would need to do just that.

I didn't want to kill this man. He was obviously not in his right mind, for whatever reason, and he needed someone to have mercy on him.

My left hand was sprained by our game of grab with the baseball bat. I couldn't fight him, and I knew that none of us out there were a match for this man's strength. I walked up behind him and fired my revolver straight up into the sky. He *had* to hear that since he was less than three feet from me at the time. He turned, and as he did, he swung the bat straight for my head. As they say in baseball, he was attempting to "take the ball downtown." I ducked just in time to hear a *swoosh* less than an inch above my head. As I hit the ground I fired my gun and hit him in the upper thigh. I just wanted to get him off of me before he killed me with that damn bat. The gunshot didn't faze him, and he was bleeding heavily now from two wounds, but he swung again and I rolled on the ground to avoid being hit.

"F!@# you! Shoot me again!" he screamed as I struggled to get up.

He turned and continued his walk down the interstate — the gaping hole in his thigh a mere flesh wound in the scheme of things. I could see that he was planning to cross the long, grassy median that separated I-40 West and East. The traffic was backing up on the other side, something we call "gapers' block." It's known in other cities as "rubber necking." Drivers in the eastbound lanes were watching all of this unfold as if they were tuning in to a drama on television.

At that moment, it was just like I had a telescope or a high-powered pair of binoculars. My eyes focused on a young lady who was stranded in her car and frightened out of her wits, with her small children strapped in their car seats in the back. Cars blocked her escape in front and others were bumper-to-bumper behind her at a standstill. This man, swinging a baseball bat, was heading straight for her and her family.

One of the correctional officers had an old prison riot stick in his hand. I borrowed it and took off after the guy. Now he was acting like a cornered animal, swinging at anything and everything he saw. As the two correctional officers worked their way toward him, I was making my way to him from the other side with that big riot stick. I knew I had one chance and one chance only to bring this to an end. Just as he was swinging toward one of the officers, I took the riot stick and struck him between the shoulder blades and the back. As my worst nightmare would have it, he just turned and looked at me again — straight into my eyes. He turned, took one more swing at the other officers, took a couple of steps, and fell flat on his face. Once he was on the ground, we all fell on top of him, cuffed him, and motioned that it was safe for the ambulance to pull up and take him away. The EMTs had begged police officers to ride with them to make this pickup. They were terrified that this guy would rise up and attack again. I sent two officers to ride along to the hospital, just in case.

This is Where It Really Gets Hairy...

In Hollywood, they close the doors of the ambulance, the lawman says, "Book 'em," and the credits roll.

In Lebanon, Tennessee, the credits wouldn't roll on this case for another year. We spared this guy to fight another day, and fight he did — in a court of law. Those few minutes of my life on

I-40 West would take months to explain in court depositions and hearings.

The troopers and I were sued for several million dollars by the family of this man — sued for shooting him in the stomach and thigh and hitting him with a "big stick" about the legs and shoulders.

God knows best, and he knows how I feel about veterans. As it turned out, this guy had walked away from the veterans' hospital thirty miles away the day before. No one from that hospital had bothered to alert law enforcement that he was missing, violent, and off his meds. He suffered from a rare brain disorder that affects the nerves and doesn't allow the body to feel pain.

I'm so thankful I didn't kill him. I couldn't have lived with the knowledge that I had killed a sick veteran.

All the parties in our defense attempted to settle this case out of court because the man was ill and we didn't think he could handle a trial. I knew it was going to be hard to explain our side, but we knew we'd done the right thing. We followed our instincts and no one was killed. I didn't want to go on trial along with the highway patrol, because I had no idea what had gone down with them before I arrived on the scene.

The plaintiffs had all the experts at the trial to testify. They were coming up with all of these "perfect case scenarios," i.e., we should have called in a fire truck and knocked him down with the water pressure.

Another expert said we should have had some kind of cannon contraption that fired a net into the air to trap him like an escaped zoo animal. Speaking of animals, another expert who had obviously watched too much "Wild Kingdom" thought we should have shot the guy with a tranquilizer gun.

Armchair quarterbacks. Gotta love 'em.

The trial didn't get off to a good start for me from the moment the plaintiff walked in. The half-naked, twice-shot slugger with the foul mouth had a name — Ethan Mullins — and he had on a nice suit and tie and smiled at all who came in contact with him. I couldn't believe this was the same guy. During the jury selection, I would catch him staring at me. I was wondering if he remembered *anything* about that October day.

Jury selection went quickly, and I had a good country lawyer on my side, Tom Peebles, who had won his share of federal cases. He was taking good care of me and Wilson County in this trial, and I trusted him completely. In addition, Peebles told me he had done a little bird hunting with the tough-ass judge assigned to the case. Just sayin.'

I thought at first that good ole' boy relationship couldn't hurt our chances with His Honor. I found out later the Tennessee Wildlife Resources Agency had cited their hunting group one day for shooting in a baited field.

In hindsight, that whole bird-hunting-brotherhood thing was not such a great trip down memory lane for the judge after all.

I was ready for trial, I hadn't done anything wrong, and I wanted to get this thing behind me. Then, the unthinkable happened. When the judge read the plaintiff's opinion to the jury, he got to the part about where I had struck the guy with the riot stick. The distinguished judge put down the paper, removed his bifocals, looked at me, and went *ape shit*.

"If I find out this sheriff struck this man with a big stick like Buford Pusser, I'll rule against him right now!" He said as he stared at me with a red face and pointed at me with his glasses.

Where the hell did *that* come from? I was wondering. He's a judge! He can't say something like that in front of the jury!

I leaned over and whispered into Tom Peebles' ear. "I want a new jury. He's tainted this one."

"Shut up!" Tom whispered back at me with a glare. "You don't make statements like that in federal court. You'll get us all in trouble!"

"In trouble, hell! He just put me in trouble with the jury." I refused to back down. "I'm paying you; you work for me. Now, I'm *demanding* a new jury."

The judge could see us talking and was getting even more annoyed than he already was. Tom had a bad knee and walked with a cane, so it took him a painful minute of silence to get up out of his chair to address the judge.

"My client wants a new jury, Your Honor. He believes you have tainted this one with your statements."

With that, the judge pounced up, slammed his chair against the wall behind his bench, and said, "This isn't going any further! Approach the bench." Both attorneys walked up to the bench to suffer the judge's wrath. I was watching the jury this entire time, and they looked as scared as I felt. After what seemed like ten minutes, Tom limped his way back to our table.

"Be careful what you ask for, because you're about to get it," Tom whispered. He was looking at his papers as he sat back down, never making eye contact with me.

The judge ordered the deputy U.S. Marshal to take this jury down to Judge Nixon's courtroom and bring the jury from that room to this one. An even swap was the perfect solution, although I've never heard of that happening before or since. The judge took thirty minutes to bring the jury up to speed — although this time he measured his words carefully — and the trial began. The trial lasted two weeks, and I was eager to tell my side of the story. The State of Tennessee had offered up tons of proof on how troopers had followed policy to the letter.

To me, the way they presented their case didn't make much sense. The trial went into slow motion, blow by blow: how the struggle ensued, and how the assault had taken place.

When it came time to tell my story, I wanted to illustrate to the jury that it didn't happen in slow motion.

"It happened in the snap of a finger." I snapped my fingers to illustrate to the jury how quickly I found myself in this life threatening situation. I looked at the jury and then I stared at the plaintiff. I told the jury how I was left out there alone by highway patrol. It was just me and that one unstable man, and I had to protect the public. I looked straight into the eyes of the man who had tried to kill me months earlier as I talked about how I had to kill in Vietnam and that I never wanted to have to kill again.

The plaintiff's attorney kept asking me why I didn't shoot "center mass" if I was indeed in fear for my life. I explained that I only shot what I could hit as I was trying to duck a ball bat swinging at my head. I also told the jury that, while I hated being on trial and sitting in that courtroom on that day, I was so thankful that I had not killed Mr. Mullins. I would have had a hard time living with the idea that I had killed another Vietnam Vet. The courtroom got quiet.

The case finally went to the jury, and after they filed out of the courtroom along with most of the audience, I sat alone at the table going over some notes. Mr. Mullins got up from the plaintiff's table and headed toward me.

Oh no, I was thinking to myself. There are no marshals here, only a few people standing around. What's this man going to do to me now? He put both hands on the table and looked me right in the eyes.

"Thank you! If not for you, I would be dead today. Anyone else would have killed me," he said.

"Why the hell didn't you tell that to the jury?" I demanded to know.

"This is just a bunch a' lawyers wantin' to make money," he said. " I'm sorry this happened. I was off my medicine and I was sick. I'm sorry, man." He looked down as he apologized.

I got up and walked out into the marble hallway of the federal courthouse. The jury was deliberating in a room just right off the hall, and with the echo, I could make out exactly what they were saying. I could hear one of the jurors asking, "Didn't you hear what the sheriff said?" The juror snapped his fingers. "It happened just that fast." My stomach was in knots. I had no idea what this jury was about to do.

Late that afternoon, we got word that there was a verdict. When the jury filed back in, none of them made eye contact with anyone in the room. That's usually not a good sign. The judge asked the foreman if indeed the jury had reached a verdict.

"Yes we have, Your Honor."

"As it relates to Mr. Mullins, the State of Tennessee and the Tennessee Highway Patrol," the judge asked, " how do you find the defendants?"

"We find no criminal intent on the part of the highway patrol, Your Honor, but we're imposing a civil penalty of 225 thousand dollars."

"And how do you find the sheriff of Wilson County, Mr. Ashe?" the judge asked.

"We, the jury, find no wrongdoing on the part of the sheriff, but we would ask that the Wilson County government pay the ambulance bill for the defendant, approximately 125 dollars."

I can't describe the feeling of relief that washed over me. It was great to know that the jury had seen my side of the story and sensed that I had testified truthfully and from the heart. I collected all of my personal property from the clerk that had been held in evidence, and Tom and I left the courthouse feeling as though a huge burden had been lifted.

Goodbye Old Standby

As we crossed the dark parking lot to our cars, I told Tom I wanted to give him something. I handed him the gun I had just gotten from the clerk — the one I had used in this shooting, the same gun I had used in the shootout with Peter Bennett Reeves on the same stretch of interstate. Tom didn't want to take my gun at first; he felt it was my good luck charm that had already gotten me out of two near misses. I explained to him how a little thirty-eight revolver was only fit for use in phone booths and restrooms, and I had been in neither when I got into my trouble, so he could have it with my blessings. I wrote him a receipt for the weapon, which would now become a trophy of sorts that he had won in a hard-fought battle. What we feared would cost me, personally, millions of dollars, was now going to cost the county government less than 125 bucks.

The gun that saved my life twice, was now in the hands of the man who saved my future as a lawman. Things were as they should be.

It wasn't until a few months after the trial that I learned an interesting fact: when I shot Ethan Mullins, I shot the nephew of one of the major gang leaders of the "Expressway Gang" of Mt. Juliet, Tennessee.

The justice the Expressway Gang members thought they were denied in the courtroom was about to be meted out in the streets. I was their target, but God had other plans.

For the Record: Three and Oh

The odds of winning the lottery are about one in fifteen million. The odds of being struck by lightning are about one in thirty thousand. A girl in Michigan was hit by lightning and went on to win the lottery the next day. She won a measly twenty bucks, but at least she got a little something for being singled out.

Me? I've been struck by lightning *three times*. I've won the lottery ... *zilch*. Any time a storm is coming up, people who know this odd little fact about my life tend to get as far away from me as possible. I can forget about being invited to play golf on an overcast day. No one wants to take that chance. Isolation is not something lottery winners experience.

The first time I was struck, I was only eight years old. I was too young to grasp the seriousness of what had happened to me, but old enough to remember it was a terrifying experience for me and my parents.

My dad milked every morning before he went to work at the aircraft factory, and my brother and I were always right out there with him. It was a race against time to milk, pour it up, and get it to the end of the driveway for pickup, which only happened once daily. In those days, the dairy sent a crew of men out to the rural areas early every morning in a little flatbed truck to collect the milk from all the farmers. I thought those milk haulers had to be the strongest people in the world; they could grab these heavy cans of milk and sling them up on the truck as if they were as light as a feather. As a young boy, I couldn't begin to lift even one side of those milk cans. Few grown men could, so Dad had this rickety old wheelbarrow with a metal wheel on the front that was designed specifically to cart the heavy cans up the drive, where they could be placed in the concrete water tank to keep the milk cool until the milk truck arrived.

One morning, we were all in our full rain gear because strong thunderstorms were sweeping through the area and the rain was coming down in buckets. We finished milking and poured the milk into the cans. Dad hoisted the cans onto the cart and hurriedly scrambled out of the barn and up the long drive.

I was wearing my raincoat, hat and boots, and thought I was helping Dad when I accompanied him up the driveway with milk every morning. This stormy day was not going to be an exception. I was walking right beside him and holding on to his back pocket, since I couldn't hold his hand.

Before we got to the end of the road, lightning struck a locust tree on the side of the driveway, ran down the tree in a straight line directly toward us, and apparently ran up the metal wheel on the wheelbarrow. The force of the hit knocked us to the ground.

Neither of us were seriously hurt, but it sure was frightening to a little boy, and I cried all the way to the house as Dad rushed us both to safety.

Oddly, that experience didn't give me any kind of phobia when it came to thunderstorms, and that served me well when I went to Vietnam. There, the lightning bolts would literally dance on the jungle floor around me and the other soldiers. In that tropical climate, it was almost a regular thing — seeing the lightning streak across the sky and hit the ground within inches of where I was standing or lying in a ditch or in a foxhole.

It never dawned on me that I might be a conductor of electricity, that I might actually be *attracting* the stuff.

In August of 1989, I was moving hay on my farm. There was only one dark cloud above me, and since it didn't look ominous, I thought I had plenty of time to finish my work before a storm hit.

I had the spear on the tractor and was moving around the giant rolls next to Leroy and Hubert Mathis' farmhouse. The Mathis boys were sitting on their back porch watching me work when they witnessed a giant lightning bolt reach down from the sky and hit me and the tractor as I was headed down a hill.

The strike momentarily knocked me unconscious and heaved my body up on top of the tractor as it was still moving forward. When I came to, the tractor was moving full speed ahead, downhill, toward a tree. It took me a minute to get my bearings and realize I had just been hit by lightning. *Again.*

This time, I had not been lucky enough to escape injury. I was hurting all over, but I was able to muster some energy, climb backward to the seat, gain control, and bring the tractor to a stop. I thought I could limp to safety and get to a low-lying area and wait out the storm until I could get help.

But Mother Nature wasn't finished with me yet.

As I started to climb off the tractor, I got hit by lightning again.

To hear Leroy and Hubert tell it, they were watching me work one minute, and then in the next minute, couldn't quite grasp what they had seen.

"Hell, I think Terry just got hit by lightning," Hubert shared his observation with Leroy as if he were just making conversation when he saw the first bolt strike.

When the lightning hit me a second time, "Well, he's a goner!" was all Leroy could manage. It was though these two were watching this transpire on a television screen.

Thankfully, these two good Samaritans wasted no time rushing into the field in their pickup truck, collecting me off the ground where the lightning had deposited me, and calling an ambulance.

I ended up in a hospital where only one doctor had ever treated lightning strike victims. He had seen plenty of them in Southeast Asia when he was a medic, and knew what type of bodily damage to look for.

Numb and partially paralyzed on one side, I was slipping in and out of consciousness and didn't quite know what was going on. I just remember waking up at one point and seeing two preachers standing at my bed praying, one on each side. I told them they looked like two vultures who were fighting over who was going to preach my funeral. Obviously, and thankfully, that coin toss never happened.

I still have some lasting effects of my lightning encounter, including nerve damage in my vertebrae, teeth and gums. Part of the gum and some of the teeth on the right side of my mouth had to be replaced. To this day, whenever I drink milk, it tastes like copper. I must have some kind of chemical imbalance after all that electricity coursed through my system, but other than that minor annoyance, I've suffered no other reminders of my close call up yonder.

Once word got out that I was going to be okay, the incident certainly got the attention of the cut-ups around town. My new nickname among insiders became "Sheriff Sparky."

Photo courtesy *Rickie Boulton*

**This picture was taken that same stormy afternoon,
about three miles from where I was struck.**

A group in North Carolina called "Lightning Strikes Anonymous" has been asking me to join their club ever since. One of the members has been hit by lightning *thirty-four* times. Time to get in out of the rain I would think, eh? At least when it comes to this organization, I'll have to be like Groucho Marx and refuse to join any club that would have me as a member.

All I can say with complete certainty after three lightning strikes is, once again, God's hand was protecting me — not only from the lightning, but from what was brewing out in the county with a large group of unsavory characters who just wouldn't go away.

The Expressway Gang

During my stay in the hospital, I received a couple of fruit baskets and several vases of flowers. The sender or senders didn't sign a card. I also got half a wreath of dead flowers, but it didn't take a genius to realize who had sent those. Obviously, my zany buddies out there on Bluebird Road who wanted me dead — those mafia wannabees who called themselves "The Expressway Gang" — were showing their hand. They had hoped against hope that God would take me out of their way with the lightning, but since that didn't happen, they wanted me to know they were cooking up a plan to get me out of their way.

After about half a dozen years on the job and two big election wins behind me, I was going to try to deliver the knockout blow to the illegal gambling, liquor, and prostitution businesses on Bluebird Road. But twelve miles to the west, those businessmen had made some new friends.

In Mt. Juliet, a sleepy old beer joint had changed its name to "Expressway," and apparently, that's where they got their name. I had dealt with them in the past, both before and after I was elected sheriff.

Selling illegal liquor and drug dealing was their main business that hid behind the front of a legitimate motorcycle club and beer joint on Central Pike. This group had strong ties in Nashville at a place known to us as "The Bottoms."

All across the county, I had closed EG down several times — using legal tactics as before — but they were going to get a private charter to work around legal avenues now. I had seen hundreds of people at this little beer joint in Mt. Juliet, blocking traffic as they had what they called a "field day" for their motorcycle gang. This so-called private club met in a building the size of a two-chair barber shop, with one pool table and one toilet. When the boys were all in town for one of these rallies, good citizens couldn't travel safely past this business on Central Pike.

Traffic would be at a standstill, which left us with no other choice than to label them a "public nuisance."

I was going to need a little help from the building inspector if this legal maneuver was going to work. That's about what I got. Little help. Everyone was too frightened of what this group might do to them or their families if they caused trouble. I learned that the County Executive and the Fairgrounds Superintendent were going to allow this group to hold a motorcycle meet at the Wilson County Fairgrounds, which, conveniently for them, has access to Bluebird Road. These are the same motorcycle meets that I had successfully blocked by court order out on Central Pike in the past few years, and now they were getting up in my face by having it in our taxpayer-subsidized fairgrounds here in Lebanon.

Dope dealers and weapons smugglers would now be parading in and out of the fairgrounds with the full blessing of the county government. Before I became sheriff they had held this meeting there, and in the process, there were aggravated assaults, rapes, and a police officer was knifed. I wasn't about to let this meet happen as long as I had a breath in my body.

I went to the Fairgrounds Superintendent, who told me the chairman of the fairgrounds committee told him it was okay to allow this group to hold their meet. He privately told me he was scared to death of the Expressway Gang and what they might do.

I then went to the County Executive/Mayor who, like a little chicken shit, blamed it all on the committee. The committee chair would not return my calls, but I wasn't surprised. These people really didn't care about what could happen if EG took over the fairgrounds.

But hey, if you've gotten this far along in the book, you know me by now and can almost guess what I did to make our guests feel … well … unwelcome.

I called the gang leader and told him that if the group showed up with booze or drugs at this facility, people were going to go to jail.

It was August and it was sweltering hot. Making this bunch go away was going to be like shooting fish in a barrel in weather like this, but these actions would add to the already long list of why this group wanted me dead. I closed them down first in '86 and again in '88 for operating a business without a license. They had ties to the Bluebird Road group, and motorcycle gangs across the country were using the Expressway building as an annual meeting place for their activities. I put a stop to that too.

Oh, and along the way, I shot — in self-defense, of course — one of the main gang members' nephew, Ethan Mullins. Remember him from the interstate melee? It's a small world when you deal with criminals day in and day out.

Expressway Gang members were always sending veiled threats to me since I had become a thorn in their side.

I was going to have to come up with something to bring this to a head sooner or later, and there was no time like the present when they were about to invade the town any day now.

I couldn't stop the meet at this late juncture, but I could plan a nice homecoming party for them when they arrived.

There was one thing I forgot to plan for, however. A few days before their arrival, I had to have jaw surgery as a result of being struck by lightning.

With me in the hospital, the "par-tay" was *on* for the Expressway Gang. Word traveled through their grapevine that I was out of the way and the coast was clear. As capable as my deputies are, they weren't about to take this on without their leader, and I wouldn't have allowed them to go it alone anyway.

No one knew my prognosis within the first 24 hours of the lightning strike; the press had already killed me off, while others had me walking on water as some kind of miracle case. What they didn't know, was that the lightning did a lot of damage and I had to have corrective surgery on my jaw once the burns were healed.

After the surgery, the pain in my neck and jaw were excruciating. On the third day, the doctor wanted me to stay in the hospital, but I had pressing business at the fairgrounds.

I checked myself out of the hospital and called my patrol commander.

"Put everyone on standby!" I ordered. "We're going to the fair, and we're going to ride the Ferris wheel!"

Rolling Out the Red Carpet

A large crowd of people and motorcycles had already arrived when we got to the fairgrounds that afternoon. They were there just in time to watch us pull up in a big, converted school bus and park it at the entrance. This makeshift paddy wagon was where the naughty ones would be handcuffed and carted off to jail, should that need arise. No one expected the law to be there; they really didn't expect to see me since they thought God had paid me back by striking me down with a giant lightning bolt.

When my deputies took their places at the entrance to welcome the hundreds of out-of-state visitors coming to pedal dope and weapons, they greeted each with a hospitable, "Come on in, boys! Have a great time!"

The motorcyclists knew what was about to happen. They could see it on our faces. Each group coming in made a U-turn after seeing our welcoming party and headed back from whence they came.

The motorcycle meet was a total flop, which put me higher on the shit list of the Expressway Gang.

Aerial photo of one of the annual meetings of the "Expressway Gang."

It got a lot of people thinking about my political demise too. Political leaders were already planning for my defeat in the 1990 election. I was organizing a fundraiser as if nothing had happened, while the boys from the Expressway Gang had other ideas. Apparently, they were already telling everyone they didn't have to worry about this sheriff being re-elected in 1990 because he wouldn't be here to run for office.

I began to hear a lot of rumors about how unhappy they were with me for spoiling their summer fun at the fairgrounds. Nothing got back to me that I considered a plausible threat. But then it happened.

Close Call

A few weeks after the fairgrounds event, detectives in Nashville arrested a man who had ties to the Expressway Gang for selling drugs. Daniel Lovell was a parolee who had just spent time in an Indiana prison for car theft. As he talked to detectives and tried to make a deal for himself, he shared what he called a "well-organized plan by the EG to kill the sheriff in Wilson County."

When I found out about this, agent Jim Harkum of the FBI and Bernie Redd of the TBI went with me to meet with Lovell and learn more about these plans for my murder. We picked up Lovell from the Metro police officers and, as we drove around, began to have a casual conversation with him. He told us a chilling story about the night we had shut down the motorcycle meet. He described how the leaders of the EG were livid that they had missed out on more than $125,000 in narcotics sales. Lovell said that in the following weeks, conversations began as to how "someone should be hired to kill Sheriff Ashe."

The group wanted the shooting to occur between the courthouse and the jail in the middle of the day, and it wanted to hire a white man to do the deed, since it would steer suspicion away from their all-black motorcycle gang.

The contract on my life had been out there for eighteen months, but they had just upped the ante. They had approached a hit man in Hendersonville — a former Vietnam veteran and soldier of fortune — offering to pay him $50,000.

We later got a lead on the man and called him in for questioning. The mercenary told us he had a conversation with the group leader, but once he found out the contract was on a law enforcement officer, he had declined to do it for so little money.

Meanwhile, I must have made quite an impression on David Lovell that day. As we started back to the Nashville jail after our discussion, he looked at me and declared, "After meeting you and talking with you today, Sheriff, *I would have hit you for fifty thousand!*"

That sent a chill down my spine. These guys were for real.

At that point, I knew which organization wanted to kill me. I knew why they wanted to kill me, but I didn't know who they were going to hire to carry out this mission. The contract was still floating around out there, and there was a hefty price on my head.

Even more chilling, David Lovell told us about witnessing a murder at the EG headquarters in Mt. Juliet. He described a well-dressed "white dude" who came in to the beer joint dressed in a cowboy shirt, big gold chains, and starched jeans to buy some dope. Lovell said some guy sitting in the corner sprang up from his seat and, without muttering a word, shot the guy in the head. Lovell said he asked the shooter why he shot the stranger. "He looked like he was all about money," was the assailant's excuse.

Lovell said they carried the body to an abandoned barn across the street and buried it in a stable.

Months later, we excavated the barn and didn't find a body, but found where lime had been used to aid in decomposition. Some unidentified remains later turned up in Davidson County, but we were never able to find out the identity of the victim.

After Lovell was released on bond, I began to think about my future. The FBI couldn't do anything until an actual attempt on my life was made. That's cutting it a little close for my money. I took it upon myself to watch out for number one, and it almost became an obsession: I put transparent tape on the doors and hood of my car to detect if an explosive might be planted there overnight. I never took the same route home each night, and I slept in the guest room to change up my sleep routine in case someone was watching me.

I continued to get feedback that the hit was still on, and that I shouldn't lower my guard.

After a few weeks of these nerve-wracking machinations, I went to the FBI and TBI again to urge them to do whatever they could to help me as soon as possible. Since they didn't want to wait until somebody actually tried to kill me, they did the next best thing: they brought agents from across the state. With all the intelligence we already had on the EG, in one big sweep, every gang member was visited in the middle of the night. Each gang member was told that we were on to the murder plot.

The agents warned that if "a hair on Ashe's head" was harmed, the EG members would be the main suspects. That still holds true today.

This tactic obviously worked. Two weeks later, we were able to bust two of the major gang leaders for major narcotics violations — drug trafficking via UPS and FedEx. One of the guys arrested went back to the same federal penitentiary where he had spent some time before.

There's something interesting to note here: our informant, David Lovell, who revealed the murder plot to us, ended up being sent back to the same facility as the EG member. He was killed shortly after being placed in prison, and I know it had something to do with his role in helping us. Looking back on how my path crossed with Lovell, I had the good fortune of his having *bad* fortune — being arrested for car theft and in turn, telling us what was going on with the Expressway Gang.

Those days still haunt me. I think about the threats all the time and have never really gotten over that terrifying feeling I had when the details of my planned murder were revealed to me.

Most of these gang members are out of the penitentiary today running free, and the old wounds don't always heal.

I sometimes see the family of Ethan Mullins, the guy I confronted on the interstate, and I've seen some of these other gang members through the years. I understand some of their children are trying to keep up the family tradition and open up the EG joint again, but so far nothing like that has happened. The original owners of the property have long since passed away, but this dangerous group was in power a long time and had many tentacles reaching into Bluebird Road.

Transitions

It was as though I was catching it from both ends — Bluebird on the east and the Expressway Gang on the west. When the EG joint finally closed up, I think as dangerous and violent as it was, the folks on Bluebird Road knew I meant business when they saw the law had fought that group and won.

It was funny to watch these same bootleggers joining forces with the churches to keep liquor by the drink from coming in. Liquor stores owners in nearby counties were pouring money into Wilson County, buying advertisements telling people to vote "no" on liquor by the drink because they knew that they, too, were going to take a financial hit.

Bluebird Road would have to go through yet another transition, and whether it would turn into a safe, clean neighborhood or a haven for prostitution and drug trafficking remained to be seen.

Photo by Bill Cook, Courtesy *The Lebanon Democrat*

"Gypsy" White is taken to jail.
Gypsy bootlegged from various locations on Bluebird Road.

CHAPTER NINE

Bluebird Rebounds

The back and forth see-saw approach to Bluebird Road was, at best, annoying. I'd get one step closer to having things cleaned up, and something else would come along to set us back. I'd close one bootlegger only to have another spring up down the street. There was some progress, but I didn't have time to marshal all my resources in this very large county with 578 square miles and all the burglaries, rapes, murders, thefts, and armed robberies which were occurring elsewhere.

This game of Whack-A-Mole was what I had to deal with every day as sheriff of Wilson County back then. Not to mention, I-40 runs right up through the middle of the county from the east to the west — from Metro Nashville to Smith County. Thirty-plus miles where everything, and I do mean everything, goes down that major highway. US Highway 70 and US Highway 231 run right through the middle of the city of Lebanon. Tennessee is surrounded by eight states, and Wilson County sits approximately in the middle of that configuration. To get anywhere, travelers almost always have to pass through here. Some bring their good money and trade with our fine merchants, while others bring dirty money and stack it at illegal poker tables or spend it on dope.

While I was making every effort to clean up Bluebird Road after I was elected, other illegal forces began to crop up in the western end of the county. The problems which sprang up there closely resembled the issues I was having on Bluebird Road. Cab companies were wide open for illegal liquor runs back in the day when this was still a dry county. A thirsty traveler could have a few bottles of booze delivered to his motel room, his business, or his home.

There has never been a shortage of beer joints in this small town, including on the square. In the outlying areas, the markets and the honky-tonks were scattered up and down Highway 70, Highway 231, and Highway 109. There was so much more to do on Bluebird Road, and now, as the sheriff, I had to "work" all of this. As I looked back at that time, after so many fatal stabbings, shootings, and robberies, I thought things were finally slowing down and getting better in that area.

After all our work, there were only about four businesses left on Bluebird Road, and they had all applied for business licenses. They had hung out neon Budweiser and Pabst Blue Ribbon signs and enlarged their parking lots and driveways just to let me know they were still in business. I was driving around one day when it occurred to me, upon seeing Bluebird Road's new look, that I had created a monster by making these establishments legal.

It was like letting your sixteen-year-old kids get a driver's license, then watching them drive ninety miles an hour down a slick road with bald tires.

On top of everything else, the little jail was full and I was having a difficult time fighting with the county court for more space and staff to keep the place going.

I was in a running battle with the county court commissioners and other elected officials. I didn't realize it at the time, but this conflict would last another twenty five years.

The federal housing projects were always a problem, and one was just a stone's throw from the entrance to Bluebird Road off Highway 70. These projects were a haven for drug distribution points. My old friends at the city police department were doing the best they could, but what goes on in the city bleeds into the county and vice versa.

Bluebird Road's so-called "legal" businessmen now had signs flashing and shingles hanging in front of their buildings. Car tags from other counties were back now, along with the fancy tricked-out vehicles and loud bands playing well into the night. But there was more brewing here now than just beer. Bluebird Road was on its way to becoming a wild and dangerous place to be once again.

Fighting the fight this time was going to be very difficult. I was going to have to bring in the big guns — a large group of legal and civic activists who were just as weary of dealing with this blight as I had become.

There are three things you learn if you spend any time down here in the South: 1) men don't like to share their wives, 2) dope dealers don't like to be ripped off, and 3) if you hurt a man's dog, you're asking for more trouble than if you had committed the first two offenses. I learned that there was a number four to add to this list: messing with a man's ability to make his living, even if it is illegal, really pisses him off.

I was going to need luck and quick wit to stay ahead of the game this time. I was about to invest both. How would I get away with what I used to do in the past — bursting into an illegal establishment without a warrant? Most of the time, I would have a warrant before I kicked down the door, but with the old houses that were running illegal businesses in the back, no one would claim ownership of the house, complicating the process.

District Attorney Tommy Thompson was my longtime friend, and he knew I was going to need his help in solving this problem legally. We began to have discussions about creating an agency that would join forces in at least five mid-state counties under his jurisdiction, and Tommy asked me to try to get the funding through the Wilson County Court. Wilson was the largest county in the judicial district, and he asked me to take the lead and head up the task force. He was tired of prosecuting murders on Bluebird Road and had even prosecuted cases in Nashville which had origins on Bluebird. He knew as well as I did that the crime there was only going to branch out and spread like a virus if we didn't stop it now.

Our plan was to hit everyone hard with this newly-formed task force, get it funded and agreed upon, and attack the problem with these fresh resources and put in play just the kind of operation that would be the killing blow to all this illegal activity. Selling illegal booze was one thing, but when the trade expanded into marijuana and cocaine, we knew we had to do something and do it fast.

Remember when...

From left are Bobby Capers, assistant district attorney general; Tommy Thompson, district attorney general for the 15th Judicial District; Eugene Murray, Lebanon Police detective; and Terry Ashe, Lebanon Police detective. The photo is from the 1970s. Since then Capers, of Mt. Juliet, served as Criminal Court Judge for the 15th Judicial District for 16 years, leaving office in 1998. Thompson continues to serve as district attorney general. Murray retired and worked in the private sector for 24 years with Toshiba. He is serving his third term as District 21 Wilson County commissioner. Ashe ran for sheriff in 1982 and has been elected to that position five times since.

Then it happened. Law-abiding citizens who wanted a drink in Wilson County, along with those who had the means to obtain a liquor license and open a legal bar, wanted to keep the money in Wilson County by making liquor stores legal. The paperwork was filed, and the "Wilson County Wet" debate began. This debate had been here years earlier, but it was difficult for the law to pass back then.

We aren't called the Bible Belt for nothing, and this liquor debate would rage on in the county for months to come, but it finally passed and much to the dismay of the illegal joints, anyone of legal age could buy legal booze at any of the safe, clean establishments in the area.

Photo by Bill Cook, Courtesy *The Lebanon Democrat*

We're not called the Bible Belt for nothing.

Romans 13

We didn't have time to lose with Bluebird Road in the crosshairs of an ongoing drug war. "Drive-by shooting" is a term we hear on the news every night these days, but it was a new way to describe murders-on-the-run a few decades ago. Drive-by shootings had become almost as commonplace in Tennessee as thistles. Automatic weapons were everywhere — especially in abundance on Bluebird Road — and I couldn't help but look around me and exclaim, "What's next?"

But then I saw the light at the end of the tunnel. It had been right under my nose the entire time! What I was going to do was fight fire with fire and use the latest and most advanced tool I had — a tough new DUI law that had just been passed. It was really strict by 1980's standards. I figured if all those people wanted to visit Bluebird Road, which only had two ways in and two ways out, and if they wanted to stay late, get drunk, get high and sell dope, they were going to have to go through my roadblocks coming and going.

I knew the good, law-abiding people who lived there wouldn't care and would probably welcome our presence. The book of Romans in the thirteenth chapter, the first through the third verse, says essentially if you're breaking the law, you need to fear the judgment of the government. Decent citizens should have nothing to fear.

I was about to give some folks a Bible lesson.

From the get-go, it worked. We were stopping people coming and going. If they were not driving correctly, or were drunk, they were going to jail. Patrol cars were passing these places every fifteen minutes. Within two months of our actions, violent crime began to fall, business on Bluebird Road was falling down, and the illegal establishments, hidden behind the legal flashing signs, were feeling the pinch. There were some very unhappy campers out there. In those two months, our arrests were up and out-of-town traffic on Bluebird was almost nonexistent.

Then, the real weakness revealed itself.

My secretary, Marie, came in one morning and told me George Walker — one of the most notoriously crooked business owners along Bluebird Road — was there to see me.

I told her to have him wait as I prepared. I didn't trust this guy as far as I could throw him, and I wanted a tape rolling for this meeting. Cassette tape recorders were the size of a couple of bricks back then, and I had to position one under my desk and run the microphone up under some papers on the top of my desk so it wouldn't be discovered. I put a fresh tape in the machine, did a microphone check, and told Marie to send in my guest.

Walker was a short, heavyset, middle-aged black man who was dressed up for that time of day; it had been quite some time since I had seen a man in a feathered hat like that. George removed his chapeau as he walked through my office door, but he still looked like a pimp. This man was no stranger to me; I had raided his business on Bluebird a number of times before when I was Chief of Detectives and had arrested him twice after I was elected sheriff.

He sat down across the desk from me and got right to the point.

"Look here, Sheriff! You puttin' a lot a pressure on us folks on Bluebird Road. You pressured me big time when I wuz in da city. I can't operate out dere on Bluebird no more."

"George, you're just gonna have to obey the law and you won't have these problems." I shot back at him with the obvious. Remember, I was being recorded too. I had to be nice.

"But you shuttin' us all down out dere by puttin' the heavy law on us! So, look here now, this is why I'm here today. I be makin' the same deal wit you dat I've had wit other folkses here and with other folkses dat runs da city."

I had suspected bribes were being offered, and sometimes taken along the line for years, but this was the first time I was going to have evidence like this on tape.

"I been payin' some of 'em a hundred dollars a week, and I'd be willing to pay you two hundred dollars a week if you'd just leave me 'lone!"

"Really, George? How have you managed to do all of that?" I wanted him to spill his guts.

"It's somethin' I've done the whole time and that's how I stayed in bid'ness. You done caught me haulin' whisky from Gallatin and Nashville in my Cadillac, you done raided my house, and I nevah could get close to ya, but now you is about to shut me down and everybody else out dere. We had a meetin' and we wanna give you two hundred dollars a week."

"George, hang on just a minute. Are you sure of what you're offering here? You want to pay me that much money?" I said, as I reached under my desk.

"Sure, that's pretty good money thea, Mr. Sheriff," he said.

At that moment, I plopped the still-rolling tape recorder on top of the desk for him to see. His eyes got as big as silver dollars.

"Can you say that just a little louder, George, I don't think I quite picked that up clearly," I chided.

George went berserk at the thought of being caught on tape offering the bribe. During his little fit of rage I told him to get his ass out of my office, and if he ever attempted to bribe me or anyone who worked for me again, I would put his ass in the federal penitentiary. George couldn't open the door and get out of there fast enough.

Da' Man's Out Here!!!

Ronnie Hancock, one of my closest friends, always called me "High," as in high sheriff. He would call me in the afternoons and invite me to come to his house for a "butterfly twist," his code word for beer. Ronnie lived out on the peaceful side of Bluebird Road not far from where I grew up, and we got together to visit as much as our schedules would allow.

It was a spring day, and Ronnie called and invited me to come out to his house after work around five thirty or so. On my way, I noticed that George Walker had a parking lot full of cars around his old house. This was long after I had shut him down for his illegal back room activities. I could see that he had cranked up business once again and was doing quite well from the looks of things.

As I continued to Ronnie's house, the more I thought about George being back in business, the madder I got. I thought back to the early days when I would just show up on the doorstep and tell them if they didn't close down immediately, "I'm comin,'" meaning, "I'm coming back to get you and haul your ass off to jail."

I went on out to Ronnie's about a mile or two down the road, and my temper was on a slow boil. When I walked into his kitchen, I turned down his offer of a beer because I was hatching a plan and needed to be "on the job" in every respect. I told Ronnie that George had cranked up his business again and that I was going to pay the old boy a little visit. I asked Ronnie to ride down there with me, but he wasn't keen on the idea. He didn't want that ornery bunch of drunks to see his face. He still had to live there and get along with everybody on that road or suffer the consequences.

I assured him that if he would go with me, I wouldn't even get out of the car and he would be safe and out of sight. With that assurance, he agreed to ride along.

We started down Bluebird Road, and the closer I got to George's place, the madder I got. When I came off the hill just before his old house, I pressed the gas pedal to the floor of my old Ford. I had the breather turned upside down on that car, and I know every one of those guys inside the joint could hear me coming. As I got closer to the house, I steered off the road at full speed, crossed over two driveways, and slid the flying vehicle into a tiny opening in the hedge surrounding George's house. The hedge gave way to reveal a water hydrant that I didn't know was there. I ran over that and opened up a geyser that shot twenty feet into the air. I kept going and pulled the car up to where my door was even with the front door of the house.

There was an elderly black gentleman sitting on the front porch, acting as George's lookout, whose eyes were as big as saucers as he surveyed the hedge-covered car and the water spewing everywhere. The expression on poor Ronnie's face was priceless as well. He was pale as a ghost and sank in the seat as I rolled down my window to address the elderly man on the porch.

"Tell George to come out here!" I commanded, as Ronnie turned to look the other way and hide his face.

"Geooorrggee, da man's out heeerrree!" The old man yelled through the screen door at the crowd inside.

George came to the screen door and cautiously stepped out onto the old wooden porch.

"George, I'm comin'!" I looked right at him and had to yell over the sound of the gushing water.

"Sheriff, now we ain't doin' nothing in here!"

"George, I'm comin'!" I said, ignoring him. I drove away, squealing my tires, and left him there amidst the weeds and the water to contemplate what was ahead.

Three weeks later, I made good on my promise to come back, just as George thought everything had cooled off and I had forgotten about him.

I hit that gambling house with seven or eight deputies. We went through the old front door with a battering ram, and the entire door frame came off and fell forward. The loose door fell onto the wood stove and knocked it over; sending sparks, hot coals and smoke everywhere. Two old "ladies of the evening" sitting by a table screamed at the dangerous domino effect we caused and ran out of the crowded room.

There wasn't a lot of liquor, but there was a real gambling operation going on. One bedroom had been turned into a cheap country casino. Money was stacked on a dining room table; a sheet that touched the floor was draped over the stash.

Everyone inside was simply shocked and didn't move as we made our way through. We lined every one of them against the wall to quickly take their names, search them, and gather and photograph the evidence. As I looked around, I noticed there were fewer people than there were cars outside, so I knew we had some people hiding in there somewhere.

Just as I was making my way to the back of the house, I heard a sneeze coming from the dining room. I jerked the sheet from the makeshift gaming table and found two terrified gamblers hiding underneath.

Three guns were under there on the floor with them and, wonder of wonders, no one knew anything about who owned the weapons or where they came from.

This raid was the straw that broke George's back. We charged and convicted him for illegal gambling and, to this day, he's never opened up another gambling house or liquor house that I'm aware of.

But then again, time marches on. And like most of the others in his group, age finally caught up with George, doing more to slow him down than the law ever could.

Miss Lillie

Not every bootlegger on Bluebird Road was a man. At least one was a woman; a seventy-something, white-haired granny who was as sly as a fox and as sweet and kind as could be. The sage advice is to keep your friends close and your enemies closer; make no mistake, I made sure I was on a first name basis with Miss Lillie. We had a very odd relationship. She was doing a booming business in the forties and fifties and would serve my Dad and his friends a drink on their way home from work back in the day.

The old boarded-up joints would come and go, but Miss Lillie ran a tight ship and was one of two businesses left standing after the riff-raff burned each other out of existence. It was easy to spot "Miss Lillie's" house; it was the neat little white cottage with the fancy paved drive way and the dead giveaway of a bootlegger: a paved parking lot out back that was usually full of cars. These cars didn't belong to delightful grandchildren who were coming to Granny's to make sugar cookies as she would have us believe. We would conduct a raid and she would meet us at the door with a big smile, wearing an apron and looking as though she just took an apple pie from the oven. As soon as she was raided, she would open up again, stronger than ever because there was never enough liquor seized during the raids to charge her with bootlegging. This had gone on for thirty years. It was getting old.

I think the elderly widow rather enjoyed this little game of 'hide the liquor when you see the Sheriff coming.' She had this down to a science.

I continued to get complaints that she was still selling booze, and then one night, we picked a guy up for DUI who promised to show us where Miss Lillie hid her liquor if we'd go easy on him. He had a deal. I'd be glad to accommodate him if he could only show me Miss Lillie's stash. What a haul this will be after all these years!

A couple of officers and I casually pulled up into the paved driveway one evening and walked to the back door very slowly, as if we were just making a social call. She had a bar set up on the back porch and greeted us with that big smile, as she had so many times in the past.

"Well, Miss Lillie, I've got another search warrant," I said.

"I always expect you to have a warrant, Sheriff—well come on in!" She seemed as confident as ever that our raid would render nothing. It never had, and she assumed it would be no different this time. She pointed at a counter that just had a bottle or two sitting on top, "This is all I've got, what's on this counter, Sheriff." It was the amount the average person would have in their bar at any given time.

"I'll just look around here, Miss Lillie, if you don't mind." I walked over to a fuse box on the wall, opened it up, and took four screws out of the corners. I lifted this fake fuse box out and behind it, was a vault full of whisky. It was just as our informant said it would be.

"Well, you've got it," Miss Lillie sighed and looked at the floor, but still didn't seem to be very upset. "There ain't no five gallons in there, so you can't charge me. Five gallons is the rule!" she warned. Miss Lillie was well versed on the letter of the law pertaining to her business.

"I'm not done yet, Miss Lillie. I'm still looking," I said as I headed down the hall. "Let's go into your bathroom." She followed me down the hall, not saying a word. There was a fake wall behind the bathtub and I walked straight to it and lifted it up. I hit the jackpot. A huge shelf held gallon upon gallon of liquor--- more liquor than I ever thought I would get off Miss Lillie. This time I was going to charge her and I was going to prove to her that I could convict her.

We got the case ready for trial.

Not So Fast...

One afternoon the district attorney called me and asked me to come to his office to talk about Miss Lillie's case. I dropped everything I was doing and rushed over there because this case was going to prove a point on Bluebird Road. When I got to the D.A's office, I was told we couldn't prosecute Miss Lillie because of what we had uncovered. Her attorney, under Rule 16, had provided the district attorney with her federal income tax return forms. On the income tax form, on the line where it lists "Type of Employment," Miss Lillie had put down "Bootlegger." She was admitting on a legal, federal form that she was an illegal bootlegger, but she was paying taxes on the revenue she was generating. In a town that had just voted in liquor by the drink, that just wasn't going to go anywhere in a court of law. All I could manage to do was look at the district attorney in disbelief. He told me we would have to go over to the courthouse and 'retire' the case immediately. When we walked in, there was Miss Lillie, standing there in the hallway of the courthouse with her attorney.

"How are you, this morning, Terry?" She was so sweet to me, sugar would melt in her mouth.

"I'm fine, Miss Lillie," I said almost under my breath. "How are you?"

"Well, I'm fine too, from what I'm hearing!" she crowed.

"Yes mam, looks like you've won again, but you know I'll be back to see you," I warned.

"Well, I'll never keep five gallons around at one time again. Besides, this liquor by the drink is coming in and I'm afraid I'll just have to go out of business."

Miss Lillie's health failed before her business, however. She passed away in her home after a brief illness a few years later, and it was a very sad time for me. She was a stately, wise woman who was doing the best she could to make a living for herself after the death of her husband, surviving on her wits and her street smarts. I seldom look at a tax return form that I don't think of Miss Lillie and how she put a good one over on us, and all she had to do was tell the truth.

I think of her only with fondness because she exuded class and cunning—even when she was caught red-handed.

One for the Road

After Miss Lillie's death, there were a few more bootleggers attempting to go into business out there on Bluebird Road, but they were short lived. The two remaining joints were hanging on by a thread with the new liquor by the drink law digging into profits and they were learning quickly that there's one little catch about trying to operate legally—you've got to follow the rules, or everybody notices.

My wife and I decided to go to a church and 'dinner on the grounds' at Saulsbury one Sunday morning. That's the country church not far from our old home place where my mother played the piano and where I was saved and baptized.

As we headed out Bluebird Road, I couldn't believe what I was seeing. One of the so-called "legal" establishments, Ned's Place, was open for business—on a *Sunday*. About a dozen cars were in the parking lot. Since my wife was in the car with me and we were running late for church, I decided not to stop then, but I was not going to let this pass. Once church was over and I got her home, I was planning on coming back for a "Come to Jesus" meeting with these dudes. I had been in tangles with the man who owned the place before and needless to say, our relationship was not in the best shape.

When the gathering at the church was over, I took the Bluebird Road route home. I wanted to see if all those cars were still parked around Ned's.

Nothing had changed and in fact, even more cars were in the lot now. After dropping my wife off at home, I went back to Ned's, eager to find out what the hell they were thinking out there. Just as I pulled into the parking lot, the doors slammed shut and were locked. I banged on the door and when no one came out, I went up the road to a small hill, near Miss Lillie's house, where there was a good vantage point. After about ten minutes, four guys came out and got into a big four-door Cadillac and took off toward Lebanon. I pulled in behind and followed them to the city limits. I notified the police that I was about to stop this car, but I didn't ask for back up. I was just going to warn Ned and the boys and let them know that I wouldn't stand for them being open on Sunday.

Little did I know, it was a little more complicated than that.

I stopped the car and walked up to the driver's side. Ned was driving and I asked him why his business was open. I wasn't surprised, but he started this whole bullshit tap dance about how they weren't open, that they were just having a business meeting. I had no warrants and no intention of arresting those men at that moment, but I wanted them to know I had noticed they were breaking the law.

There were two passengers in the back seat. I had never seen either of them before and I asked them their names. I knew Ray, riding in the seat next to Ned. I'd never had any problems with him in the past. He had an odd look on his face. After conducting an impromptu refresher course about the new liquor law and the rules he must follow, I gave Ned a warning and he drove away.

Several days later, Ray called me at my office to tell me I was lucky to be alive.

"Sheriff, you nearly got your head blowed off on Sunday."

"What do you mean?"

"Those guys ridin' in the back had a sawed off shotgun up on the armrest pointed out the door and when you pulled 'em over, they wuz worried cause they had a lot a cocaine on 'em. They said that they wuz gonna blow your head off if you tried to arrest 'em cause they wadn't goin' back to jail!" Ray said.

I thanked Ray for sharing this information and when I hung up the phone, my heart was pounding out of my chest. This is how quickly someone in law enforcement can die. For me, it was just going to be a conversation with Ned, someone I knew, about keeping a liquor store open on Sunday. For two total strangers sitting in the back of Ned's car, this was war. I would have never known what hit me. To go through all I've gone through on this road, to shut down the businesses and watch the area begin to prosper again, just to be gunned down by the last of the trash to ride out of Dodge—what a pisser that would have been!

It was unnerving to think that I was conducting a routine stop and this was going on in the back seat. But, more officers get killed doing the mundane, routine part of their job than at any other time. Sheriff Harold Griffin's death comes to mind.

I had no warrants, I had no probable cause, I had no idea there was cocaine in the car. I just wanted to have a conversation with the driver. It could have meant my demise. I was really glad I had the forethought to take my wife home before I made that stop. Both of our lives could have been in jeopardy. Guys like this—don't leave witnesses.

Rising from the Ashes

With all these things happening at once, the shutting down of the Expressway Gang, liquor by the drink getting passed, and years of solid enforcement, the illegal activity on Bluebird Road was beginning to wind down. Finally being able to say we had hit the ball out of the park took a lot of hard work, a lot of luck, and a lot of determination to make a difference. When I ride through that area now, I have a sense of pride. Most of those old joints, all of those bad reminders of what it used to be, are gone. It's a safe neighborhood and there's progress all around. People who have to pass through there every day in their course of business thank us for cleaning up the area. I promised I would, and with the help of some dedicated and determined law enforcement professionals, I was able to keep my promise to the voters. The shootings, killings and stabbings that were Bluebird's reputation for more than fifty years, are no more. God's Hand on my shoulder, and a bit of luck in being in the right place at the right time brought us to this point. By voting in liquor by the drink, the community did its part to shut down the illegal operations. Nothing works like drying up the source.

There are only two beer joints on Bluebird Road at the present time, and I have a good relationship with those owners. Ironically, after my first re-election, and then after the next six elections, some of my biggest percentages of votes have come from the black precincts. There's a mutual respect from the church going, law-abiding people, both black and white in that community.

I did what I promised I would do when they elected me. I'm grateful the voters gave me the opportunity to make a difference.

CHAPTER TEN

My Heartbreaking Job

Lisa Murphy did a pretty good job of hiding her pregnancy from her parents and her classmates at Watertown High School. She wore tight undergarments to bind her belly, and tried to hide the rest of her changing body with oversized tops and loose pants.

One teacher wasn't fooled; she had taken Lisa aside during that last trimester and offered to help. The woman told Lisa that she knew she was pregnant, but Lisa vehemently denied it and thought she had gotten by with her subterfuge when the teacher stopped asking her about it.

Only one classmate knew the truth. Lisa had told her friend Janie long before her pregnancy started to show. And she shared another secret with her friend; she told Janie that this wasn't her first pregnancy. She had lost a little girl — stillborn in the seventh month — early in 1994. She had kept that secret from her parents as well. Her boyfriend buried the child's body out in the country somewhere, and no one ever found out.

Lisa's boyfriend, Billy Stockwell, worked the night shift at a Lebanon factory, and she was concerned: what would happen if she went into labor while he was at work and she was home alone with her parents? She told Janie that she didn't know what she was going to do with this baby when it came, but that she and her boyfriend would "take care of it."

When Lisa missed school on Thursday, May 4th, Janie became worried and confided in a teacher about the situation. The teacher called UMC Hospital to see if Lisa went there to have her baby, but no one by that name had been admitted that day. Lisa didn't show up for school the next day either.

Lisa Murphy served four years; Billy Stockwell was given a life sentence.

On Monday, Lisa came to school looking pounds thinner. It was obvious to Janie and the concerned teacher that Lisa had given birth. Janie sat with her friend at lunch to try to get to the bottom of this mystery.

What she learned, and what Lisa Murphy would later tell our detectives, would become by far one of the most heartbreaking cases I've ever worked in all my years of law enforcement.

Lisa's water broke at four o'clock on Thursday morning, just as she had feared, when she was at home with her parents.

Two hours later, she called Billy when he got off work to tell him she was in labor.

Billy picked up Lisa and her sister under the guise of taking them to school, but once the little sister was dropped off, he took Lisa to an abandoned camping trailer, which was parked behind a barn on his father's property.

There, in that rat-infested trailer on a germ-ridden, ragged mattress, sometime during that next night, Lisa gave birth. She said she had a difficult delivery because he was a very large baby boy — so big, in fact, the child ripped her genital area and she needed medical attention. She was still wearing an adult diaper that day because she was bleeding so heavily and was in pain.

The baby, according to Lisa, was dead when it was born. In her words, the umbilical cord was "wrapped around its neck."

She said she only got a glimpse of the baby before it was "disposed of." She added that the baby had lots of hair.

Janie couldn't listen to another word. She was hesitant to talk to anyone about this, but she had to do the right thing. She went straight to the principal, who called us. Janie's mother brought her to our office to give an official, detailed statement.

With her parents' permission, we put a wire on Janie the following Monday to record another lunchtime conversation with Lisa Murphy. We needed to learn exactly how this child's body had been, in Lisa's words, "disposed of."

The tape was inaudible because of all the background noise from the cafeteria, but Janie relayed the most important information to us: the baby was buried in a barn just off Beech Log Road in Cherry Valley.

A quick stop at the property assessor's office confirmed that property belonged to Billy Stockwell's father. Everything was beginning to add up.

Now we needed to talk to Lisa, but since she was a minor, one of her parents had to be present. We called Lisa's mother and told her we had picked up her daughter in connection with an investigation, and that we needed her to come to the Sheriff's Office in Lebanon at once.

When Lisa's mother arrived, seemingly perplexed at all that was going on, we took her to Lisa, who was waiting in the interview room. Lisa was read the Miranda Rights and signed a paper indicating she knew what it all meant.

She wanted to talk to us, but she didn't want her mother in the room. The mother agreed to leave, and Lisa Murphy began telling us pretty much the same story she had told her friend Janie.

I asked Lisa where her first child was buried and about the circumstances of its death. She told me it was also "born dead," and that she had put it in a Walmart bag and stuffed it in a groundhog hole next to a rock fence.

Sometimes you've just got to wonder what the hell is going on in somebody's mind. I've often wondered if that first child, so carelessly tossed away in a shopping bag, had indeed died at birth.

She signed a copy of her statement. She didn't flinch. No remorse, no shame. *Amazing.*

Billy Stockwell, meanwhile, was being questioned in another room. There were some twists in his story. First, Billy told us that after the baby was born, it was crying as he took it back to the truck. Then he went back to the story of the child being stillborn. Lisa told us Billy buried the baby in the barn immediately after its birth, then loaded her up in his truck and took her home.

After questioning, Billy drew us a diagram of the barn and the exact stall where he admitted burying the child. Billy's dad, who owned the barn, consented to a search of the property within minutes after we interviewed the couple.

The old camping trailer where Baby Murphy was born was parked deep in the woods twelve miles from Lebanon.

The Investigation

When I saw the old camping trailer, I could hardly fathom a young girl going *near* it, much less giving birth inside. The couple had admitted taking with them string and scissors — things they would need to deliver the baby. However, it was obvious that they had made no plans for the baby's survival in this desolate place.

They didn't take diapers, milk, or blankets. Thrown outside the back window, bloody adult diapers, soaked from a recent rain, were scattered among the weeds. Less than a hundred feet from the trailer, a shovel was lying atop wet leaves.

Once inside the barn, it wasn't difficult to tell where a shovel had been used; freshly disturbed soil mixed with manure was piled in the middle of a stall — exactly where Billy's diagram indicated the grave would be.

Baby Murphy was buried alive in the hallway of this dilapidated old barn.

**The baby was found buried under dirt and manure in one of the stalls.
He was still alive when his father put him in his grave.**

Detective Don Hamblin and I knelt down and began to sweep the soil away with our fingers to preserve evidence. We wiped away less than four inches of dirt when the baby's tiny hand was revealed. It looked like the hand of a doll. My eyes welled with tears.

At that moment, the thought rushed through my mind: *Could the baby have been crying, raising his little arm and kicking his legs as the dirt and manure were shoveled upon his healthy body? Was his last movement on this earth an attempt to survive the murderous act of his own father?*

We carefully brushed away the remaining soil, and the entire body was uncovered. He was a perfectly formed child and looked to be full term, with the umbilical cord still attached and hanging below his knees. There was certainly no evidence of it being around his neck as his parents had wanted us to believe.

It was a devastating sight. The saddest thing imaginable.

We didn't move the body until the medical examiner got there to take it to Nashville for an autopsy.

> I agonized over sharing here a crime scene photo
> of Baby Murphy, because I felt it was important to
> underscore the heinous nature of this act.
> Because of its graphic nature, I decided instead
> to use this empty frame as a symbol of the precious life
> and future he never got a chance to live.
> His is a case that will always haunt me.

The autopsy revealed that the baby died from suffocation; all evidence showed that the baby was alive when it was born, and was *buried alive*. Traces of dirt and manure were found in the infant's trachea and stomach. Lab tests confirmed our worst suspicions: the infant was crying when he was put in his grave.

This story is haunting on so many levels, but what continues to bother me to this day is the lack of remorse on the part of this young father and mother, although I hesitate to call them parents in any sense.

They were so matter-of-fact. I could see nothing from this couple that showed me that they intended for this baby to live when they made the trip to that camper.

I can't imagine a man callously carrying his crying newborn son in his arms, all that way into the barn, to bury him alive. There was a lot of time to reconsider — many steps to hear that child screaming for its life and for its mother. What kind of cold-hearted bastard can be deaf to that? That was the question everyone was asking.

Lisa Murphy's case never went to trial. In the community, there was so much hatred for these people and what they had done to this helpless little child, the district attorney said he doubted she could have gotten a fair trial anyway. She was sentenced to ten years in prison for her part in the baby's death, and was released after serving less than five.

District Attorney Tommy Thompson presented Billy Stockwell's case to a jury; Lisa Murphy testified against him. He got life in prison for burying that child alive. And this was their second child to die. The first one will never be found.

The community rallied around Baby Murphy, and churches joined forces with our department to ensure the little child received a proper memorial and burial.

The heartbreaking case was an emotional setback for everyone who worked in this office, read about the case, or saw the story on the news. For months afterward, I received letters from caring people who just needed to mourn the loss.

One young mother in Watertown wrote a poem about Baby Murphy and sent it to me with her condolences.

In her letter, she echoed the sentiments of the community and those of us in the department: so many people who are unable to have children would have given everything they had to hold this perfect, precious baby in their arms. This child deserved a loving and caring family down here on earth, but he was denied that.

Our only comfort is in knowing who holds him today.

,   5-21-95   4-6854

Baby Murphy
34 ——— Judy Hasan

In the world he arrived in fear,
Greeted with abuse as death grew near.
He reached out — Mom and Dad take my hand,
And felt the coldness — of the woman and man.

Baby Murphy left never to feel love,
And his first caress will be in heaven above.
Baby Murphy had a life to share,
Yet he left this earth — with no family to care.

Baby Murphy touched hearts — of people like me,
Wondering why this had to be.
I can't image how this baby felt,
to plead with cries — with no one to help.

The sheriff must have been torn apart,
to dust the dirt from the tiny heart.
Buried alive this newborn boy,
to so many people — he would have been a pride and joy.

As the tiny hands reach to heaven above,
I hope his little soul — is filled with love.
I pray as Baby Murphy — rests in God's arms,
Please keep all children safe from harm.

CHAPTER ELEVEN

Terry Ashe. Unplugged. If I were making a country album, that's what I'd call this next song ... or ... chapter. It would take an entire book to tell everything about my personal life, so I'll just hit on the highest highs and the most incredible lows of life when I'm not wearing the badge. I can't decide what's harder — exposing my inner thoughts for everyone to see, or re-living it all as I reflect on a life smoked down like an unfiltered Camel, all the way to the end.

But I've got to write about it if I expect anyone to read this book. The readers are going to expect the truth, and that begins with telling the truth about Terry Ashe, warts and all.

Everyone I know who has something wrong in their life always wants to blame it on something that happened to them in their youth. They look for something traumatic in their childhood that triggered the bad habits, bad conduct, or hard feelings that made them who they are in a relationship. I'd like to be able to blame my multiple marriages and numerous failed love affairs on someone else, but I can't. Okay, I'll take 60/40 in most of them, except for one, and that one was 50/50.

I could probably get away with saying that losing my dad early on and watching my mother remarry many times after that had a negative impact on my view of holy matrimony, but that would just be a damn lie. I've been married...a lot. Insert your best Minute Rice joke here. I'm not proud of it, but that's just a fact of my life.

I have a great deal of respect for all the former Mrs. Ashes out there. Can't say they feel the same way about me, but as time goes by, I see that I've mellowed and can let bygones be bygones. I couldn't have said that when I was going through each of the divorces because there is no such thing as a *friendly* parting — especially not where passionate people and a couple of farms are involved.

In the divorce, the wife gets the friends. People tell you they're going to stay neutral, stay in touch and not take sides, but they always manage to keep their distance out of respect for her. I don't know, maybe it's a Southern thing. Many times I didn't miss the wife, and I didn't miss the stuff — and I lost a *lot* of that — I just missed the friends who left me after the divorces.

Gossip, Gossip

I wrote this little mantra several years ago: *Best friends, your secrets know. Someday that friend becomes your foe, then* **all the world** *your secrets know.* You might want to remember this so when it happens to you, and it will, let me be the first to say I told you so.

I've had indiscretions and I've had wives who had affairs when I was out working a case. The rumor mill has been busy about me throughout my political career. But with people's imaginations always being more titillating than what really happened, I'm not about to confirm or deny anything. There are two types of gossipers I've learned to recognize through all this. First, your *friends* start the gossip out of concern for you. Then the second type of gossiper, your *enemy*, takes over. By the time the gossip gets back to you, like in that old game we played in elementary school, the story is unrecognizable.

The amazing thing is that the public has never held my disheveled personal life against me — the real one or the fictitious one — when they stepped into the voting booth.

I'm sure if they wanted the Pope to be sheriff, they would have elected him. But they didn't. They elected me, the imperfect man, the sinner, the renegade. They pulled that lever beside my name all the while knowing that I've failed miserably in my marriages.

From a political standpoint, the people know how hard I've worked and have been gracious enough to put all that aside and elect me nine times, counting my win as constable.

I'm not proud of the mistakes I've made, but I don't look back with gut-wrenching regret. I read somewhere that regret is what we feel when we're not happy with where our lives are at the present time. I'm certainly experiencing true happiness at this stage of my life, and I'm not looking back except as a learning experience. If nothing else, I want my romantic missteps to serve as a cautionary tale to young men and/or women who want a family life as well as a career in politics or law enforcement.

Looking back and not being a self-critic would be a mistake on anyone's part. I harshly critique myself when it comes to my personal life, but when it comes to my career and what I've tried to accomplish, I've given it my all, and I make no excuses for that.

Purpose

The Bible says you can gain the world and lose your soul. That's not going to be me.

I'm still that little boy who first trusted Jesus when he was sitting in the top of a plum tree. I'm the same kid who was saved in the country church and baptized in a creek. I might have gotten off course many times, as we all do, but my values — my sense of right and wrong — have never faltered. Guardian angels have been constantly by my side since birth, never allowing me to forget my spiritual roots.

I find that people with all kinds of personal problems come to me for advice. I must have that trusting, father-figure face. I think they know I'll never divulge their names, their circumstances, or violate that trust. I believe they come to me in the first place because they know that what I haven't been through, I've heard about, and I can give them an honest opinion or a shoulder to cry on.

My grandfather wanted me to be a preacher, and the thought did cross my mind on occasion. I was given a gift of feeling comfortable in front of large crowds and making speeches, so it stands to reason that I would feel right at home in the pulpit. But I think I've served the Lord where he needed me the most — out in the trenches. I think the outreach purpose is the same: save people's lives, hold those accountable who need correction, and share the faith. I've certainly tried to do all of this in my mission.

I do believe my calling was to serve the people of Wilson County, Tennessee as their sheriff. That little boy who looked up to Sheriff Griffin, the child who lost his father and his home, the young man whose life was forever changed at war — all these stages of my life brought me to where I am today — closer to God's purpose for me.

There's even a purpose for this book somewhere, for somebody, in one of these stories. Who knows what might jump from these pages and make an impression one way or another?

I've lived my childhood dream and annihilated my personal life in the process. Somewhere between those two is/was my purpose. I guess I'll learn for certain what that purpose was, in the sweet bye and bye.

A Work in Progress

Looking back, I do wish I had made more of a commitment to a normal marriage when I was younger. Whenever I open up the newspaper and see a photograph of an elderly couple celebrating their fiftieth wedding anniversary, I'm touched. These are my heroes. They've managed to maintain their lives together and their love for each other through whatever life throws at them. That amazes me. When I read an obituary and see where a man is survived by his wife of forty years, I tend to reflect on my own marriages and think perhaps if I had tried a little harder, had been more committed to the marriage and family and less committed to the job, maybe then I could have experienced a love like that. I was simply committed to the wrong things and didn't make the right choices to have this kind of outcome. That's painful to admit, but it's a reality.

I was always ready to cut and run, or someone was ready to cut and run on me when times got tough. Maybe at this point in my life, I've learned to stand still and listen.

My daughter Jesse once told me when she was a little girl, "Dad, you're just a work of God in progress!" I certainly hope he isn't finished with me yet. I do know that he never gave up on me, even when I was making all of these bad choices that weren't part of his plan for me. Just like an earthly father, my heavenly father has always found a way to bring me back to center.

During one of my divorces, I was going through a particularly tough time and I asked Mr. Albert Jewell, the preacher who baptized me, the question that was burning in my heart and in my mind: "Brother Jewell, how does a person know they're still saved?" I asked. "I still believe, of course, but I haven't always lived the right way."

The answer Bro. Jewell gave me was so profound that I've never forgotten it. "Terry, we all sin, but the test is simple; when you sin — and we all do — and you feel bad about it and you're sorry you did it, then you're still saved. It's when you sin and you're no longer remorseful that your soul is in trouble."

I've had many tests of my faith, many occasions on which to feel bad about something I've done.

I speak to the graduating class at the Tennessee Law Enforcement Academy on a regular basis and try to give them some simple advice, because I know how hard this career can be on a marriage. I know about the temptations out there. I know the latitude an officer has within the community and how it can affect the ego. I tell them that if they want to be a successful law enforcement officer, if they want to be the next chief of police or the next sheriff, there are three things they need to do: number one, put God first. Second place goes to the family. The job gets third place.

Unfortunately, I've never followed my own rules. I ask them to do as I say, not as I do. I always managed to put my job first, and that's what caused all my problems.

There is no doubt in my mind that this is the reason my personal life sucked. I've missed too many Christmases with my family. I've butchered Thanksgiving meals by jumping up and running when a call came in instead of allowing the people on duty to handle the situation. I've been on the street on holidays and on a child's or wife's birthday helping other families with their issues instead of tending to my own. And you haven't been in the dog house until you've missed, or even completely forgotten, your wedding anniversary. Trust me on this. I've paid the price for ignoring family, and I won't do that again. Family is all we have when it comes right down to it.

He's Got My Back

All my life I've heard the expression, "A friend will stick closer than a brother," but I never understood it, perhaps because my older brother has stuck closer to me than anyone I know. He's not only my biggest supporter, he's my dearest friend. He knows me better than anyone and can give me reality checks when no one else can get through to me. Most brothers grow up as adversaries, but not us. Our hardships brought us together as a loyal, united front. When I count my blessings, I'm counting how lucky I am to still have my big brother who knows me inside and out and can practically finish my sentences for me.

Beth

I'm lucky to have the love of a good and understanding wife these days. I've been married to Beth for eight years, and I think I'm getting the hang of what it takes to make a successful marriage meld with a busy career. She's taught me how to do that. She's had an extensive career in law enforcement – serving as sheriff in

Lake Charles, Louisiana; she was the only woman elected to that post in the history of the state. Beth can go toe to toe with me on any job related issue. She understands the stresses of the career and has been a stabilizing influence in my life through all the pressures of politics these past few years. I think that the other women in my life loved the idea of being married to a lawman more than they loved the reality of it. Beth knows the reality since it's her career path as well. Passion and a genuine friendship are two ingredients that were missing in my marriage recipe before, and I didn't realize that until I met and married Beth.

I was thinking recently, as I sat in my office looking through the newspaper, it might not be too late for me after all, since I'm still a work in progress. I have this lovely bride at home — one who keeps me straight, challenges me, laughs and cries with me, and most importantly, is willing to stick around for our fortieth wedding anniversary celebration. I've already promised her I wouldn't be working late that day. And I've sworn that I'll *never* forget the date.

My beautiful daughter, Jesse, and my wife, confidante and best friend, Beth.

222 ASHES OF BLUEBIRD

Jesse

I'm so thankful to have the love of my only child, my beautiful daughter, Jesse, who is now 25 years old and is a successful, happily married businesswoman.

I'm so proud of her, and I know I'm sounding like a typical bragging dad, but she's a dynamo. She looks just like my mother. I'm amazed when I look at a photograph of my mother when she was in her twenties and compare it to a photo of Jesse.

She is the blessing that came from all the turmoil in the past, and if I had to go through all of that to have her in my life, then it was worth it and I would do it all again. Like Beth, Jesse is my confidant and friend.

I'm so lucky to have a daughter who understands her old man's flaws and loves him unconditionally in spite of his checkered past and warped sense of humor. I hope someday she can forgive me for putting each of her suitors under the microscope when she began dating. But hey, that's what dads with daughters do. It's just that dads who happen to be lawmen take that interrogation thing a little too far sometimes. These days, I'm trying to be very nice to Jesse because she will someday choose my nursing home. Or not.

Happy Hour

When I have something on my mind, nothing soothes my soul like working on my farm and being around the horses, the cattle and the dogs. For me, farm time is happy hour. I suck at golf even though I do manage a game now and then, but relaxing on the farm is my idea of going to the country club.

Being around the work horses and the mules and smelling the sweet hay was pure heaven when I was growing up, and since buying my own farm, I've raised horses and even showed a few at the county fair. Old Buck was the best horse I ever owned, and all of his former owners could say that about this grand animal as well.

Me and Old Buck on one of our days off.

Two different people owned Buck, sold him, and then bought him back immediately because they missed his gentle temperament. Back in the early 90's, I bought him for keeps and took up trail riding as my pastime. We went everywhere together: The Smoky Mountains, Big South Fork, East Fork, Kentucky, Mississippi, West Tennessee. Anywhere there was a trail worth riding, Old Buck and I were there.

I loved that horse because he was somebody I could talk to. On those evenings when I got home from a tough day, I could go out to the barn, look into that horse's eyes, and tell him my troubles.

In the spring two years ago, my trusty old friend and equine confidant died at age 27. I cried like a baby. He's buried on my farm where I have a small cemetery dedicated to my animals. To fill the void left by Buck's death, I bought two more horses; Beth and I enjoy caring for them, even if I don't ride much these days.

"Saddley Missed"

Dogs have always had a warm place in my heart, and we have a couple of labs keeping us company these days. Before I bought the farm I live on now, I had an Irish setter named Rebel, who lived to be almost 18 years old. The night he passed away, I called the man who runs an old cemetery not far from town. He had been drinking and probably thought I had been too, when I began bawling like a baby into the phone. The conversation went something like this:

"Jim … (sniff, sniff) … my dog … died."

"Who is this?"

"It's the sheriff, Jim … (sniff, sniff) … my dog died!"

"What do you want me to do about it?"

"Well, you run the cemetery and I need to give my dog a proper burial."

"I can't bury a dog out there! Forget it! I'll get in trouble."

"You can bury him in one of the plots I own out there."

"Forget it! I'll get in trouble if you bury a dog there!"

"I'll give you a hundred dollars."

"Bring him out there at 6 A.M."

The next morning at six, as planned, I showed up in my truck with Rebel, laid out in a beautifully lined and sealed plywood casket with his favorite toys, wrapped in his soft blanket. Jim couldn't believe what he was seeing.

"There are *people* buried out here not laid out as nice as that," he admitted.

Jim had dug up a nice plot for Rebel at the foot of my grave site and we laid him to rest there, complete with a granite grave marker the tombstone carver had screwed up with the misspelled tribute: " REBEL — SADDLEY MISSED." Rebel would have liked that I used the imperfect marker. He got his warped sense of humor from his dad.

Rebel – Saddley Missed

CHAPTER TWELVE

I first met Jerry Mundy back in the early 80's when he came to my office looking for a job. He had been laid off at AVCO — the same aviation manufacturing building where my dad had worked so many years before. Jerry wanted to change his career direction, and since he found himself in this awkward position, he felt this was the perfect time to try something new. Being a lawman had always been in the back of his mind, a little unspoken dream, so I didn't have to talk him into coming to work for me as a deputy.

Jerry worked with us for three years in Wilson County and did an excellent job before going back into manufacturing. He began to miss the challenges of his old career, and before long, was enticed back into law enforcement. This time, he went to work as a police officer in Mt. Juliet. This nice-looking, muscular guy was built like an athlete and was very energetic — active in coaching ball teams and always working toward advancement within the department.

His hard work finally paid off; he reached his goal of becoming Sgt. Jerry Mundy.

Jerry's good friend, John Musice (pronounced mew-sic), worked with me sixteen years and was a great leader within the department. He came from good stock, as we like to say about quality people here in the South.

Long before John was born, I had met his dad, Luther, when I was just a kid with an after school paper route in Lebanon. The senior Mr. Musice was the maintenance man at Castle Heights Military Academy, and stopping to chat with this wise, kind man was a must when I made my deliveries of the Nashville Banner every afternoon. I'd pedal my bike to the tiny shop where he kept his tools and lawnmowers alongside half-used cans of paint and cleaning solutions of every description.

He was always tinkering with something at his work bench, but he would take time to visit with me each day. We'd talk about our lives and the times, and he'd give me a Coca-Cola in exchange for one of my newspapers.

John, the quiet, shy man I would later hire as deputy, was just like his dad in so many ways — very active in his church and dedicated to raising his children in a safe community.

He was a graduate of the prestigious Castle Heights Military Academy where his dad had worked, and on many occasions, I offered to promote him to supervisor due to his excellent work ethic, discipline, and character. He turned me down every time. He wanted to be an officer on the beat. Not only did he enjoy dealing with people and helping them solve problems out in the community, he loved his days off with his family more than he relished the idea of being the 24/7 boss.

I really didn't blame him for turning down the promotions when he told me his reason.

John had a great sense of humor, especially about some of the more mundane, daily grind aspects of a job in law enforcement. One afternoon, after months of answering dozens of calls about an escape-artist, pet potbellied pig roaming around and annoying everyone in the neighborhood, John drove up to the station with the animal in the back seat. We had joked over the radio with him all morning about how he should arrest the old sow for loitering and bring her in.

He turned the joke on us by doing just that. He loved telling the story to anyone who would listen about the look on our faces as he prepared to book and process a potbellied pig.

Tragedy Strikes

July 9th of 2003 was a terribly hot, humid day. The entire summer had been unforgiving to the crops and the livestock, and it was especially tough on any officer on detail outside in the searing sun.

I was called into the dispatch room around 9:30 that morning because we had received a number of BOLO (Be On The Lookout) calls from law enforcement officials in Maryville and Knoxville in East Tennessee.

The calls warned us about two women in a stolen Mercedes-Benz speeding toward us down 1-40 East. Truckers had already called to tell us that the young driver was driving erratically, at nearly 120 miles per hour. She was weaving in and out of traffic, passing cars and trucks on the right, with the tires squealing on the hot pavement as other vehicles were bullied off the road and into the ditch.

This driver had already assaulted a Knoxville police officer and rammed a patrol car before escaping that jurisdiction at breakneck speed, so this was not just a youngster on a harmless joyride coming toward us.

Two of our units spotted the car as it left Smith County and were racing to catch up with it as it crossed the Wilson County line. The airwaves were full of reports from officers in Lebanon and Mt. Juliet on their way to help us intercept this reckless escapade.

I had a *really bad* feeling about this situation, as I worked the radios and the telephones to coordinate our response from point to point. This had started out as a full-out high speed chase way over in East Tennessee.

Now it was approaching our jurisdiction, and hundreds of innocent citizens out there on the highway could be hurt or killed. We had to try anything and everything in our arsenal to stop it.

Defense attorneys would later ask me to define my "bad feeling" in court. Why this was important to them, I can only guess. I could only compare it to the way a farmer smells rain coming when he's working out in the field.

While my analogy came from the farm, my instincts from years in the military and law enforcement were kicking in at that moment, and somehow I knew this was not going to end well for any of us.

9:48 A.M.

When the Mercedes reached Lebanon, several officers tried to set up a roadblock by fashioning a bottleneck of cruisers with flashing lights and blaring sirens. It failed to even get the attention of the driver. She flew by, barreling westward as though they weren't even there. The car was going so fast, there was very little time to prepare for what any of us would do at the next mile marker.

Now, of all times, the Old Hickory Boulevard exit off I-40 West was backed up with traffic as far as officers on the ground could see — directly in the path of the chase. Mt. Juliet Sgt. Jerry Mundy and Wilson County deputy John Musice had to work quickly. They stretched a "strip" — a long, flexible strip of metal spikes — across the highway from edge to edge, designed to blow out all four tires of a vehicle as it passes over.

Musice and Mundy took their places, from what they thought would be a safe vantage point, near a patrol car on the grassy shoulder of the highway; we aren't sure exactly where they were positioned.

Officers on the tail of the Mercedes were warned about the spike strip up ahead and backed off in an effort to create enough distance to stop and save their tires.

In the next moment, cacophony took over the radio.

"They've hit Jerry Mundy! They've hit Jerry Mundy!"

I ran from the dispatch room, jumped into my car, and headed to the area where the spike strip had been deployed. As I continued to listen to the radio traffic and make my way down I-40, I was thinking that Mundy's *vehicle* had been hit by the speeding car.

SGT. JERRY MUNDY

If his patrol car had been hit at that high speed, I fully expected the officer would be hurt, perhaps critically.

"Mundy is 10-7, Mundy is 10-7." The radio fell silent for a moment after that dreadful transmission.

Mt. Juliet Police Sgt. Jerry Mundy, my former deputy and friend, had been killed. I couldn't believe what I was hearing. The silence on the radio gave way to confusion and panic.

"We can't find John!" shouted the next voice, and my mind raced as I tried to figure out, John … John … John … Who could that be? I called my dispatcher to see if anyone could tell me exactly who had been sent down there.

"John Musice's car has been hit, but we can't find him. He isn't in his car."

John Musice was my deputy and was in the Mt. Juliet vicinity when all units were called to help. I frantically tried to get in touch with someone, anyone from our office at the scene, to call me on the cell and fill in the details. All the while, I was behind the wheel, driving the twelve long miles down I-40 to get to the accident. I remember very little about that drive, except that it seemed like it took forever, and I was caught in the traffic which was already backed up for miles, starting at Highway 109. I carefully weaved my way — still practically *flying* — back and forth, on the shoulder and into the median.

It was all in slow motion, as I think back on it today.

All the while, I could hear officers begging for help on the radio. They were choking on tears as they tried to talk. There was the eerie sound of people keying the radio to speak, but they never spoke. Only background sounds of total chaos were coming through.

What the hell has happened out there?

It seemed as though time stood still, and as this lump in my throat grew, I began to pray.

I asked for the strength to handle what I was about to find. I knew I was going to need divine intervention to maintain my composure and help everyone else through this, so I asked for His guidance in giving me the right words and the appropriate actions for the task I had in front of me. The radio keyed again. There was a bit of background sound, and then, the horrible news:

"Musice is 10-7, Musice, 10-7."

That transmission hung out there in space for a while. Two veteran lawmen, two men I knew very well, were dead.

I had worked homicide. I had been first on the scene of so many car wrecks and had witnessed so much death and destruction during my career and my tour in Vietnam that I should have been hardened to seeing dead bodies by now; but nothing in my past would even come close to what I was about to encounter. I loved these guys

and their families. Ten children would have to grow up without a father. Two widows were left behind. It didn't make any sense.

The thought of the wives and children of Sgt. Mundy and Deputy Musice reminded me to order our dispatch center to switch channels on all radio traffic coming from this scene to a priority channel for our ears only. All transmissions about the deaths must be blocked from the assignment desks at the Nashville television stations, all of which were equipped with police scanners.

We couldn't let the families learn about these deaths from the media.

I continued to say a prayer and took a deep breath as I arrived and parked my patrol car in the median. Officers rushed toward me with tears in their eyes, embracing me and sharing their feelings of disbelief. They walked me to the area where dozens of officers and emergency workers were gathered.

Nothing could have prepared me for what I saw when I got there. I never expected *anything* so brutal. The carnage was similar to what I had witnessed in Vietnam.

It all happened in a flash, but the first officers to arrive described what they had determined so far: apparently, Musice and Mundy had gotten out of their patrol cars and were standing at what they *thought* was a safe vantage point shortly after they secured the spike strip across the road. Fallon Tallent, the woman driving that Mercedes at 118 miles per hour, spotted the spike strip and the officers standing on the shoulder of the highway beside it.

What happened next was unthinkable, as we would later hear from the passenger, Debbie Cash. Tallent *intentionally* steered toward the officers, vowing to Cash that they would "never take her to jail." As Cash later testified in court, Tallent then squealed, "Watch this!" as she chased the officers down, crushing Jerry Mundy against a patrol car and throwing John Musice several hundred feet into the air through the tops of some tall trees, where his decapitated and dismembered torso dangled until it finally came to rest near a fence on the side of the interstate.

He had been thrown so far from the point of impact that officers initially reported they couldn't find Musice.

The violent impact had ripped the uniform, gun belt, and bullet-proof vest from his body. His badge was found several yards away — a tiny, twisted, unrecognizable piece of metal. John's eyeballs had been torn from the sockets. I was the one who found them, about ten yards from his body, completely intact, looking up at me.

I fell to my knees. The emotions were just too overwhelming.

Jerry Mundy's body was mutilated — decapitated and dismembered, scattered in pieces in the middle of I-40 West. His cell phone was still intact and continued to ring and ring and ring less than fifteen feet from his remains the entire time we stood there. It was chilling. I knew it had to be his wife, or perhaps one of his children, who heard about the car chase on the radio or television.

They were calling to check on him.

My thoughts wandered to the grim duty ahead of me; how am I going to tell these families that their brave officer is never coming home — much less, that they won't be able to view the body of their loved one at the funeral? How will they find closure? How will it ever seem *real* to them?

I had to get it together for the fellow officers of these brave men, and I would have to put those thoughts aside for now. I took a few beats to regain my composure, wipe away the tears, and try to get the painful lump out of my throat.

Mercifully, the answer to my prayer request for strength and my military persona kicked in simultaneously. We had to get to work. This was a crime scene and we needed to mark it off, take measurements, and begin the investigation.

We owed a precise investigation to Sgt. Mundy and Deputy Musice, even if it took all night.

Traffic was backed up all the way to Nashville on one side of the road and almost to Cookeville on the other. The wreckage and carnage was scattered across nearly eight lanes of interstate highway. Getting traffic rerouted while preserving the crime scene for a delicate investigation was going to be a major operation indeed, but a minor job compared to informing the next-of-kin.

The television stations were already setting up their trucks to go live with breaking news on the nearby overpass, and reporters were watching our every move. Notification of the families was something that we couldn't put off much longer.

Meanwhile, from high atop their vantage point, the news photographers were getting video of the driver, Fallon Tallent, who was being cuffed and loaded into a Tennessee Highway Patrol car and taken to the Wilson County Jail. Her passenger, Dorothy Cash, was being loaded into a helicopter ambulance amid Tallent's loud cursing and scuffling. Tallent only had slight scrapes and bruises, while Cash had a broken leg.

I assigned specific investigative duties to my deputies and found power in taking control of my anger. The only way we could help these dead officers now was by making sure justice was served. We were damned determined to do that.

Once the investigation involving the bodies was complete, every officer at the scene gathered around for an impromptu prayer service as the remains of our comrades were loaded into the ambulance. The doors had barely closed when the city manager of Mt. Juliet burst on the scene, his little police badge around his neck, announcing that he was going to hold a news conference.

The Mt. Juliet police chief was out of town, and apparently, this guy was trying to fill the chief's shoes in the spotlight. We were still in the middle of this delicate investigation, were in a devastated emotional state, and were in no mood to be dealing with somebody like this. I told Mr. Manager that if he wanted to hold a news conference before our investigation was complete, he could do so from the Wilson County Jail, because that's where I would be locking him up for the afternoon. I ordered him, his long hair, and his skinny ass, off the crime scene and out of our way.

That move brought a hearty thumbs-up from some of the officers who were within earshot of our heated exchange.

A Wild Child

As bad as these horrible moments were, the worst was yet to come in the hours ahead.

The focus had to shift immediately from losing these two great friends and officers to the paperwork, the fingerprinting, and everything that goes along with processing the people responsible for this crime. Fallon Tallent had been taken to jail, and when she was allowed to make her telephone call required by law, she went berserk and assaulted two officers with the telephone receiver. As they took her mug shot, she flipped the camera a couple of birds, saying there was "one for each of the officers," referring to the police officers she had run down in cold blood.

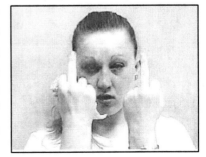

The warrants were drawn up with speedy precision, and she was put in a cell before someone else got hurt.

She was young and petite, with stringy blond hair, blue eyes, and a blank stare that made her look like a clueless little kid in many ways. But there was a hardness about her that made everyone uneasy. Years in and out of trouble had aged her and given her a cold indifference.

As required by law, I personally read the arrest warrant to her as she sat in jail. Her face was frozen in an emotionless pose as she kept repeating — almost in a chant — that she wasn't even there when the officers were killed.

It was all I could do to keep my composure, but I was on camera and my every word and gesture was being recorded for this legal process. I had to be on my best behavior. I couldn't say one word to mess up the case we had against her. I knew I could somehow restrain myself and maintain my decorum, but I wasn't so sure about the heartbroken men and women who worked with me. And who could blame them?

This woman was acting like a wild animal. In the best case scenario, this was not something I wanted my people to be exposed to, nor did I believe it was a good idea to hold someone so unpredictable in an emotionally charged jail staffed by the devastated friends of her murder victims.

Arrangements were made to move her to the Macon County Jail in Lafayette, Tennessee, until she could be transferred to Nashville.

I sat at my desk until almost midnight — praying, crying, thinking, and trying to organize my thoughts and my action plan for the days ahead. When I finally made it home, I walked in the back door and prepared to hang my jacket in the closet when I shoved my hand into the pocket and stuck my finger on something sharp.

I reached in and pulled out what was left of Deputy Musice's twisted badge that I had found on the pavement not far from his partial remains.

That tiny piece of metal and the unrecognizable form it had now assumed seemed to symbolize everything that had happened in the first awful hours of the day. The realization that two fine men were gone for absolutely no reason came crashing down on me like an avalanche.

I broke down and cried, one last time, in the darkness and privacy of my living room. No one was there to see, and I didn't have to be strong for anyone. Not for one more minute. I gave myself permission to wrench at least *some* of the despair out of my gut.

I didn't sleep a wink that night. I just stared at the ceiling, revisiting the surreal images of the day, finding it hard to believe that any of it had happened and wondering what we could have done to prevent it.

Those Left Behind

Sgt. Jerry Mundy had four children. Deputy John Musice had six. These children were now without a father because of a selfish young woman's wild crime spree and joy ride. These two young fathers — the sole breadwinners of large families — were struck down in the prime of their lives and at the top of their career.

Two wives, their ex-wives, and all their youngsters were depending on the incomes of these men, and they were all looking for answers along with moms, dads, brothers and sisters who didn't understand what happened to their loved ones.

But sometimes, out of great tragedies come great triumphs. We were going to be triumphant in prosecuting this case; we simply couldn't allow ourselves to believe otherwise.

I became totally focused on two things in the next few days: keeping the office running smoothly in spite of the high emotional toll these deaths had taken, and getting us all through the funerals.

Jerry Mundy's family chose to have a traditional memorial. Thousands of people turned out for his service at one of the largest churches in nearby Donelson. After the church services, the flag-draped coffin was brought through Mt. Juliet as an entire town said goodbye to their fallen hero, the first officer to be killed in the line of duty in that city's history. Hundreds of people lined the streets and waved American flags as bagpipers played "Amazing Grace."

At the burial site, law enforcement helicopters flew over in a show of respect. The service with full honors ended with the dispatcher calling one last time over the radio of a patrol car, parked by the gravesite.

"Mt. Juliet to car 406, Mt. Juliet to car 406. End of watch 7-9-2003."

Deputy John Musice's service was held at the largest Baptist church in the city of Lebanon. His family had chosen to cremate his remains. John's brother rode in the front seat of a patrol car to and from the service, holding the urn in the seat beside him as thousands lined up along the roadside to pay their respects and say goodbye.

Now the difficult reality for the families was setting in: how will the bills be paid? How will these ten children be fed, clothed, educated?

From the department's standpoint, working through this was going to be a logistical nightmare.

I would have one wife coming through the front door asking about insurance benefits while an ex-wife and her kids were going out the back. They were hurting and, on top of all the pain, had to worry about income for their families.

The officers had been dead one week, and already we were wringing our hands with all the paperwork, trying to complete all the necessary forms to get funding for the families before they lost everything. Mundy and Musice didn't make a lot of money. No one does in this job. At the time they sacrificed their lives, they were making about $14.50 an hour.

Charlie's Call to Action

Out of the blue, the phone rang in my office. It was Charlie Daniels. Charlie had known Jerry Mundy and John Musice personally, and he wanted to do a benefit concert to help the families they left behind.

This superstar from Mt. Juliet would put his busy schedule on hold as the event was planned. The Wilson Central High School auditorium would be the venue, and all the proceeds would be split evenly between the two families.

His offer was a Godsend.

Charlie's tender heart is legend in these parts. He and his wife Hazel, a strong woman who is his rock and soul mate, take a genuine interest in their neighbors and have been exemplary citizens. They're always there and ready to roll up their sleeves and work for those in need.

Charlie and Hazel were the first to step up when we were raising money to start the home for underprivileged children in Wilson County. So far, that home has helped hundreds of needy children because their names were attached to the cause.

The violent way in which Mundy and Musice were killed hit Charlie Daniels personally. He wanted to perform this benefit concert because he feels the death of any law enforcement officer — like the deaths of so many Americans on 9/11 — is an assault on our peaceful way of life in this country.

July 31st, less than three weeks after this tragedy, the auditorium at Wilson Central was packed with Charlie Daniels fans for a sold out concert. Charlie called it a "Middle Tennessee project," since donations poured in from Nashville and surrounding counties. The Charlie Daniels Band was joined in this effort by another Wilson County resident, country star Daryle Singletary, who took time away from his tour for the cause. Lee Greenwood was there to sing his hit "God Bless the U.S.A." So many stars showed up to share their talent for this event simply because Charlie called and asked for their help. That's all it took.

Charlie and Hazel wanted to meet backstage with the family members of the slain officers before the band performed. It was a tender moment as they met with each grieving person — holding the children, hugging the wives, comforting the moms and dads, brothers and sisters of the officers. Charlie told them how much he loved them, was praying for them, and how he wished he could do more. He felt every word in his heart, and I could tell he was hurting for them.

An entire community came out to show their love and support for those families that night. When CDB appeared on stage, it was a proud moment for all of us, especially for me. I was so proud to be the sheriff for this fine man — a legend in every sense of the word.

I was standing beside Hazel as CDB took to the stage. There were tears in my eyes.

Not only do I think Charlie is the greatest entertainer of all times, but he's one of the most generous people I've ever known. He took a burden off the department, buying us the time we needed to apply for the proper grants to ensure the families would be secure for the rest of their lives.

In recent months, Charlie Daniels and his family have suffered tragedy, loss, and health challenges of their own, and throughout, he and Hazel have maintained a strong faith that's inspirational to us all.

I'm happy they consider me a friend.

It goes to show us all that one simple idea can make a difference. More than 60 thousand dollars was raised that night for those two families. The efforts of Mt. Juliet's favorite son meant life could regain some sense of normalcy for those left behind. They no longer had to worry about the daily necessities; a few of the kids were even able to attend college as they had planned.

Using the skills and the good heart God gave him, Charlie Daniels gave peace of mind, comfort, and hope for the future to those who had lost so much. Our community may have been knocked down, but it had not been knocked out. Charlie's gesture kick-started an entire community's healing process.

For those of us who lost our brothers in law enforcement, healing could only begin when we saw justice served. The work to make that happen was all ahead of us, and it wasn't going to be easy.

The pain of reliving this entire ordeal was still ahead of all of us.

Meanwhile, Fallon Tallent, the woman accused of the coldblooded murder of our comrades, continued to be a belligerent, defiant, overbearing headache for anyone unlucky enough to deal with her, and I persuaded the Attorney General to move her to Nashville — for the sake of our sanity — as we continued the long process of preparing the case for trial.

Charlie Daniels with friends backstage at the tribute.

The Tallent Trial

Twenty-one-year-old Fallon Tallent, according to her own relatives, was no stranger to trouble. She had been in custody a number of times since she was around fourteen and had lived in a state-run facility for delinquents until she turned eighteen. She had been charged with stealing a car in Davidson County and had led authorities on a high-speed chase as late as March of 2003; but on that occasion, she finally stopped for the flashing blue lights, ironically, in Wilson County.

Charges were still pending in that arrest less than four months later, when Tallent stole that Mercedes-Benz in Knoxville on July 9th and sped down I-40 at about 120 miles per hour. Her escapade ended when she spotted a spike strip, laid out by veteran Wilson County lawmen John Musice and Jerry Mundy, swerved to avoid it, and intentionally aimed her speeding vehicle directly at them.

I've seen evil before. She truly is an evil, sinister being. I hesitate to use the word human. Sending Fallon Tallent to the penitentiary reminded me of Brier Rabbit saying, "Don't throw me in the briar patch!" She thrives behind bars because she's the young star with the "alternative lifestyle" among her fellow inmates.

She's callous and cold. It was all I could do during the trial to keep from getting my mitts around her neck and squeezing until her eyes bugged.

To this day, these families are suffering. The children miss their dads. The wives are raising kids without their husbands to help

them. As for the people who worked with Musice and Mundy, we're haunted by memories of that horrible day every time we drive down I-40 and see the two white crosses on the side of the road erected to honor the fallen officers.

My mind flashes back to that day and the way Tallent was acting as she was being cuffed and put in the back of a police cruiser. She was laughing and cursing and making jokes about what she had just done.

Part of me wishes this cold-blooded killer could be stood up in the middle of the interstate while the slain officers' family members do a demolition derby and knock her against a patrol car at 120 MPH.

Another part of me wishes she would find the right path and get right with her maker. She simply wasn't brought up to live in a civilized society.

During the trial, she laughed and smiled and mocked her lawyers. We were required to take food over there to her at the courthouse, and nothing we took was ever good enough. She pretended to be throwing up for the audience in the courtroom to disrupt the proceedings, and once we got her out of there, she started laughing and acting like a fool. We all just wanted her to disappear. Trouble was, we each wanted to be the person who made her go away.

She acted up so much behind the scenes with us at the trial, I went to the judge and got the permission to put a shock belt on her. I figured it was all we could do since the female guards at the penitentiary were no help in controlling her.

They treated her more like a BFF (best friend forever), and that just burned me up. A male guard who was shock belt trained was brought up from the penitentiary to be with her at all times while she was wearing this device. The judge was the only one who could give the order to shock her. The trained guard kept his eye on the judge at all times, and when the order came, he was ready to administer the shock to whip her ass back in line. The stress of the trial was bad enough, but for the entire last half of it, we had the added stress of managing this out of control idiot. As it turned out, just the presence of the shock belt kept her in line in the courtroom.

One morning before the trial started, I walked into the holding area where Tallent was waiting to be led out, and it looked like backstage at the Miss America Pageant. There was one of the female prison guards applying makeup to Tallent's face while the other was holding the mirror for the prisoner as she made sure her hair and lipstick were perfect. I couldn't believe what I was seeing. I asked them why the hell they were pampering her. "We like Fallon. She doesn't cause us any trouble," was their answer. Fallon Tallent's guards had become her groupies, and it was *sickening*.

I would have volunteered to put a black cloth bag over her head and be done with it, if you catch my meaning. Others in our department would like to see her hang on the public square in Lebanon. Some suggested we quietly put her to sleep. But none of those fantasies can come true. This evil wench will simply live out the rest of her life as a pampered pet behind bars. Fallon Tallent's trial had indeed turned into a bizarre media circus, but we were triumphant in the end. It didn't matter how she acted, how disrespectful she was, or how indifferent she was to the process. She received two consecutive life sentences, and can giggle and shoot birds and be obnoxious in there for the rest of her life. We got justice for John and Jerry, and that was all that mattered.

Rock Star at the Rock

Some of the women from the women's penitentiary that I've happened upon in court tell me Fallon Tallent is like the Queen Bee of the cell block. She has her designated "bitches" running her errands and doing her bidding. She's "sweet" to the ladies, as are some of the guards I'm told, so they're quite fond of her. That's one thing that just makes me furious. She's living it up and making the best of everything inside the walls. I predict that she'll run up on the wrong person one of these days and her reign as cell block queen will be over. Some rough old battle ax of a convicted murderer will clean this confrontational youngster's clock.

Something else really angered me as we all tried to put some closure to this Fallon Tallent thing. In 2007, before we got the new Criminal Justice Center built here in Lebanon, I went to the county commission with the request to name the building after John Musice who gave his life for Wilson County. I couldn't believe it, but I actually had opposition to this idea. What's wrong with people? How short can a memory be?

We were finally allowed to put Musice's name on the building, but when it came time to install the lettering on the front facade, no one knew anything about it. I had to personally meet with the builder and make that happen as though it were some kind of afterthought. The project manager was kind enough to pay for the lettering out of his own pocket.

I was fit to be tied. To top it all off, the County Court back then didn't even have a dedication ceremony for the building, which I thought showed a blatant lack of respect for all of us and what we had gone through as a department and as a community.

I'll never understand it, nor will I ever forget it.

One positive remembrance for the officers came later that year in Washington, D.C., during Police Week, when families, friends, and fellow officers come together to remember their fallen comrades. The Mt. Juliet police chief and I escorted Mrs. Musice and Mrs. Mundy to a ceremony at the capitol where they placed a rose in a large wreath in honor of their husbands.

IN HONOR OF
PFC MICHAEL H. BIA
2ND SQDN. 17TH. CAV. 101ST ABN DIV.
KILLED IN ACTION IN HUE IN THE REPUBLIC OF VIETNAM.
HE DIED FOR OUR LAND AND FREEDOM.
ANUARY 4. 1947 TO JUNE 06. 1968

CHAPTER THIRTEEN

In November 2009, I looked up the 101st Airborne Division's web site on the internet. There's a bulletin page on there where you can post a notice if you're trying to get in touch with a fellow soldier who was in your division. I was reading through all the posts to see if I recognized any names, and one came jumping out at me that was written back in 2003:

"I would like to talk with some family of Michael Bia. I was with him when he was killed in Vietnam. Please contact Art Corley." This guy's contact information gave an address and phone number in Newark, New Jersey.

Who the hell could this be? There were only three of us in the gun Jeep that night in June, 1968. I was the only one who survived the ambush. I scrolled down the page and noticed that this same guy had posted yet another notice that stopped me in my tracks — this one, from 2002:

"I would like to meet with family members of Samuel Boyd. I was with him when he was killed in Vietnam. Please Contact Art Corley."

Not only did this pique my interest as someone in law enforcement, it also pissed me off because this guy was an obvious fraud who might be trying to take advantage of Michael and Samuel's families. But what did he have to gain by this? I was going to call this guy out and make him tell me what the hell he wanted.

The number was probably old, but I gave it a shot and made what turned out to be, a very important phone call in my life. I dialed the number in New Jersey. A man answered and I asked to speak to Arthur Corley.

"Junior or Senior?" the man asked.

I thought for a second and did some age calculations.

"Senior," I said.

"This is Art Corley, Senior."

"This is Terry Ashe in Lebanon, Tennessee. I was reading on the 101st Airborne Division's web site where you were looking for the families of Michael Bia and Samuel Boyd."

There was a long silence and then he said, "Who did you say you were?"

"Terry Ashe in Lebanon, Tennessee."

"I thought you were dead, Sarge!"

Art Corley went on to explain that he was friends with Michael and Samuel because the three of them had arrived in country together. Corley was riding in another recon convoy that our gun Jeep was leading that evening and witnessed the ambush from his position of safety some distance away. He told me he had tried to find Samuel's family in New Jersey, but had no luck, then, he explained that he had been in touch with Michael Bia's widow and his brother Gabe in Window Rock, Arizona.

Apparently, according to Corley, everybody in Michael's family thought I was dead.

Corley told me he had been planning a trip out to Window Rock to meet with the family, who somehow believed Michael was still alive and lost in Vietnam. Corley believed that they needed some closure and felt that perhaps if they could talk to me, Michael's commanding officer, they would understand that Michael indeed did not survive that ambush. He shared the numbers and addresses he had for the Bia family, and I promised to get back in touch with him after I made contact with them.

This had to be done delicately. If this family had spent this many years believing Michael wasn't really dead, then it was going to be traumatic for them to hear otherwise. I had been in the position of delivering this kind of news to people throughout my career, but somehow this was different. I was Michael's superior officer, and he died under my command.

The old familiar survivor's guilt was kicking in for the first time in years as I clicked on the "Compose" icon to write an email to Gabe Bia, Michael's brother. I thought I had worked my way through this, but now, making contact with these people who were still in so much pain was going to be very tough. Or so I thought.

Once I began to write, the words poured from the heart. Somehow, the good Lord gave me the right words at the right time, and I felt a sense of peace as I clicked "Send." By that afternoon, I received an email from Gabe that brought me to tears. Gabe and his family were so happy to hear I was still alive and well and willing to share with them what I knew of Michael's last moments on earth. Over the next few weeks, as I was corresponding with Gabe, Michael's widow Lula reached out to me — first through an email, and then in a phone call with both Lula and Gabe.

As I talked to Lula, I remembered that, just before the ambush, Michael was talking about how she was expecting their first child and he was wondering if he was going to be home in time for the birth. I asked her about the baby that Michael never lived to see. Lula told me that, unfortunately, Michael's son only lived to be 36 years old. He had died of alcoholism, as many young American Indians do today.

I remembered Michael telling me about being raised with an alcoholic father, and that was the reason he never drank a drop. How terribly painful it must have been for Lula to lose her son in this way.

Lula invited me to come to Window Rock and celebrate Michael's life in a small memorial ceremony, telling me it would mean so much to all of them to finally meet me. They could now move forward with this since I had given them the information they had sought for so long.

The family had about eight months to plan everything for the service, and they chose Veteran's Day as the day we would all pay honor and tribute to Michael.

November 11th, 2009, my brother Ron and I boarded a plane to Window Rock, Arizona. I was so apprehensive about meeting with Michael's family that I had butterflies in my stomach for the entire flight. Window Rock was a couple of hours from the airport where we landed, so we rented a car and drove the rest of the way. As we got closer to our destination, Ron and I were saddened to see the extreme poverty surrounding the reservation. In many ways, it reminded me of the old Bluebird Road — old shacks, rusty tin roofs, no running water, and outhouses. It was just pitiful.

Lula was a school teacher and Michael had held some kind of prestigious ranking for Bull Riding for that area, so I was wondering if that had helped them have a better standard of living than all this. I was eager to see the home where I knew Michael's heart had been on that last day.

Michael Bia on "Buster"

I found it odd that the reservation was designated "dry." All the liquor is in the city, some distance off the reservation, and that's why so many young Indian men are hit by cars as they walk down the highway or hitchhike to get back and forth to the beer joints.

We drove straight to the hotel on the reservation where we were scheduled to meet with Michael's brother, Gabe. We would meet with Art later in the afternoon. Gabe would then take all of us out to where the rest of the family was gathered. Ron and I went in and waited in the lobby where I alternated between pacing the floor and checking at my watch, looking at everyone who came through the front door.

Then I saw him. The exact image of Michael Bia stood before me. I must have looked as though I had seen a ghost. I certainly felt like it. Gabe was just a young boy when Michael was killed, but now he had grown into a handsome young man who looked almost identical to his big brother right down to his big, contagious grin.

He embraced me and — quite unexpectedly for me — there were tears. We stood there in the lobby, and it seemed that he was bursting with dozens of questions he wanted to ask. He was in awe of what I had chosen to do for a living and wanted to know all about my duties as sheriff. But first, he wanted to take us out for a beer. I reminded him that his reservation was dry, but I should have known, there is no such thing as not being able to get a beer when you want one. "Follow me!" Gabe said. Ron and I followed Gabe and his old pickup truck down a dusty, narrow gravel road to a little beer joint. It looked like any of the dozens of beer joints that used to line Bluebird, except there were horses tied up out front and dogs were hanging out on the porch like some kind of Western movie set.

We all bellied-up to the bar, and before we ordered, Gabe looked at me and said, "I'm an alcoholic." He said it in a matter-of-fact way and pointed to a sign behind the bar that read, "Limit Two Drinks." This regulation was probably instituted because of the alcoholism that was rampant on the reservation. "Tiny," a 250-pound Indian woman with bright red lipstick took our order. It didn't take us long to drink our limit, catch up on our conversation, and get out of there.

We got back to the hotel just in time to see a mountain of an African-American man climbing from his car in the parking lot. He was about 6 foot 5, weighed a good 300 pounds, and was wearing a Vietnam Veterans baseball cap. When he turned to face me, I knew immediately that I was looking into the eyes of Art Corley — a man I hadn't seen in forty years. He smiled and approached me with outstretched arms. We hugged and gave each other a big pat on the back, while breaking out in tearful laughter.

"I would have recognized you anywhere, but I don't think you would know me, Sarge!"

"I've changed quite a bit since those days. How did you know me?" I asked.

"Sarge, I would recognize your eyes anywhere. When you came back to the unit after the ambush, you had that thousand-yard stare, and your eyes today look exactly as they did back then."

We caught up there in the parking lot until Gabe told us it was time to caravan over to where the rest of the family was going to meet us on the reservation. Gabe pointed out some interesting landmarks along the way. The rock formation with the big hole through it (hence the name Window Rock) can be seen from the side of the road. He showed us the road to the National Veteran's Cemetery, where Michael and others were honored.

When we arrived at Lula's home, I was relieved to see that her home was very much like the homes in middle class areas in Tennessee. It was a neat, stucco home surrounded by sparkling white gravel and was about 1,300 square feet. Lula had been a school teacher all these years and had managed to carve out an existence for herself without the love of her life. She never remarried, and I believe that had something to do with an Indian custom. Until she believed in her heart that Michael was dead, she could not move on with her life. It was sad to think that she now was completely alone after losing her son to alcoholism as well.

Lula believed that her son's drinking and disruptive lifestyle was a direct result of never knowing his father and feeling cheated by life. After Lula shared this with me, I began to wonder what would have happened if I had only tried to find the family sooner. Could I have helped Michael's son with his difficult transition and the demons that haunted him? Could my presence at the 2002 lodge ceremony have made a difference in this young man's life? I'll never know. Lula had told me in her correspondence that it was not meant to be.

It was getting dark as we pulled up in Lula's driveway, and as I got out of the car, I felt those butterflies in my stomach again. We had all been corresponding via email, so it shouldn't be awkward, but I didn't know what I would say at a time like this or how I would say it.

My brother and I followed Art up the sidewalk, and the front door swung open. Lula stepped out and hugged Art, then took one look at me and burst into tears as she wrapped her arms around my neck and embraced me as she cried. She led me into the living room where dozens of area residents and family members had gathered to meet Sgt. Terry Ashe — the man they were calling a hero.

Michael's uncle, Kenneth White, was the first to chat with me. He's Chief of the Dene (pronounced de-nye) tribe and a psychologist at the Window Rock Veteran's Hospital. He introduced me to some of the other people in the room, and the more of these highly intelligent and sophisticated people I met, the more I felt totally out of my element. This was not what I expected at all, and I was amazed.

Lula then had me follow her down the hall to her office, where the walls were filled with large photographs of the two of them on their wedding day, shots of Michael coming out of a chute on a bull, Michael in his airborne uniform, and Michael just being Michael. As I looked at candid photos of this young man who held so much promise for the future, who was so talented and loved his wife and family so much, I broke down and cried again.

I presented her with one of my purple hearts to display in this special room she had dedicated to Michael. I thought she deserved it more than I did, because there are wounds deeper than what bullets can make sometimes. She indeed had a wound that would never heal. I had her name engraved on the outside of the box as the recipient since it was her heart that was forever changed on June 6, 1968.

Giving Lula a Purple Heart

To the group of local veterans who had come to meet us, I presented a 48-star flag on behalf of my dad, Joe Ashe, in honor of their dads and granddads who fought the Japanese. This flag honored the "Wind Talkers," the brave Navajo Indian soldiers who frustrated the Japanese during WWII by speaking their own centuries-old language, an intricate code the enemy couldn't figure out.

An Amazing Tribute

In the backyard of Lula's home stood a "tee-pee lodge," a tent that could seat twenty-five or thirty people in a circle. This lodge was completed the first Veteran's Day after Michael was killed (November 11th, 1968), and ever since that day, two-day-long ceremonies have been held on the holiday to honor Michael and all those killed fighting for freedom. In those ceremonies, they pray to Jesus and spirits that they believe still roam the earth and have a profound impact on their lives. They've done this for more than forty years without ceasing.

In all those years, one question remained that permeated their every prayer and thought. They wanted to know how Michael died. Their prayers were for someone to be sent to them who knew every detail of Michael's final hours in this life. They felt I was the answer to those prayers.

I was shocked to learn that Lula had not opened Michael's casket for his funeral, even though I knew his body was intact and could be viewed. She was seven and a half months pregnant, and in the Indian culture it is bad luck for a pregnant woman to view the body of the dead because it might cause irreparable harm to the unborn child's spirit. Since Lula didn't see Michael, she couldn't be sure that it was indeed his body in that coffin, so she didn't get the closure she needed. For the next seventeen years, she watched every homecoming, every prisoner of war release, scanning anything she could view on television or read related to war, always looking for Michael's name because there was a part of her that didn't believe she had buried him. For whatever reason she chose to believe Michael was still alive, she clung to that notion for forty years. Now, in my presence and upon hearing me tell my story in the coming days, she would have to let go of any hope, even though that hope had gotten weaker as time wore on. Before I left that night, I looked into her eyes and told her that indeed Michael was killed in the ambush and that I was the last person to talk to him. She broke down as if she were hearing about his death for the first time. I guess, in a way, she was.

Lula asked Art and me to participate in the community awareness ceremony at the lodge over the next two days, an intense ceremony which required the two of us to essentially become Navajos. This would be the whole "Dances With Wolves" thing, with full costume, spiritual chants and readings, and would be our venue for telling Michael's story to the community. It was a Navajo version of a memorial service forty years after the fact.

Lula knew we had traveled a long way and were exhausted, so she sent us back to the hotel with the advice to get plenty of rest because the next two days were going to be intense.

Art had brought his sister-in-law with him, and I had brought my brother, but neither of them would be allowed to participate in the first eighteen hours of the ceremony.

I didn't sleep a wink that night even though I was exhausted. It was partly because of my nervous energy, but mostly because I hadn't slept in the same room with my brother since I was ten years old. I forgot he snores like a buzz saw. The next morning, I was at Walgreen's buying earplugs for me and a nose strip for him. I wasn't going to sit in lodge all day tomorrow and come back to sleep under these conditions again.

But God love him for coming with me. I couldn't have made the trip without his support. We had some good brother time and were able to catch up like we haven't been able to do in a long time.

Early the next morning, I headed back out to Lula's house and the lodge, which was then packed with dozens of dignitaries and residents from all over the area. After breakfast, we filed groups of the townspeople into the lodge, a few at a time, and sat with our legs akimbo around a huge fire. This fire, according to custom, must be kept burning for two straight days. They assign a young Indian brave for that task.

We began the ceremony with my telling of the story about Michael, then Art's telling the story from his view point of being Michael's good friend.

Since the lodge could only hold about 25 people at a time, and there were close to a seventy people who showed up for this event, it meant we had to tell our stories over and over, in shifts, so as to accommodate everyone who came to honor Michael. We were there until 3:30 in the morning on the first day.

I don't know how long it's been since you've sat Indian-style on the hard ground for that long, but I'm here to tell you, it's painful. My legs fell asleep to the point that I couldn't feel them under me. Art was in real pain because of his size. We would have made for some moody Indians if not for some of the more interesting aspects of the various customs that came later the next day.

The drums were beating and we wore the feather headdress as Michael's closest family members were led into the lodge later in the evening. More history behind what we were doing in this long ceremony was explained to us.

Then, well into the evening, the chief pulled out some big corn shucks from an old worn leather pouch, and explaining what he was doing as he went along, proceeded to roll an "ancient tobacco" joint of sorts. I had never smoked dope, but had been around tobacco all my life and learned how to roll a cigarette when I was a boy. I could do this.

Starting at where the chief was sitting, at approximately twelve o'clock in the circle around the fire, the corn shuck pouch and the pouch containing the "ancient tobacco" mixture was passed around with each person taking out a pinch, placing it on the corn shuck, rolling it, licking the edge, and twisting it into a tight cigarette. I was cautious and only put a few flakes of the mixture in my corn shuck because I didn't know what I was dealing with. I fumbled with the papers and rolled a tiny one, then passed the pouch to Art who proceeded to roll a perfect joint the size of a burrito in a matter of seconds. He didn't exactly grow up in a tobacco barn in Newark. What was the deal with him?

It was time for Lula to tell the sweet story of how she met Michael and what their lives were like before they married. When she finished talking, there wasn't a single person there who didn't have tears rolling down their cheeks. Michael's friends came forward to tell stories about his bull riding days and what a character he was. Michael's uncle, the Chief, told us about Michael's childhood and how, even then, he showed the promise of doing great things in the future.

I was going to be the next one up to tell my story, so I lit my corn-shuck ciggy and took a couple of drags for courage. It worked. Away went my nerves, and my story flowed as I started with some lighter moments about being Michael's commander. I paused before I began to work my way gingerly into the night of the ambush and what happened there. I had prayed that I would be able to tell this story to Michael's family without completely losing it. I wanted to maintain some control and get all the words out. Most importantly, I wanted them to know I had seen Michael's face in the light of the explosions shortly after he died and fell over me. On his face was a look of pure peace. I told them that it was sad they didn't view his body when it came home, because they would have seen that peace and would have been comforted by it. He died instantly, and he died a hero — a brave warrior for this country. When I finished, just as it had been after Lula's story, there wasn't a single person who wasn't crying.

Art told the story about what he saw of the ambush — about how we were caught in the crossfire with all the tracers and grenades and bullets he saw flying through the air. He told about how he had a tough time getting over the deaths of his friends, Michael and Samuel, and how he was severely wounded and almost lost his arm in an ambush four months later.

When we finished telling our stories, the Chief ceremoniously closed a small gap in the circle of fire which had been a symbol of a piece missing, of something not known.   From now on, the circle would be an unbroken one. They had finally been led to the people who could tell the story and fill in this gap.

**Art Corley and I prepare to raise the flag
that had draped Michael's coffin in 1969.**

The next day was emotionally charged as Art and I raised Michael's flag, the one that had draped his coffin. It had never been flown before. We also raised the 48-star flag in honor of the "Wind Talkers" of WWII. It was a touching way to cap off two days of intense, emotional memorials — not only for Michael and the community that loved him, but for all veterans.

Art and I went with the family to visit Michael's grave before we headed home. It was heart wrenching. It was an emotional time for everyone as we silently stood at his tombstone and prayed.

As we pulled away from the dusty, hilltop cemetery and headed to the airport, Michael's family stood at the cemetery gates, waving goodbye. We felt as though we were waving to our own loved ones. We felt that we had just buried our brother.

I shiver when I think about how, if I had not been noodling around on the internet that day, if I hadn't been to the 101st Airborne web site, if I had not called Art Corley and emailed Lula and Gabe, this family would still be sitting in that lodge, forty-two years later, praying for God to send them someone to give them peace about their hero. These are loving people who love God, their country, and Michael. How heartbreaking it is that they were under that kind of stress for so long about his whereabouts.

I was so thankful that I could play a part in helping them close the broken circle. I can't help but think Michael had a hand in getting me there. What are the chances that a little sheriff out of Wilson County, Tennessee, ends up in Window Rock, Arizona decades later, ready to tell the story of an American Indian's heroism to his chief, his wife, and his family and help his people find closure? Any healing they were receiving by my presence, I was getting it back twofold, so I'm thankful I was led out there to be of service.

These are dear people who love and care for me. I call Lula my sister and Gabe and Art my brothers. I have an extended family out there, and I think of them every day. I'm so proud to be associated with the Navajo nation. Before we left, Lula presented Art and me with a Navajo blanket that has a feather symbol woven into it. This is a sign that we've been adopted into the Navajo tribe.

It's one of my most treasured possessions.

Laid to Rest

For the family, my trip to Window Rock meant they could finally lay their loved one to rest. For me, the trip laid to rest years of second guessing myself, my actions, and my abilities as a leader. Since June 6, 1968, I have been reliving that awful day and retracing my steps. What could I have done differently on that mission to avoid the ambush and save Michael and Samuel? Samuel's remains saved my life since the carnage splattered all over my body led the enemy to believe I was dead. Michael's body was lying on top of me, shielding me from more of the crossfire. Sometimes I think playing dead was a chicken's way out for me, but I didn't have many options at the time. I did what I thought was right. I was outnumbered and outgunned. I was caught in crossfire, and my Jeep was being stripped of weapons. Had I not played dead, that group of VC would have executed me on the spot.

Still, I wonder what would have happened if I had continued to argue with that little Lieutenant back at the camp and avoided that ill-conceived mission for our small group altogether. I've thought many times that a court martial for refusing an assignment would have been better than putting my men in a no-win situation like that. Then, I think that the Lieutenant would have just sent another commander with Michael and Samuel and the outcome would have been the same. I guess I'll always be playing the what-if game on that point.

It was the most tragic event of my life. One I've had to live with in my most private moments for a very long time.

I began the journey to Window Rock feeling burdened, vulnerable, and weak and couldn't have made it out there without the help of family — big brother Ron, who has lifted me up and helped me get through more tough times than I can count.

I ended the journey as a member of another loving and forgiving family, which helped to lift the burden of that day in 1968 and helped me find a way to forgive myself. That guilt is gone, and I can look back on the tragic event with a different perspective.

When I left the cemetery that day, I was at peace with myself and with my God, and I was finally reconciled with what my service in Vietnam meant to the country.

Just as he did the day he died, Michael Bia has helped me live.

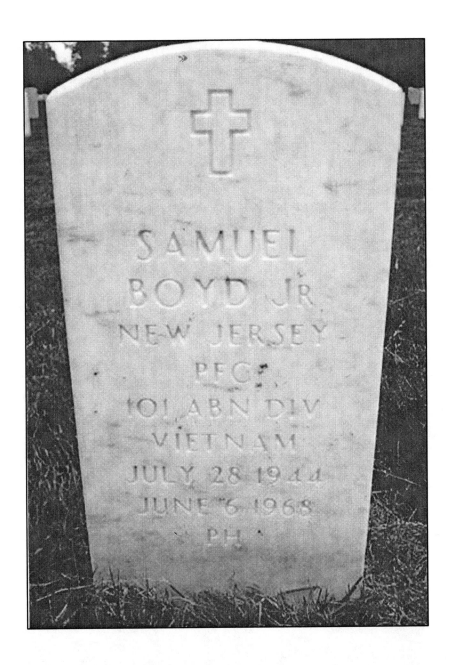

**Samuel Boyd was buried in Beverly, New Jersey.
I haven't yet contacted members of his family, but I'm still trying.**

CHAPTER FOURTEEN

The Coldest Case

The backhoe made its first bite into the grave as the cameras rolled and the grieving sisters began to cry. Connie and Sue Cooksey had brought their own cameras and, as they dried their tears, they began to document the removal of their brother's body from the grave as seamlessly as any of the professional journalists who were working this big story. My heart went out to these devastated ladies. I had known Connie since the first grade, which certainly put a strange twist on this already bizarre event. As the backhoe continued its slow and methodical work, I made eye contact with her as she walked around the grave snapping the photographs. Though she was trying to stay busy, I could tell she was in a great deal of pain.

With its seventh pass into the grave, the blade of the backhoe struck metal with a loud thump and a grinding noise. It had finally hit the steel vault. This backhoe operator never had such an audience, and I could tell he was as nervous about being on television as he was about performing such a delicate extraction. I walked to the foot of the grave and peered over the edge. I could see years of rust on the vault top, and after noticing the condition of the container, I wondered if the body on the inside had been preserved after so long. This was certainly not the first time I had been involved in exhuming a body, but never had I viewed one that had been buried for *four decades*. We had been warned that the only remains we would find inside would be a bit of clothing and bones because the badly mangled body had not been embalmed.

Dr. Jantz and I watch the vault and casket being removed.

The backhoe stopped and a cemetery worker jumped in the grave on top of the vault and began to remove the rest of the dirt with a small shovel. No one was buried on either side, so he dug a wide swath around the protective container to prevent any further damage. I could see an entire side of the vault had already begun to rust through. The vault was slowly lifted above the ground, and funeral home personnel opened it and removed the casket. Within minutes, the rusted vessel was placed into the waiting funeral home vehicle and was whisked away as TV cameras rolled. The news media began to hover around the family like a swarm of bees as they all stood next to the now empty hole in the ground.

I followed the vehicle to Ligon and Bobo funeral home, where the casket was placed on an elevator and sent to a small embalming room on the top floor — the same room in which this body had been prepared for burial forty years ago. There was just enough space for me and Assistant Chief Robert Bryan and Cheif Larry Bowman, an embalming technician and his assistant, and Dr. Jantz and her colleague from the University of Tennessee's Anthropology Department in Knoxville. Several police officers lined the hall just outside the door to keep the media and any other onlookers far away.

As we crowded closer to the platform, it was evident that time had taken quite a toll on the once beautiful bronze coffin.

It had been so lovingly picked out by the devastated family but was now covered in rust from the deteriorated vault. The steel pins holding the lid together had rusted and sealed it tightly shut. After struggling with it for several minutes, the funeral home director left the room and came back with a metal saw to perform a bit of surgery on the rusted lid. Witnessing all the effort it was going to take just to get it open, I began to have my doubts that anything we would see today would render the clues we needed. But I was determined to try. We had reopened the cold case after this long, and it was too late to turn back now.

We owed justice to the dead man and closure to his family.

The saw blade buzzed with an ear-piercing shrill against the rusted metal pins as I looked at Asst. Chief Bryan, wondering what he was thinking at this point. His dad, who was sheriff back in 1969, had viewed this body as a hit and run fatality as it lay in the middle of the road.

Now the sheriff's son was about to view the body so many years later as part of a murder investigation.

Saturday, June 14, 1969

It was 4:30 in the morning when Wilson County Sheriff Cecil Bryan got the call that a body had been found in the middle of Highway 70 North near the Spring Creek area. A nurse from Carthage who traveled this almost deserted road every morning came upon the carnage as she was on her way to work at McFarland Hospital. A badly damaged body of a half-clothed, partially decapitated and dismembered young man was scattered over both lanes. The victim looked as though he had been crushed by not just one, but several vehicles that had apparently struck him and left him in the road to die. The entire area where the body lay was covered with blood and body parts.

When Sheriff Bryan got to the scene, he was met by Tennessee Highway Patrolman Ishmael Wood. Trooper Wood was a seasoned officer who had been to many death scenes, while Sheriff Bryan was in the first year of his first term, with no prior law enforcement experience.

Wayne Barrett from Ligon and Bobo funeral home pulled up in his ambulance behind the sheriff. As the three men were viewing the mangled remains, Mr. Neal Blackburn, the newspaper photographer better known by his nickname "Snapshot," arrived.

Blackburn was Johnny-On-The-Spot back in those days, taking photos of murder scenes, car wrecks, and house fires. He had seen it all. Unfortunately, Snapshot didn't take very many pictures of this crime scene or the area surrounding it, which was unusual because he was famous for always taking more pictures than he needed. A lack of detailed photographs would hinder our investigation in the years to come.

Sheriff Bryan closely examined the bloody clothing of the young man, looking for some kind of identification. He found a brown wallet with a Tennessee driver's license inside, bearing the name of 19-year-old Charles R. (Butch) Cooksey. This was the only son of a well-known and highly respected businessman, Charles Cooksey Sr., who ran a general store just down the road on Highway 70. The sheriff flipped through the wallet, finding pictures of girlfriends, some medical insurance information, a draft card, and even an election card with Sheriff Bryan's name and photo on it. Sheriff Bryan remembered giving Butch this campaign card and asking for his support in the election when he was running for his first term the year before.

Photo courtesy *The Lebanon Democrat*

**Trooper Ish Wood, Sheriff Cecil Bryan, and Wayne Barrett,
at the crime scene.**

Butch was a fine looking young man, standing more than six feet tall, with dark hair and dark eyes. He had three sisters who adored their brother and they had made it their responsibility to look after him because he was known to drink a bit and live a carefree life.

The first impression of Sheriff Bryan and Trooper Wood was that this had been a hit and run, but something told them this didn't look right. They just couldn't put their finger on it.

The lawmen and the ambulance driver meticulously picked up every skull fragment and every bone they could find, which helped us tremendously in later years as we resumed their investigation. The body was removed from the highway and taken to the funeral home.

Trooper Wood and the sheriff then had to notify the Cooksey family that their only son had been found dead in the middle of the highway, apparently the victim of a hit and run on Friday the 13th.

The body had been at the funeral home for several hours before Dr. R.C. Kash, the Wilson County Medical Examiner, came to conduct his investigation. He determined that there was no need for an autopsy, since it appeared this man was the victim of a "traffic accident." Unfortunately, only in obvious homicide cases did autopsies receive the highest priority back in the day since they were so expensive.

When the Cooksey family arrived at the funeral home to meet with Wayne Barrett, they were devastated, as expected. For Charles Cooksey to lose his only son was unbearable.

Barrett and the funeral director explained to the heartbroken parents that there was not much that could be done to prepare the remains for viewing. They made the decision not to embalm their son, and they planned a quick service that would take place the next day at the funeral home. He would be buried in a plot at the Wilson County Memorial Gardens next to his favorite uncle, Benjamin Cooksey, who had been killed two years earlier in a traffic accident on Highway 70, not far from where Butch's body was found.

Word traveled quickly about Butch's death. The Cooksey family was beloved and had been in the country store business for generations near the little Tucker's Crossroads community where I was raised. In the 1930's, Grandpa Cooksey had been killed in a tornado that wiped out his store in the same community.

I had just been home a few months from Vietnam and drove by the funeral home the Sunday afternoon of Butch's funeral. The parking lot was packed as mourners came in to pay their respects. I wanted to offer my support for the family, but I didn't go in because I had been around so much death and carnage in the past few months and didn't think I could bear to see any more sadness.

Over the next few days, state troopers kept a close watch on Highway 70, keeping an eye out for any vehicle that seemed suspicious and looking for any sign of blood or cloth fragments when they stopped cars with obvious damage to the front. Sheriff Bryan called in the Tennessee Bureau of Investigation, and Bob Fortner was the agent sent in to help with the case. Car lots and body shops were searched as Fortner looked for any vehicle that had recently been put up for sale or had been repaired. The search around and underneath the carriages of suspicious vehicles continued in the area where the body was found for several days.

In spite of all the TBI could do, there were no suspects in this apparent "hit and run," and Mr. and Mrs. Cooksey spent the next few decades in deep sorrow. It appeared their son's killer would never be brought to justice. The anniversary of their son's death —which in their minds was any Friday the 13th on the calendar — would always cause them pain.

Thirty-six years later, Charles Cooksey died, followed by his wife shortly thereafter. They never learned who was responsible for taking their only son's life and causing their family a lifetime of despair.

An Unforgettable Case

I started my law enforcement career in 1972, when I went to work for Sheriff Cecil Bryan. From there I worked for Sheriff King, then as Chief Detective for the Lebanon Police Department. I was elected Constable in 1976, and then, in 1982, I was elected sheriff, where I'm currently serving my eighth term. Throughout my entire career, whenever this cold case came up and someone asked how Butch Cooksey really died, it was a hot topic among investigators and everybody had a theory.

For years, whenever the former Sheriff Cecil Bryan talked about Cooksey's death, he wondered aloud what he could have done differently to solve the case. He always felt that if he only had more investigative experience at the time, he might have noticed something out of the ordinary. Until the day he died, back in 2000, Cecil told me there that something "just wasn't right" about Butch's death. I was never able to get the case out of my mind either.

In forty years, no names ever surfaced of anyone who might have seen Butch on Friday, June 13th, 1969. Now it was my turn to ask some questions. I had been successful in the past at solving tough crimes due to my experience as Chief Detective and with so many difficult cases as sheriff. I was eager to see how I could make a difference for the family Butch left behind.

The Sisters

In the late summer of 2009, two of Butch's sisters called and asked if they could meet with me at the Sheriff's Office because they had some information they wanted to share concerning the death of their brother. Sue and Connie Cooksey came into my office and began to tell a wild story about a man named James Crawford and their step-uncle, Benny Page, both of whom lived in the Bellwood community only a few hundred feet away from each other.

James Crawford

The sisters had learned that Crawford and Page, who were eight years older than Butch, had been with him the night he died. Butch was running around with them because he didn't have a car. The sisters admitted they got this valuable information long before their parents died, but didn't want to reopen the investigation with their loved ones in failing health.

Connie Cooksey said that when she arrived at her grandmother's house to console her family the night Butch died, she noticed that her step-uncle Benny had a black eye. On the morning of the funeral, she said the black eye was really obvious, but he offered no explanation about what happened to him. Benny served as a pallbearer for his step-nephew, black eye and all.

Benny Page

She said Benny seemed to change after the funeral that day, getting quieter and having no interaction with the family whatsoever. Apparently he and Butch were very close, but he never spoke of Butch again after the funeral. She said that Benny lamented several times in her presence that he "wished he could have done more to help Butch the night he died."

The sisters told me they had learned from their grandmother that Butch left in the car with Benny at dusk that evening, and when Benny came back home around midnight, Butch wasn't with him. No one was ever questioned about this. I find that amazing.

The other man, James Crawford, had a reputation for being a bad ass back in the day and was known to be very violent. The sisters learned from several sources that, through the years, James

Crawford would get drunk and show his potential adversaries a small box full of what he called "Butch's teeth," to warn them that if they ever messed with him, the same thing would happen to them. This was an incredible story.

I was determined to look into this, but I didn't want to give the Cooksey sisters any false hope before I had a lead. I called in my Chief Deputy Larry Bowman and my Assistant Chief Robert Bryan, son of the late Sheriff Cecil Bryan. We didn't assign any other detectives to this because their case loads were so great and we didn't know yet if we had anything to work on.

We began by digging through old records and files. There wasn't much there — only one old newspaper photograph of the crime scene. Throughout the files, there were no notes made about teeth missing, nothing out of the ordinary, and nothing concrete. I spent weeks going through old crime scene photographs and found nothing from the morning of June 14th, 1969. I looked at negatives until I was cross-eyed, taping them to my office window and looking at them through a magnifying glass in hopes of finding something that looked like the Cooksey crime scene.

The good news was, Trooper Ismael Wood was still alive, in good health, and had a great memory. When I contacted the retired lawman, he was more than willing to help. We interviewed him extensively about what he remembered of that night, the day after, even the months and the years after, the death of Butch Cooksey.

I also interviewed the ambulance driver, Wayne Barrett, who described the condition of the body when he first arrived on the scene that night. He talked to us about how badly the head was injured, how they worked tirelessly to retrieve all the brain matter, bone, and fragments scattered up and down the highway from where Butch Cooksey's body lay that morning. He didn't recall picking up any teeth.

It seemed that what we lacked in photographs of an old crime scene, we were making up for with live witnesses. Sue Cooksey, the youngest sister, has been running the family's store for years, but she would have made an excellent detective. She told me that a truck driver who used to drive from Lebanon to Carthage every morning on that road might have some information in the case.

I located that now retired truck driver who told me he traveled Highway 70 early in the mornings during that time because there was absolutely no traffic and he thought it was a better road than the new interstate. He remembered the morning of June 14th very well. He said he remembered that there was no traffic on the road, and that he would have been passing by the area where Butch's body was found around 3:30 A.M. He said he met no other cars on the road on his 21-mile trip to Carthage.

As far as I was concerned, that ruled out the theory that Butch was struck several different times by several different vehicles.

It seemed to us that Butch's body was probably left in the road sometime after four in the morning. The carnage was found by the nurse thirty minutes later. We looked for the death report filled out the night Butch died. It didn't exist.

We decided that we needed to visit Butch's step-uncle Benny and tell him that we were reopening the case. It was the best decision we could have made.

September 23, 2009

Benny Page was in his late sixties now. He was finishing up his country ham and biscuit breakfast when Chief Bowman and I knocked on the door of his house. He let us in and sat down to finish his breakfast. I didn't waste any time getting down to business.

"Thought you'd never have anybody ask you about the death of Butch Cooksey, did ya?" I asked right out of the batting cage.

"Well ... uh ... no," Benny looked at both of us as he answered. "But I will tell you, I didn't kill Butch."

He then launched into a bizarre story of how he picked up Butch on Friday the 13th and they rode around and drank beer with some other guys. They went over to James Crawford's house, then left to get more beer at a package store, where they met and befriended a "stranger" who went by the name of Gomer. They picked up Gomer and went back to Crawford's house, and when he and Crawford got out of the car, Butch left with Gomer.

Benny told me that was the last time he saw his nephew alive. Crawford's house was less than a mile from where Butch's body was found.

I asked him about the black eye he was sporting at Butch's funeral. He tried to explain that away by saying Crawford had hit him the night before because he had told him that his wife, Sue, was sleeping with another man behind his back. He said that Sue Crawford had quite a reputation involving young men, and apparently that information was a sore subject, even though James Crawford liked to fool around with other women.

None of this explained what happened to Butch Cooksey. Who was this stranger named Gomer, and was Benny Page telling us the truth? I wasn't convinced. He could have at least come up with a better name for the stranger than Gomer. Please. This whole story stunk.

He said the next thing he remembered was that his stepmother, Butch's grandmother, had answered the phone on that Saturday morning, and when she learned that her grandson was dead, she dropped the receiver on the floor and began crying hysterically. Benny said it woke him up, and shortly after that the police came to the house to pick him up for questioning. He said they already had James Crawford in the backseat of the patrol car.

This was odd because all these years I had been hearing about this case, never once did the name of a single suspect come into play. Sheriff Cecil Bryan would certainly have mentioned that these men were brought in for questioning in our discussions about the case.

Benny told us that he and Crawford were taken to the Sheriff's Office, where they were questioned for several hours. He said they told the officers about Gomer and were released.

He mentioned that he seldom talked to Crawford anymore. We would find out later that this was another one of his lies.

For days after we interviewed Benny Page, I spent hours and hours talking to everyone involved in investigating Butch Cooksey's death. Out of twelve law enforcement officers who were still alive from back in the day, no one had heard of any suspects being questioned in the case, and no one had heard of anyone being brought in for questioning.

Chief Larry Bowman worked for several days trying to track down the illusive "Gomer" from Benny's story. To my amazement, he found a man known by that nickname back in the 1960's, whose real name was James Glover. He stood over 6 foot 5 and weighed close to 300 pounds. He wasn't well educated, but seemed to be the gentle giant type, as Chief Bowman gathered after a sentence or two came out of Gomer's mouth. The chief asked him if he knew anything about the death of Butch Cooksey.

"Yep, sure do. I'm Gomer and I gave the boy a ride that night."

Chief Bowman was relieved to see that this man was going to be cooperative. Bowman brought Gomer over to the office where we could question him further. As we expected, what Gomer had to tell us was nothing like Benny Page's story.

Gomer said he never knew a Benny Page or a James Crawford as far as he could remember. He said that on Friday the 13th he went to the old Rock House beer joint on Highway 70 in an old white Nash Rambler car. He had worked all day at the flour mill in Lebanon and wasn't feeling well due to a bad cold. Around ten thirty, he called it a night after drinking three beers. He said it began to rain as he pulled out of the parking lot, and he spotted a young man hitchhiking at the foot of the hill below the beer joint. He felt sorry for him, stopped, picked him, up and asked him where he was going. The man told him he would show him where to drop him off. Gomer said he thought he said his name was Butch, but he couldn't remember. He said the man might have been drinking, but it seemed he was more nervous than drunk.

After traveling a few miles, Gomer said, he asked to be dropped off at Highway 70 and Rome Pike — directly across the street and less than a hundred yards from where James Crawford and his wife Sue lived. As the hitchhiker opened the car door, he asked Gomer if he owed him anything for the ride. Gomer told him he didn't, and the man got out and walked away. Gomer said that was the first and last time he ever saw him. He said when he heard about a young man being killed the next morning, he contacted the police and told them about giving a ride to someone fitting that description.

Gomer later took a polygraph test for us and told his story. According to the test, he was telling the truth. Forty years of memory is a hard thing to bring back, but he promised us he would do his best and he did; he was very helpful, and we were now closer than we had ever been to connecting the dots in this case.

Now we were more convinced than ever that Benny Page's story was full of lies and he was only trying to protect his friend James Crawford. Once we put the word out to the public that we were reopening the Cooksey murder case, the phone started ringing off the hook.

Through various tips, we located James Crawford's sister, who lived in Florida. She told us that when she was growing up, her entire family was "sick and twisted". She explained how her older brother, John, and possibly James as well, had an "unusual relationship" with their mother and father and that James grew up to be both physically violent and sexually abusive not only with adults but also with minors. According to her, after James had fathered five children with his wife, Sue, he got a fourteen-year-old girl pregnant twice. We investigated this and found it to be true. We got busy looking for ways we could charge James Crawford with statutory rape four decades after the fact.

The sister left one of her most valuable tips for last. She told us that Crawford used to beat his wife and shortly after Butch Cooksey's death, Sue left James forever. The sister said if we could find Sue, she could perhaps shed some light on Butch's death.

She ended the conversation by saying she had no doubt that her brother had something to do with the murder. All of the Crawford sister's stories checked out in our investigation.

According to birth records, James had fathered two children with his children's baby sitter at the same time he had fathered two children with his wife, Sue.

One of the many tips from the public we got over the phone came from a hairdresser in Carthage who told us that when she was much younger and lived in the same house that James and Sue had lived in, she was helping her mother paint and came across a cigar box. Inside that box was a newspaper clipping about the Butch Cooksey murder case and some teeth. She said she'll never forget how frightened she was of those teeth. Her mother told her never to look in that box again because the box belonged to Uncle James. She said that she had always been scared to death of Crawford because he had a nasty reputation for being very mean and violent.

We began our search for Sue Crawford and found her contact information through the visitation records at the state penitentiary, since one of her sons was in prison and she came to see him regularly. She had remarried, and her name was now Sue Crawford-Flatt. When I dialed her number, I put the call on speaker phone so that the detectives in my office could listen in. It became one of the most important phone calls I had ever made in an investigation. Here's her story:

Sue Crawford told me that on the night of Friday 13th, 1969, Butch came to the house in Benny Page's car. They met up with James, he followed them in his old 1956 Ford, and they all headed toward Lebanon to drink beer and ride around. That night around eleven, James came home in his car, with Butch slumped over in the passenger seat. He was perfectly still, and when James stopped the car, Butch didn't climb out as he usually did. She said James got out of the car "mad as hell" and stormed into the house. He grabbed what looked like an old police night stick and told her that he "was going to teach Butch a lesson because he had tried him earlier" — she said she didn't know if that meant sexually, or that he had tried to fight him. James then drove away with Butch still slumped in the seat, and she never saw Butch again. When James returned home alone around 4 A.M., Sue said she watched

James throw the night stick across the fence into a sink hole. His car was soaking wet, and she asked him where he had been. He told her he had to wash his car in the creek. The couple got into an argument at that point because he had been out all night.

The next morning before breakfast, James said "Let me take you to where they found Butch's body!" She said he took her down the road toward Lebanon about a mile or so and showed her where the body had been lying earlier. When they left the scene, she looked at him and called him a killer. He told her that if she said anything to anyone about this that he would kill her, too.

A few days after Butch's murder, James threatened to cut off all her fingers with a butcher knife just for calling him a killer. She took the children and left while he was at work that night and was smart enough never to go back. James married their babysitter, Brenda, after that.

I asked her about the alleged fight that Benny Page had gotten into with James that night. She said there was no fight at her home. The last time she saw Benny was when she watched him get into the car with Butch and head toward Lebanon. Sue had never heard of anyone named Gomer. She added that if Benny Page said Gomer was at her home at any time, he was lying.

Sue Crawford had kept all this information to herself for forty years as a couple mourned the death of their only son and a community was baffled by the violence of his death. I asked her why she didn't come to the police. Her answer didn't surprise me. She said she was too afraid of James. However, in the last few years, she had been sick with cancer and had decided she couldn't die with this secret. She wanted to tell what she knew. Before hanging up the phone, I scheduled a time to visit her in person to get her statement on record.

The investigators crowded around the phone were speechless when I ended my conversation with Sue Crawford-Flatt. After so long, we had a witness and were going to solve this case.

Now we needed to find out how Butch Cooksey really died, which was going to be difficult since there was no autopsy and therefore no records to review.

Attorney Jack Lowery got word that we had reopened the Cooksey murder case around the same time that he got a phone call from Benny Page and James Crawford. He asked us not to question them unless he was present. He wanted to know why we had not interviewed former TBI agents Bob Faulkner or Bob Goodwin, because apparently they had picked up Page and Crawford before Butch's funeral to question them.

Here we go again with the story of the illusive suspects.

We contacted Faulkner and Goodwin, who were still very much alive and in excellent health. They also had a very good memory of the events surrounding this unusual murder case. Both former agents confirmed that there had never been any suspects in the murder of Butch Cooksey. For the record, Faulkner added that he had never even been inside the Ligon and Bobo Funeral Home where these suspects were allegedly picked up.

Benny Page and his buddy James Crawford had forty years to get their story straight, and we were still finding big holes in it. But then again, these guys never expected the TBI agents to be in such good health and have such a great memory after so many years.

We asked the Cooksey family to bring us any papers they had from the funeral home, any information that could help us. They brought us the guest registry. Benny Page was there that day. He had to be because he was a pallbearer. But if James Crawford was there, he didn't sign the guest book. Also, if Benny and Crawford were picked up by the TBI, or any law enforcement at the funeral home before the funeral, the family would have been short one pallbearer, and they would have noticed that!

And the Tips Keep Pouring In...

We got a call from a woman in Murfreesboro who had briefly dated James Crawford's son. She said one evening when she was visiting him at his dad's house she got into an argument with the elder Crawford. In the middle of the argument, James Crawford went to another room and came back with a ring box. He put it in her face and opened it. There were human teeth inside. Crawford told her that if she "continued to mess with him," her teeth would be in a box just like these, which "belonged to Butch Cooksey." She said Crawford then warned, "Butch got what he had coming to him." We now had someone who could confirm the teeth. Someone who could testify that they saw them and they heard James Crawford admit that the teeth belonged to Butch Cooksey. After that encounter, the woman said she broke off the relationship with the Crawford boy because she was scared to death. Smart move.

It was also a smart move by the Cooksey sisters to visit attorney Jack Lowery around this time to remind him that he had represented their family in a case a few years back, and if he represented Benny Page and James Crawford, it would be a conflict of interest.

Jack had to withdraw from the case after checking his records.

As the investigation wore on, it became clear that we would have to exhume the body of Butch Cooksey. It had been in the ground for so long. No one in this area had ever attempted anything like this before.

We were looking for evidence of Butch being shot, stabbed, or beaten to death. We also needed to see if teeth were missing to confirm the "teeth in the box" story that kept coming up. The death certificate signed by Dr. Kash, the medical examiner in 1969, only listed "trauma" as the reason for death. That didn't help us very much. We only had one crime scene photo. In that, the body was covered with a sheet. We were hitting dead ends here. We had to exhume the body.

I called the University of Tennessee's Anthropology Department. UT Knoxville is the home of Dr. William Bass' famous "Body Farm," where bodies in various states of decay are studied. I asked one of the experts if the department would be willing to conduct an autopsy on some un-embalmed remains that had been buried for four decades. I told them what we were looking for, and they were confident that they would still be able to find clues.

Once Connie and Sue Cooksey agreed that we could exhume the body of their brother, we coordinated our efforts with Ligon and Bobo Funeral Home, which had prepared the body for burial so many years before.

We also had to coordinate everything that was bound to happen the day of the exhumation. Digging up a body after forty years is a big story, and it could turn into a media circus if we didn't plan accordingly.

I went to Butch Cooksey's grave the afternoon before the exhumation and actually prayed about it. I prayed that we were doing the right thing, and I asked for guidance in what we were about to do. Tomorrow was going to be an emotionally charged day for the family and for everyone who had known Butch. This was part of my job — one of the most unpleasant parts imaginable.

I had given a lot of thought as to how I was going to involve the media in this bizarre case. What I was going to release and when I was going to release it was vital to how this entire exhumation would happen. This large cemetery can be viewed from three different roads and the Cooksey plot was right in the middle. No pun intended, we set up a "media dead zone," where photographers could shoot the exhumation of the body from a distance.

The University of Tennessee experts were set to arrive at the cemetery at eight o'clock. We weren't going to dig an inch into that grave until they were standing there.

The sisters were going to make the best of this emotional event by moving their brother's remains to Bellwood Cemetery, where their parents were buried, once our investigation was complete. Ironically, that cemetery backs up to James Crawford's house.

I planned to videotape the exhumation and had a detective standing by to make still photos of the event. I got to the cemetery early to make sure the media lines were roped off and the deputies were clear on the plan.

The backhoe crew arrived, followed by both the Cooksey sisters. They prayed over the site as the attendant from the funeral home arrived with chairs for them. There was a lot of tension in the air and a lot of uncertainty, but the sun was up and it was a beautiful, crisp, cool day. The media set up their tripods and began shooting what would possibly be their lead story for the five o'clock news — the exhumation of a body in a decades-old murder case. The backhoe dug until the steel vault was reached, then hand shovels were used to complete the task.

The rusty vault was lifted from the ground, and the coffin was removed and taken to the funeral home, where we planned to open it to inspect and x-ray the contents. It turned out to be quite an experience.

Back to the Embalming Room

As the power saw made its final cut, the rusted steel pins released the lid on the coffin with a hissing sound. The room became engulfed in a smell unlike anything I've ever experienced when exhuming bodies — a mixture of rotting flesh and strong ammonia that almost knocked us down. A large amount of body fluid poured out of the bottom of the casket onto the floor. The casket had been sealed tightly enough to preserve these fluids for four decades. Usually there is a catch basin built into caskets just for this purpose, but apparently it had rusted through.

There was obviously more to this choking smell than just a decomposing body. The strong odor of embalming fluid filled the air, but according to our records, he had not been embalmed. Officers standing in the hallway gagged and coughed. I tried to hold my breath. As we opened the top of the casket and looked inside, we didn't find anything we thought we would find.

There was a big black mass lying in the casket, covered in the metal flake from the rust on the coffin lid. Like archeologists, we had to take a paint brush and carefully remove the brown rust particles layer by layer to examine what was beneath.

It was soon obvious to any of us who had been around back in the sixties that this was one of those old, black rubber body bags.

This was a good sign for us because it meant the body parts were kept together. Inside the bag, you could see the outline of a person because the zipper had rusted through and it was gaping open. We peeled back the bag and were shocked to find so much of the body intact. Apparently, the funeral home technicians had made an attempt to embalm the remains before they decided it was futile. The head of the corpse was wrapped in a sheet, but from the neck down, the body was intact. The other dismembered parts were put in a smaller bag and placed between the corpse's legs.

This goes without saying, but I'll say it anyway. This was a horrifying sight, topped only of course, by that gagging smell. The UT experts were shocked because they were expecting a body that had not been embalmed. As a result, none of us were wearing the protective hazmat suits that we were supposed to wear in times like this. Who knew what we were breathing or how it would affect us all later?

This autopsy would have to be conducted as if this were a fresh murder. We had to find out if Butch Cooksey had been shot. We had to find out if his teeth were missing. Wayne Barrett, the ambulance attendant who had removed the body from the crime scene, was right when he told me the body was nearly decapitated. There was very little left of the top or the back of the skull.

We removed the body from the black plastic bag as if Butch had passed away just a few hours ago, and placed it on a stainless steel table. We had a portable x-ray machine brought in for the autopsy, and the technician, who wasn't quite sure what he had gotten himself into, did an excellent job under trying circumstances. He x-rayed every part of the body. A makeshift viewing room was set up in a kitchen down the hall and we were able to see instantly the extent of Butch Cooksey's injuries. Nearly every bone in his body was broken. I was so thankful that the funeral home had done what they could to preserve this evidence.

As I looked at each x-ray, I thought of how it was meant to be that his killer could be brought to justice by all of these elements working together for the best possible outcome.

We searched the x-rays looking for a possible bullet. We didn't find one. Sue Crawford's theory on what happened that night began to make sense. The night stick that James grabbed when he said, "I'm gonna teach this boy a lesson," had apparently done this extensive damage.

The person who beat this young man really set out to teach him a lesson.

As we looked at what was remaining of the back of the skull, the upper part of the jaw was still intact. I had to know if he had missing teeth. If so, which ones? A search of his dental records showed that all of his teeth had been intact when he was alive, except for one. One tooth had a bridge attached to it. According to his sister, Butch carried this bridge in his pocket until he went out socially, then he would put it in.

Our part of the autopsy was finished. Now, it was time for the experts at UT to take over with their complete re-construction of the body at their teaching facility. Butch Cooksey's remains were loaded into a temporary coffin furnished by the University of Tennessee, taken downstairs, and placed in a van for its trip to Knoxville. Dr. Jantz told me it would be several weeks before she could finalize any of her findings from the examination on the body.

Just a few weeks after we exhumed Butch's remains, one of the medical examiners at UT became ill, and Robert and I both came down with some nasty respiratory problems, breaking out in hives and rashes. There was some concern that perhaps what we came in contact with during that autopsy was the cause. My doctor told me I had obviously been around some unusual bacteria, but he couldn't pinpoint the exact cause for my breathing problems, which continue to this day.

With the exhumation out of the way, it was time to go back to work on our witnesses as the UT experts completely reassembled every piece of the skeletal remains they could find to come up with the actual cause of death.

Dr. Kash so long ago had listed "trauma" as the cause, but trauma can come from a lot of different things. I had a theory that James Crawford had beaten Butch Cooksey to death and had taken him down in the middle of the highway to stage what appeared to be a hit and run.

Sue Crawford was ready to give us her official statement, and when she did, she remembered some very important details she had forgotten when she talked to us before. She said when James said "Let's go down and see where they found Butch Cooksey's body," she couldn't figure out how he knew Butch was dead. She said they did not have a television set or a telephone at that time. How could he have known that Butch Cooksey was lying dead on Highway 70?

We scoped out James Crawford's current house on a regular basis and found out he had a woman staying there with him and his wife. We had heard that he had gotten involved with selling prescription drugs. Big surprise. This new woman friend of his had numerous convictions for using narcotics in several other counties. We staked out Crawford's house and followed this woman back to Smith County, where she was living out in the middle of nowhere in a rundown duplex apartment. One afternoon, we stopped her as she was leaving.

We told her we had reopened a murder case involving her employer, James Crawford, and his wife, and we told her that we thought she might be involved in covering up evidence in the case. She started talking, telling us things we really needed to know, but she wanted to be paid for her information. That didn't go over well with us.

She told us about some late night phone calls between Crawford and Benny Page. She had overheard them trying to get their story straight. She told us that Crawford had often promised that when his wife "passed away," he wanted *her* to move in with him and be his wife.

It looked as though Crawford had become a hypochondriac. He couldn't walk one day and needed a breathing machine the next. He was seen at a doctor's office requesting pain pills for his "bad back." The stress of a murder investigation might not bring him down, but his bad health certainly would in the end. Bad karma was catching up with him, as my hippie friends used to say.

A few weeks into the investigation, the Crawford clan had a death in the family. All of them were gathered at a funeral home in Carthage when a huge, full-blown fist fight broke out. Several were arrested, and it caused so much bad blood that some of these relatives became witnesses against James in our case. Our moles on the inside told us that the fight at the funeral home broke out because of the Butch Cooksey murder investigation. Witnesses were coming out of the woodwork. Now, relatives who had been treated to James Crawford's little "show and tell" with the box of teeth were ready to spill.

And what about ole' Benny during all of this? It's one thing to be a liar, but to be a dumb-ass liar is another. Benny Page had filed a false police report and had given us a false statement in a murder investigation. If we never got another thing on him, we had that much.

Our interview with either one of the suspects would have to wait until we had all of the autopsy results back from UT. Crawford was fair game because, to our knowledge, he had not put another attorney on retainer since Jack Lowery discovered he had a conflict of interest. We heard rumors that Crawford was going to claim that he took his wife to a movie on that Friday 13th. We checked old movie ads from the drive-in on Highway 70. Teenage slasher movies were playing that night — everything from "Eye of the Cat" to "I Was a Teenage Frankenstein." We got the list and were ready for Crawford and his bogus alibi.

The forensic team at UT told us that Butch Cooksey's body was traumatized as badly as any they had ever seen. As we requested, they reconstructed and photographed each body part recovered from the casket and put the body back together one bone at a time to identify all the major breaks. It was obvious that his lower body had received tremendous trauma since he had been run over several times by a vehicle. There was no traffic on the highway, so that left only one possibility: someone had intentionally put him in the street and run over him, back and forth, numerous times.

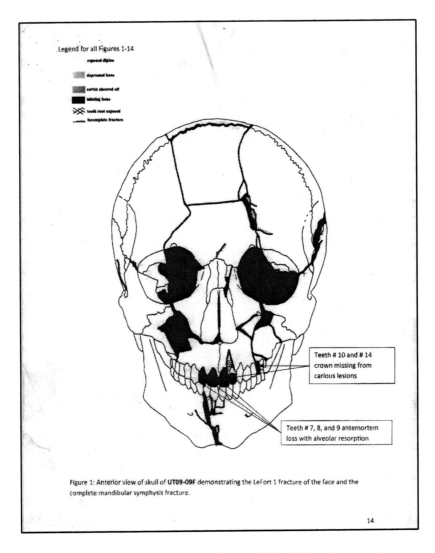

Figure 1: Anterior view of skull of **UT09-09F** demonstrating the LeFort 1 fracture of the face and the complete mandibular symphysis fracture.

14

The three front teeth were missing. All of his other teeth were accounted for. With our testimony from his ex-wife, Sue, we knew James Crawford had done it. We thought perhaps Benny was covering up for James because they were, well, closest of friends. With the crazy lifestyle of James Crawford, anything was possible. This was a man who had knifed his own sister at a beer joint one night because he thought she was "looking" at his wife.

My Theory of Friday the 13th

Here's my theory: Gomer Glover gave Butch Cooksey a ride to the intersection of Rome Pike and Highway 70 on the night of Friday the 13th. That intersection is less than two hundred yards from James and Sue Crawford's home. For whatever reason, I think Butch was about to pay a visit to Sue. He had been at the beer joint with Benny and James, and they could have had a conflict of some type in there. We later learned that Butch knew James was going to dump Sue so he could marry Brenda. Perhaps Butch was going to tell Sue what was about to happen. Perhaps he felt sorry for her and it was a social call. Whatever Butch's reason for visiting Sue, I think it was Butch that gave Benny the black eye that night. Butch was not known to ever run from a good fight.

I believe that after Gomer let Butch out of the car, Benny and James came upon him walking on the side of the road and perhaps resumed their fight with him. Benny left and James finished Butch off with the night stick as Sue described, took his teeth as a trophy, and put him out on the road to run over him time and time again to make it appear that he had been the victim of a hit and run. Butch's blood and flesh had to be all over the front of Crawford's car. That's why he washed it in the creek off Bluebird Road.

Our meetings with Crawford's girlfriend/maid continued to render more leads. Without being prompted, she mentioned that she had found some human teeth in a tin box when she was cleaning the house. When she asked him about the teeth, he told her that he "couldn't talk to her about them," but he said, "it goes to show you how bad I am!"

We thought we'd take one more shot at Benny Page, who had already hired another attorney. We asked the attorney if his client would be willing to take a polygraph. His attorney said he would get back to us. When he didn't call us after a week or so, we called again. The attorney said that Benny would indeed be willing and would be at our office the next day to take the test. We had the technician standing by and everything was ready. Then Benny dropped the bomb.

"Oh by the way, I have health issues," he said.

He knew we couldn't let him take a polygraph with health issues, and his attorney knew that as well. It was just another ploy by Benny, who just wanted to look cooperative. As Benny got up to leave that day, I said, "I'll be seeing you, Benny. This ain't over."

He just looked back at me with a sheepish grin and walked toward the parking lot.

A few weeks later, I got a call from the nursing home where James Crawford's brother, J.B. Crawford was living out the rest of his life. We had been by to visit him early on in the investigation, but he didn't have much to add that we didn't already know.

This time, our visit was going to be very different.

"Terry, come down here and see me," he said. "I got something to tell you and I can't tell you over the phone." I promised him I was on my way, and I brought Chief Bowman with me. When we arrived, J.B. was standing at the door to greet us and walk us to his room. We barely had time to sit down before the old guy started talking.

"I might as well tell you," he said, "James was up here Sunday, and he told me he killed Butch Cooksey."

"Really?" I said. "Why do you think he told you that, J.B.?" My heart was pounding.

"Well, I think it has just been on his mind so long that he wanted to confess. He's on a lot of pain medicine and wasn't thinking straight. He claims he took a ball bat and beat Butch Cooksey to death."

"Did he tell you why he did it?" I asked.

"Not really, but I think it's got something to do with his old ex-wife, Sue," he said. "She was a pretty good woman, but nobody could live with my brother, James."

Now we had enough to put James Crawford away. We had to move in on him at his mobile home near the Bellwood Cemetery when he least expected it. Larry Bowman and Robert Bryan kept his home under surveillance until we had all the necessary elements in line. About two o'clock one afternoon, the officers caught Crawford sitting on his porch, so they pulled into his driveway, approached the porch and introduced themselves.

"Do you know why we're here, James?" they asked.

"I've heard," he said.

As Larry and Robert began to question Crawford, his car alarm kept going off. It was clear that someone was inside the house setting it off with a remote, knowing that we were probably taping the interview. Within a few minutes after all the cacophony started, his wife came out on the porch and wanted to know what we were up to. She told Crawford he was wanted on the phone. The moment the officers had stepped on the porch, Crawford's wife was on the phone with his lawyer. The interview was over.

Meanwhile, I'd had a belly-full of Benny Page riding his truck up and down the road, trying to keep an eye on us and what we were doing, so we put the wheels in motion to arrest him for giving a false statement to police.

Coming home from church one Sunday, I got a call from former Trooper Ishmael Wood, who found some old photos when he was cleaning out his garage. One of the photographs was of Butch Cooksey's body. I couldn't believe it. It was a picture of the uncovered, mangled body lying in the road. He said he only had two pictures, and those were from Neal Blackburn. I sent an officer to Wood's home within minutes to pick up the photos and bring them to me.

They were certainly graphic. More so than my imagination had been all these years.

There were tire tracks in blood on the pavement and over the body. The top of his skull was lying a few feet from the body. I knew that with this photograph, I could have a traffic re-constructionist come in and give me some idea of how this man ended up on Highway 70. The team came out to the crime scene, set up survey stakes and measuring points, and determined after studying the photographs, that the same vehicle ran over Butch

Cooksey's body several times. The tire tracks were the same all the way up and down the road, and there was no way he could have been struck by any other vehicle. The body had been run over and backed over three times. The next time Larry and Robert visited James Crawford, they laid the photograph of Butch Cooksey's mangled body on a table right in front of him. He refused to comment.

By now, the problems within Crawford's family had exploded into a court hearing. I sat in on one of those hearings, and I've never heard so many people lying under oath in my life. The judge simply declared a mistrial on both sides and ordered them to stay away from each other.

We were able to indict Benny Page for filing false information in a murder investigation. The media outlets in Nashville were all there to plaster Benny's picture on TV and on the front page of the paper. Whether he liked it or not, Benny was now about to take the full rap — or believe he had — for a murder that James Crawford had committed. Meanwhile, Crawford hired the Lannom Law Firm as his attorneys. We found this out in a convenient way.

There's a camera on the square, and you can see a lot going on if you want to. Crawford pulled up in front of the attorney's office with his wife *and* his girlfriend in the car, and went in to meet with Lannom as we expected. Once the meeting was over, I called Lannom and told him we were about to indict James Crawford in the murder of Butch Cooksey. He told me he was officially representing Crawford and requested some time to talk further with his client before I did any indictments.

Not long after that, I talked to Lannom again, and he asked me why we were focusing our investigation on Crawford. I related some of the lies Crawford had told. For instance, he told others he had received a phone call about the murder, but we later learned from his ex-wife that there was no phone in the house. Lannom told me that apparently we hadn't done a complete investigation, because Crawford did have a phone. That was easy to check. I went to the library and looked at the old phone books from

1969-1970. James Crawford was listed in that one, however we were unable to check further, because the library didn't have a 1968-1969 book. I went to South Central Bell and searched through their archives.

In June of 1969, James Crawford did not have a phone in his home at the time Butch Cooksey was killed. He had one installed a couple of months after Cooksey's murder, after his wife left him. This was just one more piece of evidence that helped us pull things together. The pressure we were applying to Crawford was yielding results in many areas. The wheels were coming off, and he knew it.

His brother told me that James admitted killing Cooksey. We had just arrested Crawford's friend and longtime alibi, Benny Page, for filing a false report. Crawford had already contacted his ex-wife and warned her not to tell anybody about the "problems" they had 40 years ago. He was too late, though; she had already told us everything we needed to know.

As we expected, Crawford's alibi for the night Cooksey died, Friday the 13th, was that he had taken his wife to the movies. (His ex-wife told us that, in all the years they were married, he never took her to see a single movie.)

We soon got bad news about the terminal illness of Sue Crawford-Flatt and began to fear this valuable witness against her ex-husband might not live to testify against him. We also got word from James Crawford's attorney that Crawford was "terminally ill." His attorney wanted to discuss who would pay his steep medical bills if he were in jail.

For the Cooksey family, the many years of anxiety and the agony of not seeing justice served in the murder of their brother was about to come to an end. The family was calling us almost daily. In 1969, there were different murder statutes on the books than there are today, and we had to explain to the family that it was going to be extremely hard to make a first or even a second degree murder case in the death of their brother. After all, Butch willingly went with James and Benny that night, drank with them at a local tavern, and perhaps even visited with Crawford's wife while Crawford was not at home.

These were a lot of maybes, but they were real possibilities that the defense might bring up in a trial. The fact that their brother didn't have the best reputation in the world didn't help. But he was their brother and they loved him. We discussed all of these scenarios because the Cooksey sisters had always been sure of one thing: their brother did not die in a drunken stupor in the middle of the road after being hit by some stranger.

The law in '69 had to be researched extensively to determine what, if anything, we could charge James Crawford with. Did we have a murder? Did we at least have a manslaughter case? There was very little physical evidence. There was a body that was missing teeth – those teeth had not been recovered, but we had witnesses willing to testify Crawford had shown them the teeth and had threatened them by bragging that the teeth belonged to Butch Cooksey.

It was clearly a circumstantial case, but it was a good one.

We had lie after lie documented from the two suspects. We had a co-defendant who had given us false information. We knew we could seek an indictment, but we needed a few more elements to fall into place to get the kind of conviction the Cooksey sisters were seeking.

Butch Comes Home

It was now time for the University of Tennessee to release the remains of Butch Cooksey back to the family. Another public funeral was planned. Everything that was being done on this case now was being covered in the media.

Ironically, the new grave where Butch's body was laid to rest in the Bellwood cemetery could be seen from the kitchen window of James Crawford's house. Every morning when he woke up and went into the kitchen to have his coffee, I hoped he would be haunted by the view of that fresh grave with the flowers on it — the grave of the man whose death he was responsible for, forty years before. The reality of that body being practically at his back door was something he was going to have to deal with for the rest of his life whether he served a day in jail or not. I was hoping he would always be in his own private hell for what he did.

The body arrived at the Ligon and Bobo Funeral Home one Friday afternoon, and I went by to see what kind of job the reconstruction team had done. All I could focus on was his mouth that was missing three front teeth.

Larry Bowman and Robert Bryan deserve so much credit for their tireless work in this case. The way we worked as a team to piece everything together was amazing. It was hard to believe that we were finally going to charge someone with this murder, but we all deserved this reward for being tenacious. District Attorney Tommy Thompson spent several days going over all the evidence and felt we had enough to go to the grand jury and indict James Crawford in the murder of Butch Cooksey. With more than a year of our time invested, this cold case was now heating up again at age forty-one. It was unimaginable to be involved in a case that had gone unsolved for so long.

Meanwhile, Crawford was jumping in and out of the hospital like a scared rabbit going in and out of a hole. He began to wear an oxygen tank, somewhat by design, to illustrate that he was "too sick" to go to prison. Benny Page hired an attorney in Carthage who told us that Benny wanted to cooperate in any way he could, but every time we asked for his cooperation, he folded. Finally, the attorney called and asked us to cut some kind of deal with his client, but Benny was one big scared weenie. He never showed up to discuss anything with us.

The D.A. quickly gave us the green light to take the case to the grand jury. I described to the grand jury the lengthy investigation, the witnesses we had uncovered, and the statements that were given to us. After all that, it looked as though the best we were going to be able to get was a manslaughter charge.

The grand jury gave us the manslaughter indictment. The family was disappointed, but it felt good to us that we were at least getting something after so long. One has to look at the reality of trying a case after so much time had passed.

All we could think about now was putting handcuffs on James Crawford, bringing him to the Wilson County Jail, and booking him for manslaughter. But after the indictment, Crawford's attorney began to make noise about how his client was so sick that he might die in our facility if he went to jail. He told the DA and the judge that he was concerned that his client wouldn't be able to make bail and would suffer and die behind bars.

The day of the arraignment, every eye was on the criminal court of Wilson County as James Crawford came in to enter a plea. Coincidentally, it was the wedding anniversary of Butch's late parents.

James Crawford was now 68 years old, and entered a "best interest plea." The plea means the defendant does not admit to guilt in any offense. It was a great feeling to book, fingerprint, and photograph James Crawford that night, and it was an even better feeling to see his mug shot in the newspaper as the killer of Butch Cooksey.

We had taped and interviewed more than 25 witnesses after reopening the case, but we could tell they were still frightened of what might happen to them. Crawford worked with dynamite as part of his construction job. Many of the witnesses in the community who could have testified against him didn't, because they were afraid he would blow up their house in retaliation. In the end, we had to take what we could get.

Crawford received a three-year sentence for murdering Butch Cooksey, but due to his alleged failing health, the judge granted him probation.

Never at any time did he refute the charges brought against him. I was ready to go to trial and was terribly disappointed. The newspaper headlines quoted me saying as much. The media also picked up on the fact that we were still looking into charging Butch's uncle, Benny Page, and were planning on going to trial with those charges. The age of the evidence was the only thing holding us back. The memories of the witnesses were as dried as the blood. This wasn't the outcome I was looking for, but it was a victory just the same.

Several weeks later, we brought 70-year-old Benny Page into the courtroom. We were staying on track with our charges of "providing false information in a murder investigation." Benny didn't enter a plea, but received a sentence called a pre-trial diversion for two years. It's a form of probation and he has to be a model citizen or he'll go to prison. In his conscience, if he has one, he'll be a prisoner with a life sentence. This loser had allowed Butch, his own nephew, to be murdered. It's something he'll have to live with for the rest of his life.

The marker read June 14,
but the investigation revealed Butch really died on Friday the 13th.

This murder took place on Friday the 13th, the unluckiest night of the year according to superstition. But when it came to solving this crime, one of the greatest teams of investigators in the country couldn't put a lot of stock in luck or superstition. They could only rely upon their instincts and tenacity — and a lot of prayer — to get the job done.

The solution of this case seemed to play out just like so many cases I've talked about in this book. It seemed that God's hand was steering me around, getting me in touch with the right people, and helping me find the right information. I took a big risk by opening up what appeared to be an accidental death and proving it to be a blatant homicide. I don't think these things happen in a successful investigation just because an investigator wants them to happen. It takes the good Lord above to help put a case like this together. I was so glad to be of service to the Cooksey family. What if someone the Cooksey girls didn't know that well had become sheriff? They might have been spinning their wheels by coming forward. There was definitely a divine hand in this. I had faith that there was no way the good Lord was going to allow this crime to go unpunished.

Miraculously Healed

Not one to suffer fools gladly, Chief Larry Bowman stopped by Crawford's home one day and simply asked him for "the teeth." He then told Crawford that the least he could do for the guy he murdered was to take the teeth up to the grave and leave them. I drove by Crawford's house a few days after that. He was out in the yard and wasn't wearing oxygen anymore. Who would have thought it? Also, he was walking without his cane. He must have found a miracle healer somewhere.

A man who had spent all his life working the system had worked it again.

But he's on probation, and if he as much as sneezes outside the law, he could end up spending three years of his miserable life in prison.

That would be poetic justice.

Photo by Bill Thorup

THE STATESMEN

Having met several dynamic leaders in our country — including several presidents of the United States, governors, and senators — I've learned that they're all just men and women who want to serve the public. They all did what they thought was right at the moment, for the time they were in office. These are the standouts that made a lasting impression on my life and my career. I was so fortunate to have had the opportunity to meet them.

Senator John Glenn

When Senator John Glenn was running for President, I agreed to help coordinate campaign efforts in Middle Tennessee. I used to always say, if we'd had "Super Tuesday" in the early 80's in Tennessee, he could have won. Our state was way down on the list of primaries back then and, as we all know, Glenn didn't win the nomination. I was crushed — almost as disappointed as I would have been if I had lost the bid for sheriff. His unique, kind demeanor and his quiet voice will always be in my memories of our meetings.

Senator Glenn adored his wife and acknowledged her at every public appearance, thanking her for her love, patience, and support during this tough campaign. I was in awe of him when I was in his presence. As a young boy in the seventh grade, our class listened to the radio as this astronaut, this American hero, was sent up to circle the planet and explore outer space aboard the Gemini capsule as a news commentator said, "God speed, John Glenn." As the rocket blasted upward, reporters provided constant updates on his journey, and we cheered every new accomplishment.

Back then, I never would have imagined that I would be involved in his presidential campaign. This man, who was about my size, seemed to stand ten feet tall. It's not often that a grown man has a superhero, but John Glenn will always be mine. He was so kind to me, and I often think the U.S. would have been better off if he had been elected president. I also think the voters weren't seeing this hero — this statesman — in the same light as I did, and that's a shame. Sometimes I thought the Vietnam War had not allowed us to elect heroes. With a bad economy and wounds from the war, I just couldn't understand why America wasn't ready to elect someone they could look up to in this way. During his last space flight, I watched in amazement at a man of his age setting out on yet another journey. There was no doubt in my mind after that; I knew this brave, mature gentleman should be in some kind of leadership role in our nation's capital.

Speaker Tip O'Neill

In 1986, I was at the National Sheriff's Conference in Washington as president of the Tennessee Sheriffs' Association. One of my duties at the time was to go to Washington and meet with the elected national officials. On one of these trips, I had the honor of sitting down with the Speaker of the House, Tip O'Neill.

Meeting past U.S. presidents might seem like the ultimate thrill to many people, but Speaker O'Neill may have been the most powerful man in Washington, D.C. I got the opportunity to sit down with him in a meeting with a couple of other sheriffs and the president of the National Sheriffs' Association. I was amazed at Mr. Speaker's size. This was no little man, literally or figuratively.

The whole time I was talking to him, it kept flashing through my mind, Is he even listening to what a small town sheriff from Tennessee has to say? He indeed heard every word.

"How's Al doin'?" He was talking, of course, about Al Gore.

My reply was, "You see him more than I do, so you tell me!"

He had a deep, hearty laugh, and his white hair gave him the countenance of wisdom. He had an "I've seen it all" kind of look in his eyes.

Something I'll never forget from that day was something he said about Congress: "Every aspiring congressman should have to serve two terms as sheriff before he can even enter an election. A sheriff's job is all about dealing with people's problems, and a congressman sometimes forgets who puts them in office; but a sheriff never does."

He couldn't have spoken a bigger truth.

Governor George Wallace

Governor George Wallace was a strong supporter of the Alabama Sheriffs' Youth Ranch. A minister who had moved to Lebanon was a good friend of Wallace's, and he sold me on the idea of building something like the Youth Ranch in Wilson County for underprivileged and abandoned boys. It was quite a challenge to get the approval on the project, and there was a lot of controversy surrounding it.

Many people in the community where the home was built didn't want it in their neighborhood. The "not in my backyard" people certainly came out in force against having these children housed near them. But thanks to some tenacious and tireless volunteers and workers within the department, the refuge for these needy youngsters became a reality and has been of great benefit to the community.

Governor Wallace assured us the home would be a great success, and he was right.

Since it opened, the Youth Ranch has helped more than 500 boys and girls find good homes, good jobs, and a happy future.

On a very hot, dry summer day in 1984, I traveled to Alabama with some local county leaders to meet with Governor Wallace to discuss the ranch and share ideas.

Toward the end of our chat, I noticed he was looking very tired, very run down. Years in a wheelchair certainly take a toll, as I learned from watching my dad. When our meeting concluded, he rolled his chair toward the large door to his office and an Alabama state trooper was standing right there, ready to open it for him. I watched this powerful man maneuver his wheelchair toward the waiting area of his chambers and thought back to the circumstances which put him in that position for the rest of his life. He was running for President of the United States, had different and controversial ideas, and an assassin wanted to stop him.

Watching him, a kind and gentle man, depend on the assistance of others just to get around his office, I was reminded of how we tend to judge a book by its cover.

His image during his run for presidency was that of an angry, little, loudmouthed racist governor from Alabama. What I witnessed that day was far from that negative image.

As the governor wheeled out into the waiting area, his administrative assistant, a very proper Southern lady, took the governor by the hand and spoke to him softly:

"There's an elderly black couple waiting to see you, and they've been here quite a long time. They didn't tell me what it was about, but they said only you could help them."

"Bring them in!" Governor Wallace gave his command in a cheerful loud voice for everyone to hear. He motioned for us to go back in to the office to help him receive his guests.

The elderly gentleman came in to the office first, his hat in his hand and his clean, pressed overalls showing signs of wear but not a speck of dirt. His white shirt was yellowed with age around the collar but was clean and starched to perfection for this very important trip. His frail little wife, in her starched cotton Sunday dress and hat, followed her husband into the office.

As the governor asked them to sit down, he introduced our little group as his old friends.

"These are my friends from Tennessee. I carried that state!" He gestured toward us and gave us a sly grin.

"What can I do for you fine folks today?"

"They won't bring us a refrigerator, Governor." The elderly man's voice was weak.

"Who won't bring you a refrigerator?" The governor was incensed at the thought of someone not giving this man the most basic of needs on such a sweltering summer day.

"The landlord of our house, Governor Wallace. He's supposed to furnish appliances, and our refrigerator has been out of order for nearly two months. We've been to the mayor, the sheriff, and the alderman. Nobody will help us. It takes a lot of ice to keep our food cold, and we're on a fixed income."

Upon hearing this, Wallace was furious. He looked up at the trooper standing near the door.

"Go right now, find them a refrigerator, and take it to their house!"

"Yes sir, Governor!" the trooper answered with an eager "glad to be of service" smile and nod to the couple.

The elderly lady got up from her chair, reached down, and hugged the governor's neck in appreciation. There were tears in her eyes, and I saw her husband wipe away a tear as well. This was the end of a long and frustrating journey for the couple, and the governor had made everything happen with one simple order. But he wasn't finished yet. Not by a long shot.

"Trooper, you go find that landlord and you get his ass up here to me as soon as you can. I want to talk to him eyeball to eyeball!"

As the couple left the office that day, they told the governor they would be praying for him and his administration. They were smiling from ear to ear with tears still glowing in their eyes as they accompanied the trooper who would carry out the governor's wishes for them.

I wouldn't have wanted to be that landlord for anything in the world that afternoon. Heaven knows how the governor made him feel for treating those elderly folks like that. Anything the landlord got was no less than what he deserved for his negligence.

A few weeks later, I got an Honorary Lieutenant Colonel Aide de Camp certificate in the mail from Governor Wallace. I still have the souvenir of that day hanging in my office.

Wallace was a man of short stature who had hoped and prayed for the biggest and most powerful position in the land. But his prayer wasn't answered — at least not in the way he had imagined. His journey, his true calling, was the governorship of Alabama. It was where he was meant to be.

Vice President Al Gore

Sometimes unanswered prayers are indeed our answer, as Vice President Al Gore might be able to attest. Gore wasn't the VP when I first met him. This was the man who, but for the "falling of a few chads," could have been President of the United States.

He became my congressman about the time I first became sheriff. When he was in the U.S. Congress, he was home all the time, holding town hall meetings. He held so many of them right here in Wilson County that I got to know Gore very well and admired his hard work. As we say here in the South, this is a man who will look at you "eyeball to eyeball" and tell it like it is.

Some friends and I used to rent a farm from him after he became VP. This is when I learned that Vice President Gore can be as tight as the bark on a tree when it comes to money. He would have made a great president just by judging on how well he can stretch a dollar.

Al Gore loved his constituents and loves his friends and family. Once he was elected to the Senate, he didn't get an opportunity to visit us that much, and then when he became VP, he was traveling the world and we didn't see him at all.

The reason Gore makes my short list of "true statesmen" has nothing to do with anything he might have said in those many conversations we had during his visits to Wilson County. It has to do with something he did as the world watched — a selfless gesture that made a difficult transition a bit easier.

In 2000, when Vice President Gore ran as the Democratic nominee for President against Republican nominee, George W. Bush, our country stood on the eve of one of the most controversial presidential elections in history.

It seemed the problems on that endless night were going to be insurmountable; lawsuits were filed in the wee hours, and talk of corruption swirled around the election process — especially in the state of Florida. There were accusations of voter fraud, uncounted votes, unclear ballots, and disenfranchisement. Each side was accusing and blaming the other.

Gore won the popular vote by 5%, but Bush won the Electoral College vote 271 to 266. It all came down to the votes in Florida, where another Governor Bush — Jeb Bush — was in office, and that caused even more controversy.

These were some very long days for all of us. As the drawn-out process continued, it was a roller coaster ride. Gore would be President one day, then the next morning, after "hanging chads" were debated, Bush would be President.

The eyes of our friends and enemies around the world were watching this mess unfold, and it didn't look good. The media was waiting for a ten round fight and, as far as the pundits were concerned, the whole thing had to be settled with a knock-out. The battle went all the way to the Supreme Court, which, in a 5-4 decision, ended the recounts and gave the electoral votes from Florida to George W. Bush.

There could have been more lawsuits and more heated arguments and recounts. Some supporters were even insisting on more action from the Gore camp. But it was not to be, and one wise man could see what the bickering was doing to this country.

I was watching the local news when it was announced that Vice President Gore would be addressing the nation. I watched as a man who was born to be President walked up to the microphone and did something very presidential. He announced that he was putting a stop to this fight — a fight which was dividing our nation. He said that if the argument over votes were to continue, it would not be good for the country, and that he had just called Governor Bush to congratulate him and wish him well.

Al Gore quietly walked off the national political stage with grace and humility because he wanted to spare the land he loved from further dissent surrounding the close election. We missed out on a great leader with great promise and ability because he put the country ahead of his own ambition that night.

That, my friends, is a true statesman.

Governor Ray McWherter

I'll probably never know another man quite like Governor Ned Ray McWherter of Tennessee. I first met him when I was President of the Tennessee Sheriffs' Association and he was Speaker of the House for the state. For thirty years he held the position of Speaker, and while not many people from other states could name our governors who came and went in those decades, just about anyone who knew about Tennessee politics knew Ned Ray McWherter — the man we always referred to with all three of those Southern names.

He was a "bull in a china shop" personality, but a no-bull, what-you-see-you-get gentleman. As Speaker of the House, he needed a sheriff's input on the prison overcrowding problem, and I worked with him weekly on prison issues and legislation. When he walked into a room, it was like the old E.F. Hutton commercial. Everyone stopped talking and looked at him. His large frame and country boy charm made you think he was as warm and cuddly as your grand pappy. But make no mistake; he wasn't.

This was a self-made man who was as tough as nails, and through the years he had learned how to make things work in Tennessee for the better. Before he passed away last year, I got one more chance to talk with him, and I'll always cherish that meeting. I wanted to ask his permission to talk about our friendship in my book. I asked him what I could say.

"Boy, I don't care what the hell you say, just tell the truth!" He looked at me with that big grin that had grown a bit weak with his illness.

This man's first race for Governor was fought against a powerhouse — Winfield Dunn — a man who everybody liked, a man who had already served two terms as Tennessee's top man. It speaks to Ned Ray McWherter's ability to lead that he won that election.

It was Christmas Eve when I went to the governor's mansion for a reception a couple of years later. Everyone was making an early evening of it, leaving before 9 P.M. to get home to their families and celebrations.

Ned Ray was a widower and would be alone for a long evening, so I stayed to have some Old Charter Ten and water with him out in the sunroom before I called it a night. Except for the maids and the butler cleaning up the mess left by the crowd, the big, drafty room was quiet and our conversation almost echoed in the empty space. It would be filled with the laughter of children, grandchildren and great-grandchildren tomorrow, but for now, it was a lonely place.

I enjoyed seeing the governor in his most casual mood, in a ratty, red cardigan buttoned up over a white shirt. He had burned a giant hole in the sweater pocket when he stowed his still-smoldering pipe there sometime during the evening.

He didn't care. He was who he was. That was his charm.

Ned Ray was a man who knew how to develop and maintain relationships and solve problems just by being himself and bringing people together. As we enjoyed our cup of cheer, I wished him a Merry Christmas and thanked him for bringing me into his confidence and into his inner circle for so many years. He turned to the bar to mix himself another drink, and I noticed his snow white hair touching his collar and that huge red sweater stretched around those giant shoulders. Santa himself would swim in this man's clothes, I thought.

Then something akin to what a child would say to his favorite sports star came spilling from my mouth: "Governor, you certainly are a powerful man!" He slowly turned and looked at me as he stirred his drink with his finger.

"Terry, let me tell you the secret to being powerful ..." He stopped, took a sip, and looked away to gather his thoughts. "The secret to power is not having to use it. It's also called respect."

I'll never forget his warning against using power the wrong way, because it came from a humble, honest, and powerful man who earned the respect of all who knew him.

Ned Ray McWherter was a wise, Southern gentleman of few words who gave me a quick lesson in life — and a good lesson in politics — with one simple sentence.

Turning the Page

Taking a ride down Bluebird Road today is a trip down memory lane, since there's not much left but memories of what we fought out here for so long. Only two places sell booze on this stretch of road now. Roofs are caving in on some old shacks next door to vacant, overgrown lots, but for the most part, give me this over flashing neon, drive-by shootings, and illegal gambling any day. I can get rid of weeds in one afternoon, but ridding an area of street thugs and drug dealers requires months, if not years, of steady police work. It also requires energy — loads of energy along with a dash of youthful naiveté.

Sometimes if I need to clear my head and leave the stress in the office, I take a ride down Bluebird Road. I stop at the place where old Legs Stinson saved me and my deputies from walking into a trap laid by contract killers out for revenge. The shack is still standing, but barely. The hedges where Legs hid until he could reach out to stop me are sparse and unkempt, and the overgrown grass and broadleaf weeds have taken over the gravel road leading to what's left of the old shack.

I shiver when I think of how this well-organized group planned my death that night. They knew I was angry and frustrated with their antics to the point of distraction, and they used that against me to lure us there.

They certainly knew which buttons to push on a young new sheriff who was on fire and eager to do the job the people had elected him to do.

Looking at this tattered lot today and going over each step in my mind, it's almost as if that near-death experience — that horror movie — happened to someone else. I'm a different person than I was that night in so many ways. Every experience I've had as a lawman since then has served to either mellow me or harden me, depending upon who is doing the judging.

I often wonder how I would handle these same circumstances as the man I am today. That night I thought I had every step well planned. Compared to what they had planned for me, I was showing up to the picnic empty-handed.

The situation with the Expressway Gang and the fifty thousand dollar price tag they put on my head was an open death threat that might as well have been broadcast on the national news. Everyone knew about it. But to paraphrase that song from the seventies, it's not your enemy who'll do you harm; *it's the man with the smiling face* you have to worry about.

The men who hid out in this shack never made an open threat and never got the word out on the street about what they were going to do. They were counting on the element of surprise to put an end to my clean-up campaign, and they almost succeeded. That's what still scares the hell out of me when I think back on it. I would have only figured it out in the last moments of life, as I lay there bleeding on that gravel path.

Cut away the excess and it came down to this: they were ready to kill a sheriff over booze and a little bit of money. I was ready to die to defend a peaceful way of life in the town I loved. I sometimes wonder about the murder plots against me that I never heard about. I guess if I worried about those, I'd never leave the safety of my office.

I have stalkers to this day whose threats get back to me. I've put men in prison who vow right in front of a judge to kill me the minute they're set free, but I can't live in a shell. I just have to be as watchful as anyone in my career. You can't become a paranoid wreck because of some loose-lipped lunatic out there.

I do know that for the rest of my life, whether I'm sheriff or not, I'll have to carry a gun and look over my shoulder. It's a lawman's version of the belt and suspenders mindset.

As I stand at the end of this gravel path and look over the top of the shack, I see in the horizon a steeple of a newly built church in this community. Apparently the 350 members felt safe when they moved their sanctuary here five years ago. They wouldn't have dreamed of bringing their children down here to worship back in the day. Remember, it was after church one Sunday when I pulled over a bar owner in his old Cadillac and was almost shot at point blank range by a couple of fugitives riding in the backseat. Watching this new church go up brick by brick in the past few years has given me a great sense of satisfaction, because it means our passionate work to clean up this area has not been in vain.

It was so damned hard. So incredibly frustrating at times. But we got 'er done. If the illegal joints didn't burn to the ground, they were torn down. If we couldn't get them out by force, we worked the system and used the laws in our favor to make life inconvenient and uncomfortable for those who would dare to break the law. It took some serious game strategy, but our side won in the end.

The poverty is still here; the public housing projects are across the main highway from Bluebird Road, but that, too, will change someday. New roads are coming through, and that means better interstate access and more businesses looking for prime real estate to develop. Nothing gets in the way of progress. A bulldozer trumps a gun-toting thug trying to protect his drug territory any day of the week.

I've done what I set out to do. I achieved my goals and, in most cases, far exceeded my own expectations that were in the stratosphere to begin with.

I can turn the page now on what has been a dream career for me with all the ups and downs and roller coaster rides that dreams are made of. I can move on to the next chapter of my life with the confidence that I kept many of those promises I made, not only to myself, but to the people who trusted me to protect them, term after elected term. The day I take off this badge forever and pin it in my display case, I know I'll miss what this amazing chapter in my life has brought me, but I have so many memories and much to share with the next young man or woman who desires to be elected to this office.

And if I ever have a doubt as to what I've accomplished in my journey, I need look no further than the backyard of my childhood — the area trying to overcome its sullied past and move forward to accommodate a new generation with positive, fresh ideas — the ever changing and ever evolving place with that innocent, happy little name... Bluebird Road.

Sheriff Terry Ashe

From busting up illegal gambling and bootlegging operations to reopening and solving cold cases inherited from his predecessors, Sheriff Terry Ashe has depended upon his sharply-honed investigative instincts to bring scores of dangerous criminals to justice during his forty-plus years in law enforcement.

He served with the 101st Airborne Division during the Vietnam War and was awarded three Purple Hearts, the Bronze Star, and the Cross of Gallantry, among many other honors for his heroic service as a paratrooper and recon scout.

After his tour of duty, Ashe came home to begin his career in public service, rising from a sheriff's deputy to Chief Detective for the Lebanon Police Department. There, he led a top-notch investigative team to solve dozens of crimes, among them, the high-profile case of the elusive "Southside Rapist," the brutal Melrose slayings, and a forty-year-old cold murder case.

Sheriff Ashe's constituents have re-elected him for eight consecutive terms since his first run for office in 1982, making him one of the longest serving sheriffs in the nation.

Terri Merryman

Award-winning writer Terri Merryman has ducked rifle fire, lived in an Israeli colony, and moved into a Russian village to anchor important interviews via satalite.

She's interviewed subjects as volatile as Shimon Peres and Newt Gingrich, and as gentle as Lena Horne and Nancy Reagan, but her belief that everyone has at least one unique and interesting story to share has never varied.

Her career has put her in the roles of news anchor, reporter, talk show host, and even associate producer for the top rated *Survivor Reunion* reality show. She was profiled in trade journals for the live coverage that put her in harm's way during the Miami riots, and the Philadelphia MOVE confrontation.

Terri's skills as an interviewer, reporter, writer, and producer were honed when she started as a fledgling television reporter while a freshman in college. Since then, Terri has anchored in Nashville, Los Angeles, Philadelphia, Atlanta, and Miami, and has reported for NBC's morning syndicated show *Real Life*.

Her work in Los Angeles placed Terri in the middle of the Hollywood action at Paramount Studios and at the famed CBS Television City Studios. It was the best of all worlds for this movie and entertainment buff who coached young Reese Witherspoon when she began her Oscar-winning acting career.

When not on camera, this author and adjunct professor serves as a media and talent coach to business executives, athletes and law enforcement personnel, helping them communicate effectively in the new media climate.

She's currently ghostwriting several books and serves as a coach, publicist, and consultant to aspiring authors, entertainers, and reporters.

Terri writes from the peace and tranquility of her horse farm overlooking the Cumberland River in Lebanon, Tennessee.